Palgrave Studies in Communication for Social Change

Series Editors: **Pradip Ninan Thomas**, The University of Queensland, Australia, and **Elske van de Fliert**, The University of Queensland, Australia

Advisory Board: **Silvio Waisbord**, George Washington University, USA, **Karin G. Wilkins**, University of Texas at Austin, USA, **Thomas Tufte**, Roskilde University, Denmark, **Zaharom Nain**, University of Nottingham, Malaysia Campus, **Rico Lie**, Wageningen University, The Netherlands, **Claudia Mitchell**, McGill University, Canada, **Jo Tacchi**, RMIT University, Australia, **Nicholas Carah**, The University of Queensland, Australia, **Zala Volcic**, Pomona College, Claremont, USA

Communication for Social Change (CSC) is a defined field of academic enquiry that is explicitly transdisciplinary and that has been shaped by a variety of theoretical inputs from a variety of traditions, from sociology and development to social movement studies. The leveraging of communication, information, and the media in social change is the basis for a global industry that is supported by governments, development aid agencies, foundations, and international and local NGOs. It is also the basis for multiple interventions at grassroots levels, with participatory communication processes and community media making a difference through raising awareness, mobilizing communities, strengthening empowerment, and contributing to local change.

This series on Communication for Social Change intentionally provides the space for critical writings in CSC theory, practice, policy, strategy, and methods. It fills a gap in the field by exploring new thinking, institutional critiques, and innovative methods. It offers the opportunity for scholars and practitioners to engage with CSC both as an industry and as a local practice, shaped by political economy as much as by local cultural needs. The series explicitly intends to highlight, critique, and explore the gaps between ideological promise, institutional performance, and realities of practice.

Titles include:

Tina Askanius and Liv Stubbe Østergaard (*editors*)
RECLAIMING THE PUBLIC SPHERE
Communication, Power and Social Change

Saba Bebawi
INVESTIGATIVE JOURNALISM IN THE ARAB WORLD
Issues and Challenges

Levi Obijiofor
NEW TECHNOLOGIES IN DEVELOPING SOCIETIES
From Theory to Practice

Pradip Thomas and Elske van de Fliert
INTERROGATING THE THEORY AND PRACTICE OF COMMUNICATION AND SOCIAL CHANGE
The Basis for a Renewal

Sonja Vivienne
DIGITAL IDENTITY AND EVERYDAY ACTIVISM
Sharing Private Stories with Networked Publics

Zala Volcic and Mark Andrejevic (*editors*)
COMMERCIAL NATIONALISM
Selling the Nation and Nationalizing the Sell

Karin Wilkins
COMMUNICATING GENDER AND ADVOCATING ACCOUNTABILITY IN
GLOBAL DEVELOPMENT

Palgrave Studies in Communication for Social Change
Series Standing Order ISBN 978–1–137–36166–0 (hardback)
(*outside North America only*)

You can receive future titles in this series as they are published by placing a standing order. Please contact your bookseller or, in case of difficulty, write to us at the address below with your name and address, the title of the series and the ISBN quoted above.

Customer Services Department, Macmillan Distribution Ltd, Houndmills, Basingstoke, Hampshire RG21 6XS, England

Communicating Gender and Advocating Accountability in Global Development

Karin Gwinn Wilkins
University of Texas at Austin, USA

First published 2016 by
PALGRAVE MACMILLAN

Palgrave Macmillan in the UK is an imprint of Macmillan Publishers Limited, registered in England, company number 785998, of Houndmills, Basingstoke, Hampshire RG21 6XS.

Palgrave Macmillan in the US is a division of St Martin's Press LLC, 175 Fifth Avenue, New York, NY 10010.

Palgrave Macmillan is the global academic imprint of the above companies and has companies and representatives throughout the world.

Palgrave® and Macmillan® are registered trademarks in the United States, the United Kingdom, Europe and other countries.

ISBN 978–1–137–45047–0

This book is printed on paper suitable for recycling and made from fully managed and sustained forest sources. Logging, pulping and manufacturing processes are expected to conform to the environmental regulations of the country of origin.

A catalogue record for this book is available from the British Library.

Library of Congress Cataloging-in-Publication Data
Wilkins, Karin Gwinn, 1962–
    Communicating gender and advocating accountability
in global development / Karin Wilkins.
        pages   cm. — (Palgrave studies in communication for social change)
    Summary: "Women are more central than ever before in visions of global development. So then why has the development industry failed to resolve gender gaps on a global scale? In this book, limitations of development are explored through research on micro-enterprise programs in South Asia, celebrity funding of girls' schools in Africa and Afghanistan, and population programs and conferences in Egypt. Concerns are raised with the overly narrow articulation of women's empowerment at the expense of gender dynamics, privileging of communication as a technological tool rather than as discourse or global industry, and assertion of neoliberal development without attention to political-economic global contexts. Critical inquiry can contribute to advocacy by subverting accountability to meet the
     demands of global social justice" — Provided by publisher.
    ISBN 978–1–137–45047–0 (hardback)
    1. Women in development.   2. Microfinance.
    3. Women-owned business enterprises.   I. Title.
    HQ1240.W55 2015
    305.42—dc23   2015023409

*To Grace Way Knudsen, Marie Monroe Wilkins, and
Karel Knudsen Wilkins*

Contents

Acknowledgments

There is more to acknowledge than I can adequately convey in this brief page. This project has been challenging, in part because I care so much about its potential contribution to our conversation on improving global conditions, not only for women but for all communities facing oppression and marginalization. First, I want to thank Pradip Thomas for his vision in initiating this publication series, which promises to offer a significant contribution to our scholarship on communication and social change. I also appreciate support from Elske van de Fliert, and guidance from Felicity Plester and Sneha Kamat Bhavnani in working with me through Palgrave Macmillan in the production of this book. This work has benefited from thoughtful discussions with many great colleagues at events sponsored by Aarhus University, the International Association for Media & Communication Research, the International Communication Association, Karlstad University, Malmö University, Roskilde University, Texas A&M, University of Oregon, and University of Pennsylvania. I appreciate insights from Leslie Steeves and Radhika Gajjala into feminist contributions to development communication; Paula Chakravartty, Florencia Enghel, and Toby Miller into the importance of political economy; John Downing, Dana Cloud, James Pamment, and Jan Servaes into politics and advocacy; and Emile McAnany into integrity and significance. I am particularly thankful to Kyung Sun Lee for her diligence and thoughtfulness as my research assistant. I wish to thank the University of Texas at Austin's Center for Women's and Gender Studies for a core faculty research grant. Special thanks to Kari Siegenthaler for working on the index to this book. My children, Katherine (Kari) and Alexander Siegenthaler, bring me great joy and inspiration. My husband, Paul Rubin, brings me strength and support. Thank you.

1
Communication, Gender, and Development

Women are more central than ever before to visions of global development: so why then do gender inequities remain? More money is being spent in development in the name of women's empowerment. More women are serving in roles of global leadership. More girls are being educated. But serious gender gaps in employment, in pay, in legal rights, and in leadership positions challenge the ability of both women and men to reach their potential. The overarching question guiding this project concerns how it is that development has failed to resolve gender disparities on a global scale.

Issues surrounding gender and women feature prominently in the articulation of the Millennium Development Goals (MDGs), which represent a "blueprint agreed to by all the world's countries and all the world's leading development institutions," according to the United Nations (UN) (2015a). Among other concerns, the MDGs focus on reducing maternal mortality, achieving universal access to reproductive health services, and improving rates of female participation in formal education, paid employment, and elected political positions. While attention to women in development is valuable, recognition of gender dynamics highlights potential concerns with the ways in which programs articulate problematic assumptions about both women and men in society.

The eight MDGs, focusing the work of the development industry, are to:

1. Eradicate extreme poverty and hunger
2. Achieve universal primary education
3. Promote gender equality and empower women
4. Reduce child mortality

5. Improve maternal health
6. Combat HIV/AIDS, malaria, and other diseases
7. Ensure environmental sustainability
8. Encourage global partnership for development

Working toward these goals, the UN declared that specific outcomes would be reached by 2015; with the passing of this year, the UN and other development agencies are presenting their visions for "post 2015" strategies, now intended to achieve significant change by 2030 (UN, 2015b).

What we do know is that although some progress has been made for girls and women, particularly in terms of increasing rates of literacy and primary education, narrowing gender gaps between girls and boys, improving sources of safe drinking water, reducing child and maternal mortality, and reducing the proportion of people in poverty,[1] many important and preventable problems remain.

Still, significant proportions of women do not have access to health and family planning services, paid employment, or political positions with power, and are dying unnecessarily when giving birth (UN, 2015a). Globally, gender gaps, particularly in terms of education and health status, have improved in most countries, though gaps between men's and women's economic attainment and political empowerment remain wide, according to a recent World Economic Forum report (Hausmann et al., 2011). Gallagher concludes, based on her reading of the 2010 World Economic Forum report, that in some countries gender gaps have actually increased rather than decreased, and that there is "[n]o country in the world [that] has achieved gender equality" (Gallagher, 2011, p. 132).

As citizens, women are lacking a voice, even if they are more visible. Although women are estimated to constitute 40% of the global workforce, women earn far less than men for the same positions and hold only 1% of global wealth (World Bank, 2012). Women are also much less likely to make it onto Forbes' wealthiest in the world lists: of the richest 100 people in the world (Forbes, 2014) only 11 are women, and about half of these are listed due to "family" wealth. When women do accrue their wealth separately from family connections, typically they do so through fame enabled by their commodification in mediated venues.

Global disparities in income by gender need to be understood within a broader context in which the proportion of those who are truly wealthy grows smaller, in sharp contrast to a burgeoning global community of those in poverty. The very richest of the global elite, at 1% of the world's population, own almost half of all global wealth (Credit Suisse, 2014). These proportions are directly oppositional when considering those who are in the poorest half of the global population, owning less than 1% of global wealth (Credit Suisse, 2014). The International Labour Organisation (ILO) reports that women are particularly disadvantaged in the context of informal economies and wage distributions (ILO, 2015). Gender inequities in wages earned are stimulated through undervaluing the work that women tend to do, the structural conditions of professions and workplaces, gendered norms about familial roles, and a lack of collective organizations such as unions (ILO, 2015). Feminist research needs to situate women's conditions not only within gender differences, but also in the context of unequal global wealth distribution (Lee, 2006, p. 191). Gender gaps are exacerbated given other conditions of marginality, manifest in concrete circumstances.

This project is motivated by my serious interest in improving conditions for marginalized communities, whether considering devastating yet preventable gaps across gender, class, or ethnicity or other conditions differentiating relative positions of power. While individual evaluations of single projects may help assess the effectiveness of particular interventions, a valuable contribution of critical research is to broaden the scope to include development interventions as part of an industry, working within complex local, national, regional, and global contexts. In this way, research is directed toward accountability in terms of social justice, rather than aiming to meet the criteria of individual donors. Situating development within an industry allows us to focus on the discourse that structures how problems are defined, how interventions are conceptualized as solutions, and what targeted beneficiaries are expected to gain.

Development discourse serves as more than a set of phrases used to explain the world and its myriad problems. This discourse structures the allocation of resources toward particular subjects as well as designated countries and communities. The first intermediary research question then concerns how development discourse constructs problems and solutions in its public narratives. Communication surfaces as a projected tool within this narrative, as a mechanism to promote social change; but critical research reminds us of the complexity of communication, as a way of structuring discourse, as well as an industry creating wealth and fame, which contribute to global development. The second intermediary research question concerns how communication works within development programs for women in the fields of microenterprise, population, and education. The final intermediary research question highlights the articulation of gender within these narratives, how women are conceptualized as actively engaged or passive recipients, the ways in which they are valued, and whether men, or gender dynamics, are recognized in this discourse.

The articulation of development, communication, and gender is explored through analysis of public discourse, within political-economic contexts. In this study, public discourse includes publications and public statements explaining programs and their evaluations, as well as published news on designated topics, including the building of girls' schools by Angelina Jolie, Madonna, and Oprah Winfrey; microenterprise programs in South Asia; and population and reproductive health programs in Egypt. In each of these cases, conditions critical to the political-economic context are explored, connecting concerns with patriarchy with the potential for a neoliberal framework to dominate the development narrative.

Next, I conceptualize development as an intervention, within a global industry structuring resource allocations. This attention to political economy resonates with a neoliberal ideology, building from earlier models of modernization. Political economy also helps guide the next discussion of communication, arguing for a critical communication approach to the study of development. As a field of study, political economy foregrounds "the power relations, that mutually constitute the production, distribution, and consumption of resources, including communication resources" (Mosco, 2009, p. 2). The political economy of development, then, building from this foundation, recognizes the power relations among agents engaged in the production and distribution of resources committed to the project of development.

The following section considers the role of feminist critique in connection to research on development as well as studies of communication. Feminist scholarship offers a valuable approach in understanding the importance of power relations, embedded in structures and norms, that limit development intervention and the possibilities for communication in approaching more meaningful work toward social justice.

Development

Development as narrative

Global development as an industry distributes resources from networks of wealthy institutions toward their approved recipient agencies on behalf of perceived publics. The narrative guiding the development industry begins with the recognition and framing of problems that can be solved through strategic intervention, feasibly funded and implemented by partner agencies, with the power to assert their institutional missions and their strategic visions. The projected purpose is to act to promote a public good, conceptualized beyond the institutional parameters of the acting agencies. This goal to benefit people outside of the donor community is critical in differentiating "development" as strategic social change, with a mission to improve the conditions not just of the individual or organization funding the intervention, but also of a broader community. What defines public benefit, and how best to achieve social change toward that benefit, is contingent upon narratives of development that structure the allocation of resources as well as the articulation of the nature of the social change process, the problem and its solution, and the people expected to receive the benefit.

Dominant narratives of development still rely on modernization as a foundational paradigm, even though for decades scholars have critiqued this framework through critical analysis of national dependencies and growing inequalities, pointing out the elitist and patriarchal assumptions made, and the lack of more open structures for participatory decision making. But the idea that nations, through their receipt of foreign aid, channeled in appropriate directions with the blessing of their donors, can improve the conditions of their citizens through strategic planning and targeted intervention relies on the expectation of modernization. Through the use of technology and the process of bureaucratic management, modernization offers a vision of how serious development problems can be solved.

The global narrative of development has been challenged not only by critical academics, but also from an entirely different angle by private agencies. The Narrative Project, designed to promote a positive message about development progress, has recently been initiated by the Bill & Melinda Gates Foundation along with partner agencies including Bond, Care, Comic Relief, DSW, The Global Poverty Project, InterAction, ONE, Oxfam, Path, Results, Save the Children, US Global Leadership Coalition, United Nations Foundation, and Welt Hunger Hilfe, which together are responsible for billions of dollars in development programming (Wilkie, 2014). Scott (2014), Director of Global Brand and Innovation at the Bill & Melinda Gates Foundation, explains that having witnessed negative attitudes through public opinion research in the US, the UK, France, and Germany, development agencies have realized that they need to "improve [the] public perception of development," countering the idea that "aid is wasted."

Two types of goals appear to be operating in this project. The first goal is to change public perceptions to support development intervention. Bilateral and private agencies are increasingly concerned with their public relations, feeling the need to justify their institutional survival by projecting the idea that they are not only "doing good," but doing it well (Kremer et al., 2009). The critical point here is that these institutions feel a need to show donor communities that they are worthwhile (Pamment, 2015). The desperate need for optimism promoted through the Gates Foundation resonates with a rather American predisposition to cloak serious concerns with layers of optimism, whether the issue is cancer or poverty (Ehrenreich, 2010). These discussions of changing the narrative declare that progress has been made, but more could be done to demonstrate actual documentation.

While the goal of this public relations intervention may be to change attitudes among donor country citizens, another goal, less well publicized but reportedly included in an internal memo, is to change the wording used in development narratives (Wilkie, 2014). Specifically, the project suggests that instead of calling people "poor" we "use terms that invoke dignity and pride." Moreover,

> The project also recommends that groups not "position donor countries, celebrities or NGOs as heroic providers of benefits and solutions for poor people." This could be difficult for groups like ONE, the charity synonymous with global superstar Bono and his band U2, as well as for the Bill and Melinda Gates Foundation, through which Microsoft founder Bill Gates funds highly publicized global health and development projects.
>
> (Wilkie, 2014)

This resolution would indeed change the development narrative in important ways, given the problematic articulation of Western, white (as well as single, heterosexual) men as heroes in relation to women of color as victims in the global South. But there may also be room for some concern here that along with this strategic shift in language is a specific interest of Bill and Melinda Gates, voiced in their videos on the narrative project, that we no longer have "poor countries" by 2035.

Critics of development models that focus on aid as a primary mechanism for resource distribution suggest that broader concerns with inequities and social justice are neglected. It is not just the language that needs to be changed, but also the way in which development institutions engage in strategic intervention (Dutta, 2011; Hickel, 2014; Quarry

& Rameriz, 2009; Thomas & van de Fliert, 2015; Wilkie, 2014). The argument presented in this book is that the language used in discourses about development helps to guide strategies, and that to promote significant shifts in development intervention we need an accountability that not only references better rhetoric but also builds on thoughtful evidence.

On a global scale, we can understand development as an industry enabled by an extensive network of organizations, including bilateral and multilateral donors, partnering with nongovernmental organizations (NGOs), foundations, corporations, individuals, and at times, civil society organizations (CSOs). Narrowing our focus, we can consider development strategies in terms of approaches to particular types of constructed problems, whether in health, poverty, education, gender, or sustainability, for example. Moving to an even more concrete level, we can explore strategic interventions, as well as their constructed assessments. These groups of interventions call into play particular narratives in justifying their focus, as well as their own ability to solve these problems.

Critics of development discourse raise concerns that these narratives tend to be asserted as common sense, yet through their articulation narrow the potential ways in which one might consider engaging in social change processes. Escobar (1995) offers an insightful critique of the managerial approaches taken by prominent development institutions, such as the World Bank. Mitchell (1991) shares this concern that the narratives of development, particularly when applied to visions of Egypt's development problems, attribute the conditions of poverty in some countries to their having too little arable land for too many people, rather than considering the many other possible ways of understanding national economic and human conditions. The implications of these dominant narratives in development are particularly problematic when situated within corporate frameworks, demonstrated in Richey and Ponte's *Brand Aid* (2011). How gender becomes articulated in this narrative will be described later in this chapter in the section entitled "Gender" (Cornwall, 2007). The importance of the development narrative is manifest in how the industry structures resources and engages in intervention (Nederveen Pieterse, 2001).

Whereas modernization emphasizes national intervention, funded through foreign sources that seem invisible in these narratives, situating development as an industry within a global network recognizes the international and transnational conditions of organizational networks, social movement practices, and climate concerns. Increasing attention to the prominent role of transnational social movements and activist networks offers an important way of understanding strategic resistance to dominant development, military, and other institutions actively engaged in managing publics. But while the ability of groups to mobilize across national boundaries enables particular moments of resistance, globalization trends, discussed in the next section, attract competing forces able to unite in promoting their own abilities to control ideologies and structure resources.

Modernization theories, particularly those promoted by US scholars such as Lerner, Schramm, and Rogers, "emphasize the role of the media in its particular vision of economic and social development," becoming known for "technological determinism and the omission of practically any interest in the power relations that shape the terms of relationships between rich and poor nations and the multilayered class relations between and within them" (Mosco, 2009, p. 8). Mosco believes that the "developmentalism" projected by "elite" and influential academics is more than an apology for capitalism, projecting a more encompassing hegemonic ideology that positions the US as caring about people in other nations (p. 98). What was once labeled modernization has transformed into a "neoliberal orthodoxy, which insists that developing countries take a market-based approach with as little government intervention as possible" (Mosco, 2009, p. 9).

Global elites benefiting from an increasingly integrated capitalist market across national boundaries are able to justify their dominance through neoliberal narratives. Both modernization and neoliberal approaches to development focus on individuals as the central actors in social change, but the former grew out of frameworks justifying national policies and programs supporting development, whereas the latter privileges private agencies and individuals in social change. Neoliberalism builds from pluralist and liberal political theories that assume individuals have equal opportunities to participate and engage in their communities and countries. In this framework, public policies are designed to encourage individuals to earn money and to purchase goods through their participation in formal market economies. Given the globalization of market economies, this approach intends for its owners, managers, laborers, entrepreneurs, and consumers to become integrated in a global network. As a model of social change, neoliberal development privileges individuals as entrepreneurs and consumers actively participating in market-based economies. Along these lines, development attention to the "empowerment" of individuals tends to be conceptualized through this structure of global capitalism. How these narratives work to justify some approaches to social change at the expense of others needs to be understood within a framework that positions development as a global industry.

Development as industry

The development industry works within a global context, in which dominant development paradigms have been shifting focus gradually from modernization towards neoliberalism (Sparks, 2007). Trends toward a more integrated market-driving global economy, along with the increasing transnational character of global concerns and social movements, engage with the global context in understanding how development is initiated, engaged, and assessed. Conceptualizing power dynamics within this global context highlights a geometry of development, through which global elites are able to control development not through their territorial positioning or membership of a nation-state, but through their access to forms of capital (Shah & Wilkins, 2004; Wilkins, 2008). Within the geometry of development, access to financial capital clearly contributes to the ability of some individuals and groups to accrue disproportionate resources. While historically development had been conceptualized along West–East or North–South axes, the concentration of wealth among elites within countries challenged by dramatic internal inequities, and the emerging economies in countries such as Brazil, India, and China, as well as regions such as the Arab Gulf, means that contemporary development industries operate in more complex ways, but still within hierarchies of power conceptualized within a global context.

The development industry, like other industries, has witnessed significant shifts brought about by trends toward globalization and privatization. "Globalization" has referenced many different human, resource, and environmental connections; particularly relevant to the development industry is the conceptualization of globalization as a trend toward integrating local, national, and regional economies into broader global markets (Jaggar, 2001; Kang, 2008). This movement toward the global disengages from the national as being the most central actor in directing strategic development. Curran's (2002) reminder that although diverse perspectives on globalization share a conclusion that these processes are "eclipsing the nation," nations "are still key sites of power," responsible for decisions to engage in military conflict, assert national policies, and maintain education, health, and welfare services (pp. 182–183). While national agencies do have key control over regulations that affect citizens and decisions that later impact lives in other countries (Morris & Waisbord, 2001), whether related to environmental conditions, military acts, or migration restrictions, it is their ability to control their own economies that even Curran believes may be eroding in the face of an increasingly integrated global market economy.

As global markets gain in relevance to more local economies, the actions of the World Trade Organization (WTO) and other multilateral agencies become more powerful, with increasing control over decisions made within countries over how best to determine public policies. Recognizing the increasing ability of the WTO to influence national financing and policies – by 2004 it was regulating 97% of world trade (Jaggar, 2001) – the political protests in 1999 in Seattle, and others more recently, have mobilized constituencies across diverse national, demographic, and political communities.

Groups resisting the control of the WTO have a challenge in resisting the dominant neoliberal ideology, which pervades development discourse through projecting individual models of social change as conventional wisdom, with the appearance of being a more humanitarian, less political style of intervention. The most serious trend in the conceptualization of global development relies on this neoliberal understanding (Dutta, 2011; Nederveen Pieterse, 2001). The development industry is supported in its neoliberal approach through the work of the WTO, the International Monetary Fund (IMF) and World Bank, "whose policies support free trade, privatization, deregulation, structural adjustment" (Kang, 2008, p. 360). On a systemic level, elite organizations act in ways that perpetuate their ability to control resources, as opposed to a Rawlsian sense of justice through which decisions are made to promote institutional policies that benefit people more equitably (Kang, 2008; Rawls, 1971). Groups organizing to mobilize resistance against neoliberal globalization through dialogue in the World Social Forum do so by considering how best to promote economic justice, human rights, ecological sustainability, and gender equity (Dahlgren, 2011).

In opposition to development approaches privileging individual empowerment and economic gain, social justice concerns focus on inequalities across groups, provoked through inequities in access to resources. Globalization trends have been dramatically increasing these inequalities, within and across countries, so hiding this as a central focus enables those benefiting from globalization to carry on without major disruption (McLaughlin, 2004; Melkote, 2012; Milanovic, 2011; Sparks, 2007). While inequality has been on the rise, so has the economic value of large corporate agencies, with enough surplus to invest in philanthropic projects on a global scale.

Private donors have become more visible on the stage of global development, even though their proportionate contribution to the development industry is still much smaller than that of bilateral and multilateral agencies (Edwards, 2009). As a broadly conceptualized group of agencies, not accountable to national governments through bilateral or multilateral channels, agencies in the private sector are quite diverse, and political agendas and economic resources range widely among these NGOs, corporations, civic groups, and individuals. Enghel (2015) finds that the rhetoric of beneficial "partnership" between private and public agencies avoids problematic power differences, given that "the ability to initiate and terminate actions lies with the funders at the expense of the citizens named as beneficiaries of initiatives, at times bypassing the governance structures of recipient countries" (p. 15). While the potential for private citizens, corporations, foundations, and other organizations for structural participation has grown, all individuals, communities, and agencies do not have equal opportunities to engage in social change planning, implementation, or assessment. Those with access to capital, able to control material as well as ideological resources, are able to dominate development geometry through perpetuating narratives that resonate with their construction of problems and appropriate solutions.

Access to global financial capital matters in allowing individuals and corporations to establish foundations to structure their philanthropic mission and allocation. Wealthy individuals in the US and other countries with low tax rates have more disposable income with which to donate to charities and establish charitable agencies (Roodman & Standley, 2006). A concentration of a few wealthy individuals, or "philanthrocapitalists," are central actors in global development. Those who applaud philanthrocapitalists welcome any contribution to development assistance given concerns that economic crises have limited the abilities and interests of national governments to invest in their own aid programs or multilateral agencies. Those who would rather see the curtains close on philanthropic performance believe that not all development assistance is equally valuable or works well.

Development assistance can take on many forms, from the type of aid – whether it is a grant or a loan with interest for example – to privileging some purposes over others, and differing dramatically in terms of restrictions on spending. Understanding that development aid involves more than a simple exchange of economic resources, philanthrocapitalism, as one mechanism, embraces a neoliberal narrative that underscores market frameworks as appropriate models for conceptualizing social change (Edwards, 2009). Thomas and van de Fliert (2015) suggest that the very act of trademarking "Communication for Social Change" by a consortium in the US implies a more business-oriented than public service approach, along the lines of "a neo-liberal model of developmentalism" (p. 68).

The neoliberal narrative justifying economic globalization is paramount in understanding the development industry, and will be discussed in more depth later in this chapter. As a structuring narrative, neoliberal globalization then works to justify economic globalization, privileging corporate and private actors in starring roles.

Even bilateral and multilateral donors, funded through governments increasingly affected by economic crises, sing the praises of their corporate partnerships, promoting the idea that private aid could substitute for individual states' responsibilities to protect citizens' welfare. This claim can be overstated, however, given that national contributions to bilateral and multilateral agencies still carry a high proportion of development costs (Kremer et al., 2009).

The political economy of the global development industry

Within the broader field of political economy, this study focuses on the institutions doing the work that perpetuates the development industry. Most directly involved are the development agencies funding, implementing, and assessing development programs, but indirectly government agencies and media industries have the potential to support and challenge the direction of intervention. The institutions funding development have allocative control (Murdock, 2005) over the direction of resources driving development practice. Relative to the importance of structural conditions in contributing to the processes and consequences of development, political economy has yet to attract significant attention in development communication scholarship (Enghel, 2015).

The global development industry is supported through public and private financing, through grants, loans, direct investments, and other resources. Official development assistance represents the most classic form of financial aid, most recently documented at US$ 134.8 billion in 2013, and while it rose slightly by 6% in that year compared to the previous one, it overall maintains a consistent level, and is more often given in the form of direct grants than loans.

Foreign direct investment has been increasing steadily, in amount as well as proportion of overall development financing, as have market-driven bonds and securities, private grants, and individual remittances from migrant workers to their families at home (OECD, 2014). When considering the total amount of external financing distributed to developing countries, development assistance from bilateral donors has actually represented a much smaller proportion in more recent years than it did in the early 2000s. The possibilities for citizens and governments to receive money directly from private contributions, through families, foundations, corporations, and other non-public sources have been steadily increasing with more integrated economic globalization.

Twenty-nine countries are members of the Development Assistance Committee (DAC), bringing together wealthy bilateral donors to assess their strategies and report on their outcomes. This group articulated the formal phrasing "Official Development Assistance" (ODA). Focusing on DAC donor contributions to development assistance, overall ODA has been steadily increasing over the last decade, propelled by increased funding to bilateral and multilateral programs.

While humanitarian program funding has been more consistent within formal ODA, at about 10% since 2008 (Tomlinson, 2014), two features are worth noting. First, according to a 2014 report, there has been an "alarming increase in humanitarian assistance delivered through defense agencies...(such that) US humanitarian space has become dangerous space, with 152 aid workers killed in 2013" (Tomlinson, 2014, p. 165). The second factor in the economics of humanitarian aid is the dramatic increase in funding by private individuals, from US\$ 4.1 billion in 2012 to US\$ 5.6 billion the following year, resulting in one-quarter of all humanitarian aid being dedicated by individuals (Stirk, 2014).

Funding for debt relief varies over time, with proportionately more funding for debt relief granted in 2005 than previously. The dramatic increase in debt relief grants from US\$ 4 billion in 2004 to US\$ 23 billion the very next year can be explained by decisions by the elite group of Paris Club creditors, who are government delegates who have been meeting unofficially and regularly since 1956, when Argentinian delegates flew to Paris to renegotiate their debt payments. This elite group decided to allocate US\$ 14 billion to Iraq and just over US\$ 5 billion to Nigeria in 2005 (World Bank, 2006). Government contributions to multilateral agencies have slightly increased over time, but not nearly as dramatically as those to bilateral aid, controlled by donor governments.

Estimates of the largest bilateral donors are calculated in different ways, with dramatically different results. If donor countries are listed in terms of the absolute amounts given, the top five in 2013 include the US (US\$ 31.5 billion), the UK (US\$ 17.9 billion), Germany (US\$ 14.1 billion), Japan (US\$ 11.8 billion, though for a brief period during better economic times it led this pack), and France (US\$ 11.4 billion).

But when considering how much a country donates in relation to its available resources, as a percentage of its Gross National Income (GNI), we witness a changing of the guard, led by Norway (1.07%), Sweden (1.02%), Luxembourg (1%), Denmark (0.85%), and the Netherlands (0.67%; OECD, 2014). While the US may be the largest donor in terms of absolute amount given, the percentage of its resources devoted to development is only 0.19%. Even this low proportion, though, represents a slight increase from 2012, with more funding for humanitarian and HIV/AIDS measures, countering an overall drop in funding by the US to the poorest countries (11.7%) and to sub-Saharan Africa (2.9%; OECD, 2014).

Financing of global development projects tends to be thought of in terms of specific foreign aid programs, such as those in the fields of health or agriculture. But spending on development infrastructure in foreign countries also includes substantial spending by military institutions, estimated at US$ 1747 billion in 2013, with even more channeled through UN peacekeeping operations, estimated at US$ 8.47 billion in 2014 (UN, 2014). Among other governments, the US channeled its human and financial resources through military programs, exceeding US$ 5.6 billion in 2015, mostly targeting Israel, Pakistan, and Egypt (US Department of State, n.d.). Military financing includes capital expenditures on military (including peacekeeping) forces, foreign government agencies collaborating with the military, as well as programs and projects deemed relevant to military operations (Perlo-Freeman & Solmirano, 2014). In descending order of total amount spent, the countries with the highest military expenditures in 2013 following the US include China, Russia, Saudi Arabia, France, the UK, Germany, Japan, India, South Korea, Italy, Brazil, Australia, Turkey, and the United Arab Emirates (UAE) (Perlo-Freeman & Solmirano, 2014). Many of these countries also contribute to bilateral aid with other countries, thus engaging in international development in multiple capacities.

When asserting that private financing in global development has been growing proportionately, it is worth defining what constitutes this source. Funding not originating in bilateral or multilateral agencies, from private sources, can be "given voluntarily and transferred internationally through formal channels without a profit-making aim" (Henón, 2013, p. 5). Considered separately from ODA, private contributions can be initiated through NGOs, foundations, or corporations, through loans, grants, in-kind services, volunteers, or material products (Henón, 2013). Estimates of the total private annual contribution vary, from an estimate of US$ 58.9 billion by the US Center for Global

Prosperity, to US$ 45.3 billion by Development Initiatives, to US$ 32 billion by the OECD using documentation of private grants originating in DAC countries. Among the organizations that may be termed private sources, NGOs with Civil Society Organizations (CSOs) constitute the bulk of this category (57.8%) by 2011 estimates, followed by corporations (18%), foundations (15.6%), and other private sources (8.6%, Henón, 2013). Among the countries hosting these organizations, the US contributes two-thirds of private assistance (US$ 39.4 billion in 2011), followed by the UK, Germany, Canada, Australia, France, the Netherlands, Switzerland, Japan, and Italy in descending order (Henón, 2013). Within these donor countries, the proportion of private aid given by corporations specifically is the highest among US donors, but notably high as well compared to other countries in Switzerland, the Netherlands, Japan, and France. Private development assistance is growing as well among organizations outside of North America and Europe, particularly from private sources in Saudi Arabia, UAE, India, Turkey, China, South Africa, and Brazil, though the *Development Initiative Report* admits that it is difficult to make accurate estimates given partial data. Overall, private donors are more likely to fund natural disaster relief, humanitarian crises, or communities with cultural or religious connections.

The countries receiving most of the bilateral ODA in 2013 included Egypt, Afghanistan, Vietnam, Myanmar, Ethiopia, Syria, Tanzania, Kenya, Turkey, and Bangladesh. Egypt not only topped this list as attracting the most bilateral aid (US$ 5506 million), but also had the highest GNI per capita, at US$ 3000 in 2012. This distribution does not neatly fit categorizations that classify countries in terms of needs: among the top ten recipients only three (Afghanistan, Ethiopia, and Myanmar) are classified as "fragile, least developed countries," and Turkey is considered an "upper middle-income country" (OECD, 2014). OECD documentation confirms overall patterns that distribution to the poorest of countries may be slowing down while financing of development in middle-income countries is actually increasing (OECD, 2014). Distribution of foreign aid is not necessarily then following a logic of documented need, despite the rhetoric of development as "help."

Development discourse offers a narrative of social change that serves a global elite benefiting from political and economic conditions that enable them to continue to accrue wealth while most people proportionately lose their access to various capitals. Foregrounding the political-economic structures of the industry helps us to understand how neoliberal narratives of development signify roles for institutional intervention. These development interventions also invoke more specific frameworks of social change that guide program interventions. Communication becomes an identified mechanism in the strategic attempt by development agencies to change individuals for the public benefit.

Communication

Development communication has emerged as a field within communication scholarship that historically has highlighted communication technologies and processes as being integral to strategic social change, and is currently known in the development industry as "C4D." The field of development communication is most widely known, within prominent development institutions as well as many scholarly homes, for conceptualizing communication, as content, technology, and process, for the purposes of development.

Critics of development, though, understand communication as a structuring narrative about development (Wilkins & Mody, 2001). Critical approaches to development have been supported by interdisciplinary work from scholars in political economy, communication, anthropology, geography, and other academic fields. Critical scholarship foregrounds communication as a discursive strategy used to explain and justify development narratives.

More recent attention to the political economy of development builds from political-economic research in the field of communication, recognizing the role global communications industries play in creating wealth and celebrity that contributes to development discourse. Attention to the global political economy reveals the importance of understanding communication as an industry in itself. Global film, television, gaming, social media, news, and other transnational media productions enable individuals to gain resources, opening the door to their inclusion in a global elite able to benefit from a neoliberal narrative.

Communication becomes relevant in this work as a perceived vehicle for social change, as a discourse justifying social change intervention, and as a global industry. These three conceptualizations of how communication relates to development strategies, discourses, and resources guide analyses in this project.

Role of communication in development narrative (C4D)

Development incorporates communication technologies and processes in intervention through the strategic creation of content, distribution of technologies, teaching of skills to use these technologies, and building of infrastructures that enable the production and distribution of communication. Whereas the US approach focuses on the strategic creation of content in programs using strategies such as social marketing, Japanese programs tend to avoid subsidizing content creation, seeing this as too paternalistic an approach, instead funding the establishment of radio stations and training in computer skills (Wilkins, 2003). Many development programs underscore concerns about access to digital technologies, such as computers with internet capacity and mobile phones.

Communication for development assumes that strategic use of communication processes, media technologies, and targeted messages has the potential to achieve social change. Many of these programs rely on social marketing and entertainment-education to motivate behavior change. Development problems often addressed through these projects can be found in health, agriculture, governance, population, nutrition, sustainable development, and other sectors. Communication intervention for social change may help to mobilize support, create awareness, foster norms, encourage behavior change, influence policy makers, or even shift the frames of social issues.

Emphases on social marketing, as well as the entertainment-education programs that target individuals, build on psychological models of behavior change structuring communication campaigns aimed at persuasion. There is a rich field of assessment demonstrating the potential as well as the limitations of these approaches (Snyder, 2002). However, in this analysis I focus on not just the evidence demonstrated through evaluation research, but also the nature of outcomes that guide determinations of success and failure, as well as the projected conceptualization of communication as a strategy within these programs and their assessments.

Much of the literature in this field celebrates the potential of communication technologies, new and old, to stimulate significant social change. Lee (2011) argues that the UN projects an unquestioning faith in the power of communication technologies by assuming their neutrality, rather than their potential commodification for profit in a global industry. In another study, Lee (2006) demonstrates how focusing on women's consumption of existing content through accessible technologies, rather than their ability to engage in production, devalues women as active participants. In this way, the development industry supports a narrative of development that highlights women as individuals who need to become empowered (and cannot do so themselves), ignoring the context of a global economy. Next, I consider communication as a discourse, followed by attention to communication as a global industry.

Communication as development discourse (C@D)

Critical scholars question how communication about development privileges particular models of social change, structuring narratives of problems and possibilities, as well as who might be appropriate participants and how (Wilkins & Mody, 2001). Nederveen Pieterse (2001) describes this approach to the study of development as a narrative that has "become a standard genre" (p. 13). The narrative of development prefers stories of heroic victory, as hapless victims suffer from villainous exploits. Women serve in this capacity as victims requiring rescue from typically Northern, Western (masculine) agencies. The justification for development as rescue builds on the assertion of devastating conditions as well as necessary remedies possible through development intervention.

Development narratives engage neoliberal agendas when privileging individuals as agents of social change best "helped" through integrating them into global market economies. An alternative social justice narrative would spotlight the structures that limit the possibilities for individuals to meet their basic needs, to lead healthy lives, and to participate as active citizens. Analyses of development as discourse explore the nature of these narratives.

While critical scholarship raises concerns with how development discourse limits possibilities for civic engagement and social change, development institutions themselves are quite aware and strategic about their public relations, caring not only about doing good but also about looking good while doing so (Kremer et al., 2009) This projection of altruism serves the purposes of public diplomacy across nations as well as of political agendas among public and private agencies. Just as celebrities might be engaged in philanthropic pursuits for the perceived public perception, corporations publicize their "social responsibility" actions, while governments promote their humanitarian programs. This is not to say that there would be little benefit to a genuine distribution of resources, but that this public promotion engages a sense of the power of the communicated narrative on behalf of the designated heroes. Development narratives as a subject of study were explored earlier in this chapter in section on "development as industry." Communication as privileged discourse can be understood within a broader political-economic context.

Political economy of global communication

This project builds from a critical political economy approach to communication research, foregrounding the ways in which dominant agencies work to maintain their control over ideological and material resources as competing groups attempt to resist, subvert or avoid participation. As a way of studying control and survival within relationships, as characterized by Chakravartty and Zhao (2008) in their introduction to *Global Communications*, an excellent edited volume on transcultural political economy, this study explores development institutions as agencies working to control development as a practice, with their institutional survival contingent upon their assertion of a neoliberal narrative.

Political economy conceptualizes communication "as a social exchange of meaning whose outcome is the measure or mark of a social relationship," according to Mosco (2009, p. 6), enabling us to theorize a connection between ideology with social practices, accorded status and possibility given particular power relations. Structures of power, differentiating access to resources, result in some groups having more control than others to promote hegemony, as conventional wisdom incorporated into the social practices of individuals and institutions. Building from political sociology, this conceptualization of structuration depicts a process through which individuals and groups create their circumstances as well as work within the limitations of their conditions. While different models of political economy shift in their balance between individual agency and structural limitations (Giddens, 1984), the shared assumption is that political engagement does not follow a pluralistic model with equal opportunities, but rather is severely constrained by geometries of power.

Development can be understood as an industry that operates within global contexts (Miller, 2014). The production and distribution of communication as a global commodity results in high profits for those in control of these industries. Global communication industries, whether packaged as news or popular culture, create wealth and manufacture fame through their production and distribution in global markets. Broadly, the global media market has an estimated worth of almost US$ 2 trillion, with rapid growth predicted (Bond, 2013). Social media and video games are quickly outpacing financial growth from global cinema, with revenue from social media expected to reach US$ 30.1 billion by 2017 (Stringer, 2013), while the video game market, including hardware, software, and games, has already hit US$ 93 billion in 2013 (Gartner, 2013).

Those who own global communication enterprises, such as Bill Gates, Warren Buffet, and Oprah Winfrey, as well as those whose fame is cycled through these productions, such as Bono or Angelina Jolie, use their wealth to participate in development, through contributing financial resources, as well as drawing attention to certain issues or programs. The Gates Foundation is clearly the most prominent private foundation in the development business, investing in global development, global health, and global policy and advocacy along with other philanthropic programs in the US. This foundation has been applauded by some for the amount it has contributed to global development and for its attention to health, but challenged by others for investing in companies with poor records for pollution, child labor, and other offenses (Filler et al., 2007). An investigative journalist adds to these concerns noting that the WTO's Trade-Related Intellectual Property Rights support the work of Gates, but harm African nations by restricting their abilities to purchase medicine at cheaper costs (Palast, 2003).

Alternative approaches to global development financing are emerging with South–South cooperation, having increased recently by 21% (Vaes & Huyse, 2013), though it would be misleading to assume these practices are monolithic, just as it would to believe that bilateral and multilateral agencies, or all NGOs, engage in development in monolithic ways. One mode of South–South cooperation takes the form of bilateral agreements for local currency swaps, avoiding global financial restrictions. Another approach is to negotiate bilateral exchanges in skills and trade. These multilateral agencies, such as BRICS Development Bank and the Asian Infrastructure Bank, bring together a new set of nations into global development. The countries engaging in bilateral assistance, through what is being termed "South–South Assistance," with the highest contributions include China, Saudi Arabia, UAE, Turkey, Brazil, India, Taiwan, South Africa, and Kuwait (Tomlinson, 2014). The top four providers listed here contribute about 90% of all South–South aid, though these numbers do need to be read with caution, given that complicated funding streams may be operating such that countries such as Turkey appear to be large donors but in effect are channeling other funds initiated elsewhere (Pamment, 2015).

Though much work has been done in the years since this initial publication, offering more nuanced theoretical approaches and stronger empirical evidence, it is worth recognizing Herman & Chomsky's (1988) work on the subject of political economy and communication. Their approach to the study of "manufacturing consent" connected structural "filters," such as ownership, advertising and sourcing, to news content concerning the assertion of which victims were worthy and which elections legitimate. While the specifics of how these filters are named and how these processes are expected to work may be contested,

the underlying assumption that those who control the economic contributions and the ability to create and enact policies have an ability
to structure the possibilities for the production and distribution of
particular narratives is crucial.

Enghel (2015) suggests that when considering how a political economic framework contributes to our understanding of development
communication we not only map the structures through which
resources are allocated and agendas prioritized, but also consider the
processes engaged through the development project. Building from
Bateson's (1972) insights disentangling maps from being seen as equivalent to territories, we envision maps as temporary constructions rendered through political struggles over boundaries, both territorial and
symbolic. Illustrating the ways in which a World Bank program in
Indonesia manifests broader power dynamics into the shaping of rules
and strategies, Li's (2007) ethnographic study of this development
project demonstrates the value of studying process. Particularly relevant
to this project is her characterization of participation and empowerment
as constructs asserted through project implementation that resonate
with neoliberal strategies, similar to historical colonial interventions,
benefiting the donor institution.

Political economy is at its heart concerned with power relations, particularly as a way of understanding inequities. Gender is one of many
conditions that allows us to understand explanations for and manifestations of these inequities. Political-economic approaches are compatible
with feminist research that foregrounds gender as central in our analyses
of how power works (Mosco, 2009, p. 197).

Gender

This project explores the articulation of gender in development discourse, conceptualizing gender as the construction of women and men
in social and political contexts. This conceptualization means that
gendered roles are considered to be more complex than a biological
dichotomization, which is problematic in its limiting categorization
into simplistic dual categories and in its asserting of heteronormative
sexuality. The central concern here is that foregrounding women in
development runs the risk of losing sight of power dynamics, in which
men are central actors. It is not that women do not deserve attention,
but that our understanding of social dynamics means that men and
women, and the potential intersections across and complexities within
these broadly based categories, need to be understood as structuring

potential for power relations within specific contexts. Gender is not just a social construction, but is necessarily linked to the attribution of and control over resources.

This project situates its approach to critical development scholarship within feminist critiques. This critical approach is rooted in concerns with differences in power, particularly gendered but necessarily connected with material resources and social capital (Baaz, 2005). Feminist concerns begin with a recognition of the patriarchal nature of development discourse, understanding patriarchy as a hierarchical relationship, which allows men to dominate women structurally, materially, and socially (Hartmann, 2004). This narrative will be discussed in relation to political-economic understandings of gender and development.

Gender in development discourse

The narrative guiding discussions of how women and gender appear historically in development discourse begins with the absence of either in US development frameworks guided by modernization in the years following World War II, as global divisions into nations were structured by the victorious, and development donors became more actively engaged in global intervention. The years in which bilateral and multilateral institutions were established focused on economic recovery following years of historical violence, administered by national governments and funded through development agencies. Over time, women became visible, though lacking voice. Subsequently women began to appear in their connection to men, through the lens of complex distinctions in relation to their access to resources depending on class, ethnicity, and other conditions of marginality.

The recognition of women's roles in development, characterized as Women in Development (WID) within development discourse, marked a critical juncture, moving from epistemological denial of women's contributions to a stronger representation in development narratives. That women's roles were more often relegated to being passive subjects or targeted objects of development intervention became a common criticism among feminist scholars, though Boserup's (1970) early attention to women as being actively involved in agricultural production offers a more engaged characterization. Her work was important in supporting an argument that development programs did not offer uniformly positive benefits, though in bringing visibility to women significant issues were avoided (Peterson, 2005). When focusing on individuals as being responsible for problems as well as solutions, development frameworks work within the WID paradigm, as opposed to conceptualizations of development more broadly constructed. What concerned feminist academics, though, was not just the limited representations of women, but, even more problematically, the absence of gender within the development narrative.

Women became part of development discourse on a formal global platform in the UN Decade for Women 1975–1985, and again with the Fourth World Conference on Women in Beijing in 1995 (Prügl & Meyer, 1999). Prügl and Meyer (1999) describe women actively shaping international agendas through their institutional work creating these events and through their intentional focus on language, shifting the emphasis from women alone to gender equality. This decade moved women from being invisible to visible, but suffered from a trivialization in mediated discourse (Gallagher, 2011).

The critical assertion within concerns with Gender and Development, known by the acronym GAD in development discourse, is that development is challenged by power differences between men and women in areas targeted for intervention. In his 2001 publication, Nederveen Pieterse writes of gender as a prominent theme in development agendas, along with "empowerment" as "ubiquitous in development management" (p. 14). While over time, the term "gender" began to appear in industry as well as academic discussions of development, it would be inaccurate to believe this shift entirely replaced WID, featuring women without men or as challenged by power dynamics.

Foregrounding power as the prominent feature marked a trend among some global feminists concerned with the broader contexts of marginality, contributing to women's oppression particularly when denied opportunities given social class, ethnicity, or other marginalized identities (Chua et al., 2000; Luthra, 1996; Mohanty, 1991a; 1991b; Sreberny-Mohammadi, 1996; Steeves, 1993). Gender-based oppression becomes accentuated through the lens of poverty and racialized inequalities. Dutta (2011) reminds us that these "structural inequities are deeply embedded in human experiences, rendering them natural and invisible," which then limits our potential for dialogue (p. 174). What McMichael (2004) refers to as the "racist legacy of colonialism" (p. 15) lives on in dominant discourses of civilization as ideal and of development as a necessary strategy. Blaming individuals for failure to modernize through the constraints of their "traditional culture," the "fictions of modernization rhyme well with Orientalism" (Nederveen Pieterse, 2001, p. 21). Feminist critiques remind us of the centrality of power in understanding gender differences, necessarily connecting these inequities to issues of race, ethnicity, and other cultural differences that demarcate those who serve as development donors from others targeted for intervention.

Cornwall (2007) adds additional layers of complexity in her insightful reflections on the imposition of "Western" assumptions about gender onto development practice in other cultural settings. Her discussion in collaboration with Harrison and Whitehead (2008) questions the

> narratives of gender and development policy as both heroines and victims: heroic in their capacities for struggle, in the steadfastness with which they carry the burdens of gender disadvantage and in their exercise of autonomy; victims as those with curtailed choices, a triple work burden and on the receiving end of male oppression and violence. (p. 3)

This critical work contributes to research agendas that highlight the politics of development discourse (Escobar, 1995), attempting to problematize more monolithic articulations of social change.

In relation to development, feminist scholars raise concerns with the lack of attention to gender, an oversimplification of women's interests, as well as an objectification of women as victims of circumstance. This objectification can be connected with commodification of women, through asserting their value as a way of promoting market-driven consumption, as well as with controlling women's sexuality and fertility, through privileging women's value as human vehicles of reproduction (Calás & Smircich, 1996; Chua et al., 2000; Meyer & Prügl, 1999; Mohanty, 1991b). Peterson (2005) connects this objectification of women, as opposed to constructions of them as strong, independent, competent agents, within globalizing economies in which geopolitical elites govern in their own interests.

These concerns are raised when development narratives assert women as victims or objects, in subservient and passive roles (Hegde, 1996; Mohanty, 1991a; 1991b; Shome, 1996; Wilkins, 2005). Moving to envisioning women with more active roles in development can become part of a participatory approach when programs recognize power differences within communities, rather than idealizing participation as a universally engaged process. But in the moments when women do become constructed in more active ways, a neoliberal narrative constrains their potential, highlighting women as individual entrepreneurs and consumers.

Building on a neoliberal narrative of development that privileges individuals as central actors in social change, women are conceptualized as actively engaged individuals who participate in free markets as consumers or as small-scale entrepreneurs. Carrying this refrain of neoliberalism further, women become visible without attention to the contexts through which gendered differences in access to resources and appropriation of legal rights matter. Women's issues become those of the individual, striving to improve her family's health and economic situation, devoid of politics or history.

Privileging gender, in terms of the contextual differences that structure women's and men's circumstances, over women in this discourse becomes more possible in a social justice narrative of development. Whereas success within a neoliberal approach is measured in terms of individual achievement, success in a social justice framework would consider resolving inequities across gender, along with other groups relevant in particular contexts. The movement to a neoliberal approach may move women from merely being envisioned, to actively creating visions, but the parameters of women's engagement are tightly controlled. The agencies that benefit from these tightly structured parameters are those that hold allocative control within the political economy of the development industry (Murdock, 2005).

Gender in neoliberal development

While a neoliberal narrative highlights individual female empowerment, attention to gender demands a comprehensive justice narrative that spotlights inequalities. And it is these inequalities across gender that have not improved. Jaggar (2001) concludes, after careful analysis, that globalization is indeed not good for most women, emphasizing problematic aspects of neoliberal approaches (p. 298). One of the consequences of neoliberal development is public cutbacks in social programs that had benefited women and those in poverty. Against the dominant neoliberal attention to women as individuals, Jaggar supports women's activist movements' work to promote the right to education, employment, and health services.

The problem with the assertion of individual empowerment within the neoliberal paradigm is that poor women are then blamed for their circumstances, rather than understanding the broader economic environment in which one loan may require several others to pay off, or the social world in which domestic violence increases with women's participation in microenterprise. Batliwala and Dhanraj (2004) describe the "neo-liberal rules for the new woman citizen" observed in their own assessments of a community in India:

to improve your household's economic condition, participate in local community development (if you have the time), help build and run local (apolitical) institutions like the self-help group; by then, you should have no political or physical energy left to challenge this paradigm. These rules sustain a sort of depoliticised activism at the local level – one that inherently does not build upward momentum. (p. 4)

They raise an important link between the unfair distributions not only across nations but also between genders, particularly harming women in the global South (Batliwala & Dhanraj, 2004). While more women may be working, their employment circumstances are detrimental, with low pay and unsafe working conditions, perpetuated by lack of union activism or protective policies. Focusing on women as individuals relegates their vulnerabilities to individual responsibilities rather than allowing opportunities for collective movements or organized unions to structure safer conditions and fair compensation.

Against the potential raised with global recognition of women and gender in development, Runyan (1999) questions how dominant neoliberal frames undermine feminist concerns. She notes the way in which free-market capitalism, assumed to be a Western "triumph," structures women's roles to their use of technologies and their participation as entrepreneurs. Gallagher (2011) offers an insightful critique of a "neoliberal vocabulary" that focuses women's interests in terms of individual choice, empowerment, and personal freedom. She cites Susanna George in determining women's empowerment to be "indispensable to a vocabulary that has been institutionalized ... related to [the] neoliberal, market-based globalization agenda of [the] world elite" (p. 137). Women hold a rather narrow ability to control their sexual assertiveness and consumption choices in this neoliberal narrative.

Social justice as a narrative, like that of development and social change, bridges academic disciplines as well as theories with practice, with the intention of improving the lives of marginalized communities (Jansen, 2011). The difference, however, is that attention to social justice recognizes politics and values as integrally connected to programs and research (Jansen, 2011), centralizing an ethics of justice intended to guide visions and assessment. Rawls' (1971) theory of justice serves as a classic reference in conceptualizations of moral justice in guiding policies and programs.

Gender emerges as one component in this framework, among other distinctions of marginality and dominance given connection with groups in power. In contrast to neoliberal models of empowerment, social justice frameworks would point our attention to questioning the consequences of structural adjustment policies and exploited labor for women's lives (Runyan, 1999) or how more significant social transformation might be inspired (Gallagher, 2011, p. 140).

Cognizant of the critical distinction raised by Nancy Fraser, separating feminism motivating a transnational political movement from feminism as a discourse, Gallagher (2011) situates feminism as one part of a broader, heterogeneous movement for social justice, working against a dominant foundation of neoliberal capitalism in a global context (p. 133). Kang (2008) proposes a transnational feminist approach to global justice highlighting "processes of globalization [that] have generated transnationalized socio-economic units as ontological conditions of justice, and in such conditions, transnational women's collectivities are viewed as agents of global justice" (p. 359). Everett and Charlton (2014) juxtapose the potential of a global justice movement with the MDGs strategy, appreciating the Goals' recognition of gender and poverty as significant yet concerned with a narrow vision of empowerment that privileges education at the expense of political and economic power. In contrast, global justice as a framework would be "organized to confront the inequalities created or exacerbated by neoliberal globalization" (Everett & Charlton, 2014, p. 65).

Both neoliberal and social justice narratives work within global contexts. Whereas a neoliberal narrative serves hegemonic purposes in perpetuating existing power structures, a social justice narrative challenges those with political power resting on economic resources.

Political economy of gender and development

Feminist critiques intersect with political economy research when gender is understood as constructed and asserted given differences in power. Mosco (2009) warns us against essentialism, reducing our understanding of social relations to that of class or gender, in favor of recognizing the combinations of identities and positions that result in our ability to navigate within our communities (p. 17). Global feminist researchers concerned with development agree that it is not just gender, but rather how gendered norms contribute to other conditions of marginality, in class, ethnicity, orientation, and other markers of identities, that create problematic conditions limiting women's and men's potential.

Referencing power dynamics, the study of political economy needs to recognize gender as a central condition, shaping the production and distribution of knowledge and commodities (Lee, 2006; Sreberny, 1996).

Feminist approaches have much to contribute to political economy, which may be recognizing "women" as a critical category in analysis but not doing enough to understand "gender" as a central condition with hierarchical implications, "privileging that which is masculinised and devalorising that which is feminised" (Peterson, 2005, p. 499). Particularly relevant in this study is Peterson's (2005) discussion of how gendered constructions of value become articulated through knowledge production and distribution, within what she refers to as a gendered political economy of globalization, dominated by neoliberal policies that support liberalization and privatization. Structural adjustment programs, justified through a Washington consensus approach to development that builds on these neoliberal principles, have been particularly harmful to women (Everett & Charlton, 2014). McLaughlin (2004) refers to an "ascending neoliberal economic orthodoxy" (p. 156) in her discussion of how globalizing capitalist economies work to restructure public spheres through excluding marginalized groups such as women. She argues that our concern should not be in making women more visible through mainstreaming into processes of globalization, but instead in struggling against gender inequality and injustice.

Feminist approaches to political economy underscore the need to recognize the potential exploitation of women through processes such as the privatization of public services and the lack of legitimation for unpaid labor (Mosco, 2009, p. 58). Conventional wisdom about what counts as productive work and political engagement is reinforced through the assertion of these hegemonic discourses, which privilege neoliberal principles of politics and economics as well as patriarchal assumptions. It is the link between neoliberal approaches and patriarchal assumptions that strengthens the broader argument that groups in power have the ability to control hegemony.

Hegemony here is understood to represent not just an ideological approach, but a broader sense of discourse situated within political and economic conditions, enabling groups in power to maintain their status through the manufacturing of consent rather than through coercion (Herman & Chomsky, 1988; Mosco, 2009, p. 207). Given that this process of manufacturing consent offers a dynamic landscape in which there is potential to shift who has access to sources of capital, there is potential for resistance, through offering directly competing or alternative narratives.

Focusing on institutional practices articulated through discourse, political economy helps us understand how gendered dynamics contribute to problems with the development project, along with the centrality of the global North, of corporate actors, and of wealthy national governments (Lee, 2011). Although the UN has expanded its development mission to focus on "human" dimensions, a welcome alternative to sole reliance on GNP, Lee argues that the programmatic implications work to expand choices for those who are poor, but not to transform the power relations that create stark differences between wealth and poverty.

Feminist critiques of mainstream development enterprises emphasize the patriarchal nature of discourse that privileges men's roles over those of women (Wilkins, 2007). Part of the problem lies in development approaches that subjugate women as passive targets of strategic communication campaigns, constructed as participants when contributions are valued in the service of imperialism, patriarchy, and capitalism. Toward imperialism, women become a prominent part of the justification for military intervention in their role as victims in need of a savior; toward patriarchy, women become targeted in population and nutrition programs as conduits for reproducing and feeding new generations; and toward capitalism, women become relegated to small-scale entrepreneurial microlending schemes within the confines of the capitalist market.

At least in name, gender is increasingly attractive to donors. A recent OECD report documents development activity that addresses "gender equality" as a "principal" or a "significant objective." For it to reach the status of principle objective, programs must be explicitly attempting to promote "gender equality;" but if the objective is not primarily about gender equality, the program is rated significant (OECD, 2012). Using these criteria, OECD estimates that in 2013, US$ 5383.92 million was allocated for activities that included gender equality and women's health as principal components.

The concentration of funding for gender equality and women's health originates in bilateral agencies from the US, Canada, the UK, Sweden, and the Netherlands.

When considering the additional US$ 24,455.21 million spent on projects with significant but not primary attention to gender equality, funding comes mostly from the UK and Germany, followed by the US, the European Union, and Sweden. Gender equality and women's health include a broad range of subjects, including reproductive health. In 2013, gross disbursements by DAC members amounted to US$ 990 million to aid projects whose *principal objectives* targeted population policy/programs and reproductive health, which is almost one-fifth of funding for all programs in gender equality; DAC members disbursed

US$ 1506.89 million to programs with *significant objectives* targeting population policy/programs and reproductive health (6% of all gender programs).

The countries attracting the most global funding for programs with principal objectives devoted to women and gender begin with Kenya (US$ 299.49 million), with more than all funding for the Middle East combined (at US$ 177.63), followed by Mali, Afghanistan, Ethiopia, and the Democratic Republic of the Congo (OECD 2013).

Countries rated though as having the greatest gender inequality include Niger, Chad, Afghanistan, Mali, and the Democratic Republic of Congo (UNDP, 2014). The countries receiving the most funding directly focusing on gender equality, estimated in 2010, include Afghanistan, India, Indonesia, Vietnam, Iraq, Pakistan, China, Kenya, West Bank/Gaza, and Tanzania, in descending order (OECD, 2012). The areas receiving proportionately the most bilateral funding in gender include education (21%), government and civil society (20%), and health, emphasizing population and reproductive health (19%; OECD, 2012). Microenterprise, another dominant approach to women's issues in development, is funded largely through NGOs and through banking schemes, representing a billion-dollar industry with high rates of return: in 2012 estimates based on documentation from more than 1000 institutions determined that US$ 81.5 billion in loans were granted to 91.4 million low-income clients (Knaute, 2014). OECD (2012) demonstrates the growth of funding for gender in development activities in the last decade, with the most prominent areas in 2012 being health (US$ 6.3 billion), governance and security (US$ 5.8 billion), and education (US$ 4.6 billion).

The Association for Women's Rights in Development (AWID) conducted extensive research, published in 2013, mapping the changing landscape of agencies engaged in international development for women and girls. Their assessment of 170 initiatives between 2005 and 2020 concluded that over this time period US$ 14.6 billion was committed to this focus (Miller et al., 2013). Their assessment charts the types of donors engaged in this work, finding many partnerships across agencies: not considering these as mutually exclusive then, NGOs (63%) and corporations (60%) feature prominently as donors, whereas government agencies (37%) and private foundations (32%) figure in about one-third of these programs. Also included as donors are women's organizations (27%), multilateral agencies (22%), academic institutions (21%), family foundations (19%), corporate foundations (15% for established and 14% for newer agencies), private individuals (8%), microfinance schemes (8%), celebrities (5%), media (4%), and crowdsourcing (1%). While this analysis is not representative of all funding devoted to gender, this consideration of current donors participating in contemporary programs for women and girls offers critical highlights of the importance of profit-driven agencies and wealthy individuals in an industry conventionally thought of in terms of bilateral and multilateral aid. While government agencies engaged in foreign assistance still contribute proportionately more to international development, global development, funded outside of national relationships and across national boundaries, feature those agencies and individuals benefiting from globalization.

Based on their documentation of these studied initiatives, AWID concludes that the most prominent theme (35%) is women's economic empowerment and entrepreneurship, followed by women's leadership and empowerment (25%). Education for women and girls is also quite visible (21%), as is attention to public health (19%), maternal health (18%), and sexual/reproductive health (18%). Important to this study is the additional importance granted to media, technology, and communication issues for women (15%). Women's rights (14%) and violence against women and girls (11%) were also documented as themes. In this project, I explore in more depth how these themes have been articulated in development discourse.

Neoliberal globalization as development discourse

The analytic approach to this project engages critical analysis of neoliberal globalization as a structuring narrative in development discourse. To explore this narrative as serving hegemonic purposes as an assertion of a neoliberal ideology, I consider the nature of public discourse in connection with political economic conditions in contexts of development intervention and assessment in particular regions.

The philosophical foundation of this work is rooted in understanding our reality as politically constructed, not simply socially constructed as suggested in classic work by Berger and Luckmann (1967). Building from the idea that we not only create our worlds through language (Rorty, 1979; Wittgenstein, 1958), but also given our particular positions in society (Hall, 1996), it is the institutional production and assertion of knowledge (Dahlgren, 2011; Said, 1971) that demands our attention. Understanding media as a contested site for the articulation of knowledge underscores critical communication theory relevant to the analysis proposed here. Before describing the specific case studies considered in this analysis, I offer brief articulations of key concepts framing this study.

Rooted in critical approaches to communication theories and critical realist methodologies, this study foregrounds discourse as an articulation of practice (Laclau & Mouffe, 2001; Phelan & Dahlberg, 2011), relevant here as a way of understanding development. Discourse can be seen as an "epistemology," emerging from a politically situated social construction of knowledge, portrayed as conventional wisdom (Nederveen Pieterse, 2001, p. 13). More specifically in this study, I borrow from Thomas and van de Fliert's (2015) concern with communication theories for social change as "epistemological understanding(s) of why and how a communication intervention will result in the required change" (p. 9). These insightful scholars agree that studies of discourse, particularly as epistemologies, need to be situated in terms of power dynamics, structuring the production and distribution of knowledge (Nederveen Pieterse, 2001; Thomas & van de Fliert, 2015). In their classic text explaining discourse analysis, Phillips and Hardy (2002) describe discourse as a set of related texts and practices in context that constitute our reality (p. 3).

Discursive practice, inherently political (Dahlberg, 2011), operates as a form of mediation, such that representation is best "understood as constitutive, rather than merely reflective, of social practice" (Phelan & Dahlberg, 2011, p. 5). This representation in the specific instance is constitutive of a broader ideology, asserted and resisted through hegemonic processes. Through discursive analysis, we "explore how the socially produced ideas and objects that populate the world were created in the first place and how they are maintained and held in place over time" (Phillips & Hardy, 2002, p. 6).

The study of ideology, relevant to this project, can be approached through observations of discursive systems, "such as neoliberalism," when it is "seen as 'all there is,' its hegemonic logic having become so naturalized and sedimented that the political – in other words, the contestable – conditions of its discursive constitution are no longer socially recognized" (Phelan & Dahlberg, 2011, p. 27). Ideology here builds on Hall's (1996) definition as the "mental frameworks – the languages, the concepts, categories, imagery of thought, and the systems of representation – which different classes and social groups deploy in order to make sense of, define, figure out and render intelligible the way society works" (p. 26). Premised on the idea that structuration is dialectical (Giddens, 1984), hegemony, describing the process through which consent to dominant ideologies may be asserted or resisted, is a central feature in critical communication research. Discourse serves as a composite of dialectic relations, given an "inherent materiality of language" (Dahlgren, 2011, p. 225). When narratives become conventional wisdom, meaning difficult to contest, the allocation of political and economic resources follows.

Situating discourse within political economy is critical to understanding development as an industry in a global context. Dahlberg (2011) suggests that "a radical political economy critique of global capitalism, and the media-communication systems supporting it, is very much needed to support critical analysis of how global exploitation is taking place and how counter-hegemonic contestation may be possible" (p. 55). Global capitalism is justified through hegemonic assertion of neoliberal ideology, which not only structures economic activity but also human relationships (Phelan & Dahlberg, 2011).

Neoliberal ideologies justify global capitalism through specific hegemonic tropes of individualization, entrepreneurship, and consumerism, linked with development success. Phelan and Dahlberg (2011) assert neoliberal capitalism as "still, despite recent speculation about its dissolution, the most hegemonic discourse in existence today" (p. 22). Chakravartty and Zhao (2008) explain neoliberalism "as a political philosophy rooted in a claim that the market is more rational than the state in the redistribution of public resources and is based on a 'return' to individualism animated by the modern notion of consumer sovereignty" (p. 4). In their edited volume offering *Global Perspectives* on *Social Justice and Neoliberalism*, Smith, Stenning, and Willis (2008) agree in their introduction with the concept that neoliberalism serves "as a set of ideas and practices, centred on an increased role for the free market, flexibility in labour markets and a reconfiguration of state welfare activities, has become increasingly predominant across the world, particularly since the mid-1980s" (p. 1). While the chapters included in this book point to the variations in the ways in which neoliberal ideologies structure practices, the overarching sense that privatization offers the best way to organize social relations prevails, with privileging of individuals, entrepreneurship, and empowerment (Smith et al., 2008, p. 3). The problem here is that the media perpetuate "neoliberal capitalist discourse" through focusing on "individuals' strategies, choices, successes, failures, lifestyles and cultures, without serious in-depth questioning of the capitalist system in which these individualistic dispositions are naturalized" (Phelan & Dahlberg, 2011, p. 28). Analyses of development discourse need to engage with this approach, considering not only what narratives privilege, but in doing so, what is missed.

Development intervention in education, population, and microfinance

In order to explore the articulation of gender and of communication in development discourse, I consider three case studies, concerning programs promoting microfinance for women, population, and reproductive health, as well as girls' education. These three subjects are central in prominent discussions of women's empowerment (Kristoff & WuDunn, 2009, p. 246). These issues relate directly to MDGs, strategically guiding interventions and assessments in global development. Within each of these cases, I consider the nature of development conceptualized, the construction of women and gender, and the assertion of communication within frameworks of social change.

Communication is proposed within this study at three different levels: first, as a tool assumed to facilitate social change; second, as a discourse structuring development ideology; and third, as a global industry creating wealth and fame. The dominant C4D model privileges communication as a technology that enables individuals to achieve material and social gain; this role for communication is evidenced in discourse about technologies in programs and assessments of microenterprise. Focusing on communication as a way of structuring discourse about gender underscores concerns with population programs, objectifying women as being of value in terms of potential fertility. Recognizing the profits accrued through global communication industries that contribute to celebrity status draws attention to female celebrities who become donors of girls' schools. While each of these case studies allows a distinct aspect of communication to be highlighted, I consider communication as a discourse, connected with political-economic contexts within each case study.

The next chapter explores the articulation of gender and communication within discourse explaining microenterprise programs in South Asia, particularly Bangladesh, home of the founding Grameen Bank, as well as India, Pakistan, and Nepal. This analysis considers how women's empowerment is featured in public and program narratives, as well as how communications devices, particularly telephones and digital media, are considered as part of these entrepreneurial initiatives. This case concludes by connecting these narratives in program and evaluation descriptions as well as news discussions, with neoliberal features of global capitalism.

Next, I consider how population and reproductive health programs articulate roles for women in development and public discourse.

Population programs assert particular roles for women, as well as a construction of problems and solutions that reflects assumptions about gender, rights, and health. Situating this case study on Egyptian development allows us to consider the particular political and economic dimensions of this country as a prominent recipient of foreign aid, with specific allegiances within the region and in connection to US foreign policy. Moreover, the 1994 International Conference on Population and Development in Cairo was an opportunity for women to be featured as leaders in development, not just as subjects of intervention. What happened with this potential is explored in analysis of news discourse since the conference.

The third case study also offers an opportunity for women to be visualized in more active ways, as wealthy donors and not just development targets. Accruing wealth and fame, through profits in global television, film and music, celebrities Oprah Winfrey, Angelina Jolie, and Madonna have each invested in girls' schools in Africa and Asia. How their contributions have been constructed in public discourse is considered in terms of articulations of gender and development. Neoliberal development offers a familiar refrain in structuring articulations of gender and possibilities for communication.

Analyses of these discourses, on the subjects of microenterprise, population, and education, focus on specific attention to empowerment as a development framework for women; the potential for explicit recognition of gender dynamics in context; and the role of communication in assumed models of social change. Women's empowerment dominates attention in global development interventions devoted to women and gender issues. Analysis of the construction of empowerment concerns not only how development is conceptualized, but also how these narratives resonate with neoliberal approaches justifying economic globalization. The basic argument is that development needs to be understood within particular contexts, and that intervention is limited when focusing on individuals without sufficient recognition of and action to shift norms and policies.

Just as development is considered to be too narrowly conceptualized when foregrounding individuals as agents of change, constructions of women are considered to be necessarily limited without attention to contexts of gender. First, moving women from symbolic annihilation to visibility may have been a critical step historically, but without significant voice, not in solo but working in harmony through collective movements, feminist interests in gender equity cannot be assessed. Even when women have the potential for more visible and vocal roles, as global leaders in development conferences or as wealthy donors to development programs, their significance is challenged given their commodification as well as the perpetuation of gendered stereotypes.

The limited focus on empowerment as development and on roles for women could be improved by enlarging our scope to include normative conditions and policy potential in development intervention. We need to consider gender and other manifestations of power differences. The third beat in this analysis inspires a similar conclusion: instead of conceptualizing communication as merely a technological device, I argue for critical research on communication as discourse and as global industry, creating financial and cultural capitals that allow private citizens and corporations more significant roles in the development industry.

Alternative visions are possible, and evident in historical reviews of development, as well as in popular representations. We have witnessed more active roles and more nuanced characters played by women over time in US popular culture. We have also observed historical shifts in articulations of women, gender, and feminism in development discourse. We recognize that development donors as well have quite varied funding structures, as well as mission statements and ways of engaging in social change. These variations across agencies and shifts over time point to the possibility for resisting dominant neoliberal narratives of development.

The final chapter offers constructive suggestions, rather than being satisfied with deconstructing narratives as a final step. Building on transnational feminist networks, it is possible to imagine how to consider gender equity and inclusion (McLaughlin, 2004). This chapter argues for advocacy, as a way of structuring development along a social justice orientation considering structural and normative conditions. Advocacy can be supported through strong critical research, focused on assessments of social problems in context, rather than evaluations of single programs. It is this need for empirical research, engaged in a different way, which guides the final section of this chapter on accountability.

Accountability appears to be gaining currency as a guiding principle not only in development, but also more broadly in public programs. Critics of this attention to accountability raise concerns with introducing outcome assessments, with quantitative indicators, too early in implementation processes, creating data that could be more artificial than genuine with great risks to people and programs. Rather than seeing accountability as a conservatively political strategy to reduce funding from government agencies for public welfare, I propose accountability within a social justice framework. Many of the initially progressive ideas of development, such as sustainability and participation, have been co-opted over time by the development industry such that ideal interests in long-term global survival or democratic governance based on equal opportunities have been overshadowed by corporate interests in avoiding regulation and political interests in ignoring corruption and injustice. Instead of seeing co-optation by the development industry, I am suggesting that those of us interested in the project of global social justice subvert the meaning of accountability. As Jansen (2011) describes an "ethics of care" bringing together "activists and scholars to engage in ongoing reflection about the challenges, responsibilities, relationships, and processes involved in representing the lives of others" (p. 3), critical research must integrate theoretical work on social justice with the experiences of people engaged in this project. We need to be accountable to our global communities if we are to make significant progress in improving the human condition.

References

Baaz, M. E. (2005). *Paternalism of Partnership: A Postcolonial Reading of Identity in Development Aid*. London: Zed Books.

Bateson, G. (1972). *Steps to an Ecology of Mind*. Chicago: University of Chicago Press.

Batliwala, S. & Dhanraj, D. (2004). Gender myths that instrumentalise women: A view from the Indian frontline. *IDS Bulletin, 35*(4), pp. 11–18.

Berger, P. & Luckmann, T. (1967). *The Social Construction of Reality*. New York: Anchor Books.

Bond, P. (2013). Study: Global media industry poised to top $2 trillion in 2016. *The Hollywood Reporter*. Retrieved from http://www.hollywoodreporter.com/news/study-global-media-industry-poised-562694. 25 February 2015.

Boserup, E. (1970). *Women's Role in Economic Development*. New York: St. Martin's Press.

Calás, M. B. & Smircich, L. (1996). From "the woman's" point of view: Feminist approaches to organization studies. In S. R. Clegg, C. Hardy & W. R. Nord (Eds.), *Handbook of Organization Studies* (pp. 218–257). London: Sage.

Chakravartty, P. & Zhao, Y. (2008). Introduction: Toward a transcultural political economy in global communications. In P. Chakravartty & Y. Zhao (Eds.), *Global Communications: Toward a Transcultural Political Economy* (pp. 1–19). Lanham, MD: Rowman and Littlefield.

Chua, P., Bhavnani, K. & Foran, J. (2000). Women, culture, development: A new paradigm for development studies? *Ethnic and Racial Studies, 23*(5), pp. 820–841.

Cornwall, A. (2007). Buzzwords and fuzzwords: Deconstructing development discourse. *Development in Practice, 17*(4–5), pp. 471–484.

Cornwall, A., Harrison, E. & Whitehead, A. (2008). Gender myths and feminist fables: The struggle for interpretive power in gender and development. In A. Cornwall, E. Harrison & A. Whitehead (Eds.), *Gender Myths and Feminist Fables: The Struggle for Interpretive Power in Gender and Development* (pp. 1–20). Malden, MA: Blackwell Publishing.

Credit Suisse. (October 2014). *Global Wealth Report, 2014.* Zurich, Switzerland: Credit Suisse Research Institute.

Curran, J. (2002). *Media and Power.* New York: Routledge.

Dahlberg, L. (2011). Discourse theory as critical media politics? Five questions. In L. Dahlberg & S. Shelan (Eds.), *Discourse Theory and Critical Media Politics* (pp. 41–63). New York: Palgrave Macmillan.

Dahlgren, P. (2011). Mobilizing discourse theory for critical media politics: Obstacles and potentials. In L. Dahlberg & S. Shelan (Eds.), *Discourse Theory and Critical Media Politics* (pp. 222–249). New York: Palgrave Macmillan.

Dutta, M. J. (2011). *Communicating Social Change: Structure, Culture, and Agency.* New York: Routledge.

Edwards, (2009). Why philanthrocapitalism is not the answer: Private initiatives and international development. In M. Kremer, P. van Lieshout & R. Went (Eds.), *Doing Good or Doing Better: Development Policies in a Globalizing World* (pp. 237–249) Amsterdam: Amsterdam University Press.

Ehrenreich, B. (2010). *Bright-Sided: How Positive Thinking is Undermining America.* New York: Henry Holt & Co.

Enghel, F. (2015). Towards a political economy of communication in development? *Nordicom Review, 36*, pp. 11–24.

Escobar, A. (1995). *Encountering Development: The Making and Unmaking of the Third World.* Princeton, NJ: Princeton University Press.

Everett, J. & Charlton, S. E. M. (2014). *Women Navigating Globalization: Feminist Approaches to Development.* Lanham, MD: Rowman & Littlefield.

Filler, C., Sanders, E. & Dixon, R. (2 January 2007). Dark Cloud over good works of Gates Foundation. *LA Times.* Retrieved from http://www.latimes.com/news/la-na-gatesx07jan07-story.html#page= 1. 15 February 2015.

Forbes. (2014). The world's billionaires. Retrieved from http://www.forbes.com/billionaires/#tab:women_page:2. 25 February 2015.

Gallagher, M. (2011). Feminism and social justice: Challenging the media rhetoric. In S. Curry Jansen, J. Pooley & L. Taub-Pervizpour (Eds.), *Media and Social Justice* (pp. 131–144). New York: Palgrave Macmillan.

Gartner. (2013). Gartner says worldwide video game market to total $93 billion in 2013. *Gartner Press Release.* Retrieved from http://www.gartner.com/newsroom/id/2614915. 25 February 2015.

Giddens, A. (1984). *The Constitution of Society: Outline of a Theory of Structuration.* Berkeley: University of California Press.

Hall, S. (1996). The problem of ideology: Marxism without guarantees. In D. Morley & K. H. Chen (Eds.), *Stuart Hall: Critical Dialogues in Cultural Studies* (pp. 25–46). London: Routledge.

Hartmann, (2004). Towards a definition of patriarchy. In L. Heldke & P. O'Connor (Eds.), *Oppression, Privilege, & Resistance: Theoretical Perspectives on Racism, Sexism, and Heterosexualism* (pp. 143–163). New York: McGraw-Hill.

Hausmann, R., Tyson, L. D. & Zahidi, S. (2011). *The Global Gender Gap Report 2011.* Geneva, Switzerland: World Economic Forum.

Hegde, R. S. (1996). Narratives of silence: Rethinking gender, agency, and power from the communication experiences of battered women in South India. *Communication Studies, 47,* pp. 303–317.

Henón, S. (2013). Measuring private development assistance: Emerging trends and challenges. Available from: http://devinit.org/wp-content/uploads/2014/08/Measuring-private-development-assistance1.pdf. 1 July 2015.

Herman, E. W. & Chomsky, N. (1988). *Manufacturing Consent: The Political Economy of the Mass Media.* New York: Pantheon Books.

Hickel, J. 2014. The death of international development. The development industry needs an overhaul of strategy, not a change of language. *Al Jazeera,* 20 November 2014. Retrieved from http://www.aljazeera.com/indepth/opinion/2014/11/death-international-developmen-2014111991426652285.html. 19 January 2015.

ILO. (2015). *Global Wage Report 2014/15: Wages and Income Inequality.* Geneva: International Labor Organization.

Jaggar, A. M. (2001). Is globalization good for women? *Comparative Literature, 53*(4), pp. 298–314.

Jansen, S. (2011). Media, democracy, human rights, and social justice. In S. C. Jansen, J. Pooley & L. Taub-Pervizpour (Eds.), *Media and Social Justice* (pp. 1–23). New York: Palgrave Macmillan.

Kang, H. R. (2008). Transnational women's collectivities and global justice. *Journal of Social Philosophy, 39*(3), pp. 359–377.

Knaute, M. (2014). A growing sector: microfinance opens the way towards financial inclusion. *Microfinance Barometer 2014/Convergences* (p. 2). Paris: Chevillon Imprimeur.

Kremer, M., van Lieshout, P. & Went, R. (2009). *Doing Good or Doing Better : Development Policies in a Globalizing World.* Amsterdam: Amsterdam University Press.

Kristoff, N. & WuDunn, S. (2009). *Half the Sky: Turning Oppression into Opportunity for Women Worldwide.* New York: Knopf.

Laclau, L. & Mouffe, C. (2001). *Hegemony and Socialist Strategy: Towards a Radical Democratic Politics* (2nd Edn.). London: Verso.

Lee, M. (2006). What's missing in feminist research in new information and communication technologies? *Feminist Media Studies, 6*(2), pp. 191–210.

Lee, M. (2011). A feminist political economic critique of the human development approach to new information and communication technologies. *The International Communication Gazette, 73*(6), pp. 524–538.

Li, Tania Murray. (2007). *The Will to Improve: Governmentality, Development, and the Practice of Politics.* Durham: Duke University Press.

Luthra, R. (1996). International communications instruction with a focus on women. *Journalism and Mass Communication Educator,* Winter, pp. 42–51.

McLaughlin, L. (2004). Feminism and the political economy of transnational public space. *The Sociological Review,* 52, pp. 156–175.

McMichael, P. (2004). *Development and Social Change: A Global Perspective* (3rd Edn.). Thousand Oaks: Pine Forge Press.

Melkote, S. (2012). Development support communication for social justice: An analysis of the role of media and communication in directed social change. In S. Melkote (Ed.), *Development Communication in Directed Social Change: A Reappraisal of Theory and Practice* (pp. 15–38). Singapore: AMIC.

Meyer, M. K. & Prügl, E. (1999). *Gender Politics in Global Governance.* Lanham, MD: Rowman & Littlefield.

Milanovic, B. (2011). More or less: Income inequality has risen over the past quarter-century instead of falling as expected. *Finance & Development,* September, pp. 6–11.

Miller, J., Arutyunova, A. & Clark, C. (2013) New actors, new money, new conversations: A mapping of recent initiatives for women and girls. *Association for Women's Rights in Development (AWID).*

Miller, T. (2014). Globalization and development. In K. Wilkins, T. Tufte & R. Obregon (Eds.), *Handbooks of Development Communication & Social Change* (pp. 20–39). Oxford: Wiley-Blackwell.

Mitchell, T. (1991). *Colonizing Egypt.* Berkeley, CA: University of California Press.

Mohanty, C. T. (1991a). Cartographies of struggle: Third world women and the politics of feminism. In C. T. Mohanty, A. Russo & L. Torres (Eds.), *Third World Women and the Politics of Feminism* (pp. 1–50). Bloomington: Indiana University Press.

Mohanty, C. T. (1991b). Under western eyes: Feminist scholarship and colonial discourses. In C. T. Mohanty, A. Russo & L. Torres (Eds.), *Third World Women and the Politics of Feminism* (pp. 51–80). Bloomington: Indiana University Press.

Morris, N. & Waisbord, S. (2001). *Media and Globalization: Why the State Matters.* Lanham, MD: Rowman and Littlefield.

Mosco, V. (2009). *The Political Economy of Communication* (2nd Edn.). Los Angeles: Sage Publications.

Murdock, G. (2005). Large corporations and the control of the communications industries. In M. Gurevitch, T. Bennett, J. Curran & J. Woollacot (Eds.), *Culture, Society and Media* (pp. 114–147). London: Methuen.

Nederveen Pieterse, J. (2001). *Development Theory: Deconstructions/Reconstructions.* London: Sage Publications.

OECD. (2012). *Aid in Support of Gender Equality and Women's Empowerment: Statistical Overview.* Retrieved from http://www.oecd.org/dac/gender-development/_CRS%20overview%20web.pdf. 13 February 2015.

OECD (2013). *OECD development cooperation report: Mobilising resources for sustainable development.* Available from: http://dx.doi.org/10.1787/dcr-2014-en. 1 August 2015.

OECD. (2014). "Norway", in *Development Co-operation Report 2014: Mobilising Resources for Sustainable Development.* Available from: http://dx.doi.org/10.1787/dcr-2014-47-en. 1 August 2015.

Palast, G. (2003). *Bill Gates: Killing Africans for profit & Mr. Bush's bogus aids offer.* Accessed from: http://www.informationclearinghouse.info/article4103.htm. [1 August 2015].

Pamment, J. (2015). Media influences, ontological transformation & social change: Conceptual overlaps between development communication and public diplomacy, *Communication Theory,* 25(2), pp. 188–207.

Pamment, J. (2015). Personal Communication.

Perlo-Freeman, S. & Solmirano, C. (2014). Stockholm International Peace Research Institute (SIPRI) fact sheet: Trends in world military expenditure. *SIPRI.* Retrieved from http://www.sipri.org/research/armaments/milex/publications.

Peterson, S. V. (2005). How (the meaning of) gender matters in political economy. *New Political Economy, 10*(4), pp. 499–521.

Phelan, S. & Dahlberg, L. (2011). Discourse theory and critical media politics: An introduction. In L. Dahlberg & S. Shelan (Eds.), *Discourse Theory and Critical Media Politics* (pp. 1–40). New York: Palgrave Macmillan.

Phillips, N. & Hardy, C. (2002). *Discourse Analysis: Investigating Processes of Social Construction.* Thousand Oaks: Sage Publications.

Prügl, E. & Meyer, M. K. (1999). Gender politics in global governance. In M. K. Meyer & E. Prügl (Eds.), *Gender Politics in Global Governance* (pp. 3–18). Lanham, MD: Rowman & Littlefield.

Quarry, W. & Rameriz, R. (2009). *Communication for Another Development: Listening Before Telling.* New York: Zed Books.

Rawls, J. (1971). *A Theory of Justice.* Cambridge: Harvard University Press.

Richey, L. & Ponte, S. (2011). *Brand Aid: Shopping Well to Save the World.* Minneapolis: University of Minnesota Press.

Roodman, D. & Standley, S. (2006). Tax policies to promote private charitable giving in DAC countries. *The Center for Global Development Working Paper Number 82.* Retrieved from http://www.cgdev.org/publication/tax-policies-promote-private-charitable-giving-dac-countries-working-paper-82.15 February 2015.

Rorty, R. (1979). *Philosophy in the Mirror of Nature.* Princeton: Princeton University Press.

Runyan, A. S. (1999). Women in the neoliberal "frame." In M. K. Meyer & E. Prügl (Eds.), *Gender Politics in Global Governance* (pp. 210–220) Lanham, MD: Rowman & Littlefield.

Said, E. (1971). *Orientalism.* New York: Vintage.

Scott, T. (2014). Changing the public conversation about global development. *InterAction Forum.* Retrieved from http://www.interaction.org/blog/changing-public-conversation- about-global-development. 28 January 2015.

Shah, H. & Wilkins, K. G. (2004). Reconsidering geometries of development. *Perspectives on Global Development and Technology, 3*(4), pp. 395–416.

Shome, R. (1996). Postcolonial interventions in the rhetorical canon: An "other" view. *Communication Theory, 6*(1), pp. 40–59.

Smith, A., Stenning, A. & Willis, K. (2008) Introduction: Social justice and neoliberalism: Global perspectives. In A. Smith, A. Stenning & K. Willis (Eds.), *Social Justice and Neoliberalism: Global Perspectives* (pp. 1–15). London: Zed Books.

Snyder, L. (2002). Development communication campaigns. In W. B. Gudykunst & Bella Mody (Eds.), *Handbook of International and Intercultural Communication* (pp. 457–478). Thousand Oaks: Sage.

Sparks, C. (2007). *Globalization, Development and the Mass Media.* London: Sage.

Sreberny-Mohammadi, A. (1996). International feminism(s): Engendering debate in international communications. *The Journal of International Communication, 3*(1), pp. 1–3.

Steeves, H. L. (1993). Creating imagined communities: Development communication and the challenge of feminism. *Journal of Communication, 43*(3), pp. 218–229.

Stirk, C. (2014). *Humanitarian Assistance from Non-State Donors: What is it Worth?* Bristol, UK: Development Initiatives.

Stringer, G. (2013). Social media revenue will hit $30.1 billion by 2017. *Accuracast.* Retrieved from http://www.accuracast.com/news/social-media-7471/social-media-revenue-will-hit-2-5-billion-by-2017. 25 February 2015.

Thomas, P. & van de Fliert, E. (2015). *Interrogating the Theory and Practice of Communication for Social Change: The Basis for Renewal.* New York: Palgrave Macmillan.

Tomlinson, B. (2014). *Reality of Aid 2014 Report: Rethinking Partnerships in a Post-2015 World: Towards Equitable, Inclusive and Sustainable Development.* Quezon City, Philippines: IBON International.

United Nations (UN). (2014). *Peacekeeping.* Retrieved from http://www.un.org/en/peacekeeping/resources/statistics/factsheet.shtml. 25 February 2015.

UN. (2015a). *News on Millennium Development Goals.* Retrieved from http://www.un.org/millenniumgoals/. 15 February 2015.

UN. (2015b). *Action 2015.* Retrieved from http://www.un.org/millenniumgoals/beyond2015-news.shtml. 15 February 2015.

UNDP. (2014). *Human Development Reports.* Retrieved from http://hdr.undp.org/en/content/table-4-gender-inequality-index. 13 February 2015.

US Department of State. (2015). *US Department of State: Diplomacy in Action.* Retrieved from http://www.state.gov/t/pm/ppa/sat/c14560.htm.

Vaes, S. & Huyse, H. (2013). New voices on South–South cooperation between emerging powers and Africa: African civil society perspectives. *HIVA-KU Leuven.*

Wilkie, C. (3 September 2014). Internal memo recommends major global charities adopt new outreach strategy. *Huffington Post.* Retrieved from http://www.huffingtonpost.com/2014/09/03/gates-foundation-memo_n_5761990.html. 28 January 2015.

Wilkins, K. (2003). Japanese approaches to development communication. *Keio Communication Review, 25,* pp. 3–21.

Wilkins, K. (2005). Constructing gender across cultural space: Japan's international development programs. *Global Media Journal, 4(6),* Retrieved from http://lass.purduecal.edu/cca/gmj/sp05/gmj-sp05-wilkins.htm.

Wilkins, K. (2007). Confronting the missionary position: The mission of development/The position of women. *Communication for Development and Social Change: A Global Journal, 1(2),* pp. 111–125. 13 February 2015.

Wilkins, K. (2008). Development communication. In W. Donsbach (Ed.), *The International Encyclopedia of Communication* (pp. 1229–1238). Oxford: Wiley-Blackwell.

Wilkins, K. G. & Mody, B. (2001). Reshaping development communication: Developing communication and communicating development. *Communication Theory, 11(4),* pp. 1–11.

Wittgenstein, L. (1958). *Philosophical Investigations.* Oxford: Wiley-Blackwell.

World Bank. (2006). Global development finance: The development potential of surging financial flows. *World Bank.* Retrieved from http://siteresources.worldbank.org/INTGDF2006/Resources/GDF06_complete.pdf. 15 February 2015.

World Bank. (2012). *World Development Report on Gender Equality and Development.* Washington DC: World Bank.

2
Communicating Gender in Microenterprise Development

Microenterprise is hailed as the solution to women's poverty, applauded by agents of the development industry, financial institutions, and public reviews. But what are the consequences of this strategy for the ways in which we understand development itself, for our projections of women's roles in development, and for the consideration of gender dynamics; and how does communication figure in this narrative? This chapter explores these questions through a study of microenterprise programs explicitly focusing on women in the South Asian region, with special attention to known interventions and conditions in Bangladesh, India, Nepal, and Pakistan. I consider the narrative of microenterprise interventions that employ communications as tools to resolve problematic conditions women face as "victims" of poverty, enabled through the "heroic" actions of men administrating formal finance institutions. This analysis is not meant to suggest that women are indeed victims or that men are necessarily heroes, but to consider how gender differentiates roles for women and men in the construction of social change.

While the ways in which this discourse limits the rhetorical possibilities for women and men is of concern, so too is the limited evidence that guides the political and economic choices made by development institutions. In relation to development goals, I consider how success is defined conceptually through these interventions, typically in terms of fighting poverty and promoting empowerment. Understanding how these outcomes are conceptualized then allows us to understand the operationalizations used in evaluations, which guide the method-ological approaches used in document assessment. The nature of the evidence is then considered in the light of broader conditions as well as unintended consequences. This chapter concludes by considering this development agenda as a contribution to neoliberal triumphs, in that through microenterprise, capitalist systems are justified and sustained, with women's roles reduced to those of consumers and small-scale entrepreneurs who perpetuate free-market systems.

In this chapter I consider how the discourse of microenterprise programs implemented in South Asia has constructed the role of communication in social change, specifically in descriptions of telephones, as well as discussing the role of women in development, and in articulations of gender. In analyzing power dynamics across gender differences, assertions of men as heroes in response to women as victims are examined. How microenterprise is proposed as a solution to the problem of development foregrounds this narrative, structuring a plot through which heroic, villainous, and vulnerable characters engage within the setting of poverty in South Asia.

This study considers published works on these programs by development professionals, as well as public discourse. To consider public discourse, this review is limited to global sources identified through two search engines for online sources: the Lexis-Nexis digital news archive and The Communication Initiative Network (comminit.com) archive of program and evaluation descriptions. Key terms were used to find texts published since 1997 on "Grameen" (the Grameen Bank in Bangladesh), "Microenterprise," or Microfinance"; in "Bangladesh," "India," "Pakistan," "Nepal," or "South Asia"; connected with "women" or "gender"; and "phone" or "ICT." Along with published industry discussions, these sources allow analyses of dominant and challenging themes in this discourse. This study of development, gender, and communication as articulated through public discourse is situated within the specific programs engaging microenterprise strategies within the context of development in the region of South Asia.

Development in South Asia

South Asia serves as the setting for the interventions explored in this chapter. The contemporary political history within the region demonstrates the permeability of national boundaries, created and contested over time within a geopolitical spectrum of global, regional, and local interests. Following more than a century of British domination in India, post-World War II political negotiations affirmed India and Pakistan as sovereign nations in 1947. Schramm (1964) and others promoted the idea that national identity could transcend many cultural and linguistic differences in the region. However, internal and regional conflicts continued despite the emergence of these national boundaries.

Among other violent confrontations in the region, war within Pakistan resulted in the establishment of Bangladesh in 1971. Political history in Nepal manifests its own complicated and diverse political constituencies within the country, but these territorial boundaries have remained in place since the 1814–1818 Anglo-Nepalese War, contracted with Britain in a 1923 treaty.

An optimistic World Bank report from 2006, suggesting that the "region will be free of poverty in a few decades" (Devarajan & Nabi, 2006), credited the economic reforms of the 1990s with the economic growth of the South Asian region, recognizing however that comparatively, East Asian economic conditions were faring better. These analysts describe poverty falling by 9–12% in Bangladesh, India, Pakistan, and Nepal from 1990 to 2004. They do lament what they perceive as a lack of integration in trade in the region, as well as corruption, civil conflict, and natural disasters. Although these countries in aggregate may be gaining in resources, inequality has been accelerated (Todhunter, 2012). The differentiation between small groups of wealthy urban elites and the poor majority is also found in Pakistan and other countries in the region.

Even compared to other regions of developing countries, as categorized by the World Bank (World Bank, 2014), the South Asian region has a low Gross National Income (GNI) per capita; its GNI was just US$ 1474 in 2013, not only lower than that of East Asia (US$ 5536) but even lower than that of Sub-Saharan Africa (US$ 1624). This means that the Gross Domestic Product (GDP) of the South Asian region at US$ 2.355 trillion is spread more thinly among its 1.671 billion people, in contrast with a higher population and GDP in East Asia (1.006 billion; US$ 11.41 trillion) and lower population and GDP in Sub-Saharan Africa (936.1 million; US$ 1.592 trillion).

World Bank statistics referring to the South Asian region include not only Bangladesh, India, Pakistan, and Nepal, the countries focused on in this analysis of microenterprise, but also Afghanistan, Bhutan, the Maldives, and Sri Lanka. The former group includes a range of circumstances, from the most populated and wealthiest among the group, India, to the smallest and least wealthy, Nepal. Despite India's relative wealth, it is the country with the most pollution (measured in CO_2), and it has a lower life expectancy at 66 than that of Nepal at 68 or Bangladesh at 70. The country with the smallest proportion of citizens in poverty (12.4%) is Pakistan, compared with 21.9% in India, 25.2% in Nepal and 31.5% in Bangladesh, where fewer rural communities have access to clean water (84%) than in neighboring countries (88–91% in the three other countries noted).

Given that microfinance has been judged "exceptionally successful in parts of Asia," more so than in Africa (Kristof & WuDunn, 2009, p. 191), this project focuses on programs implemented in the South Asian region. Most of the mediated discussion of the microenterprise model as a development approach focuses on the Grameen Bank in Bangladesh, despite the vast replication of this model in the region and in many diverse global settings. With reference to Bangladesh as the initial location of microfinance services in the region, Henry Kissinger, with an insensitively derogatory tone, declared that microfinance had helped a country once branded as a "basketcase" (Wahid & Hannah, 2014). Through the work of the Grameen Bank, Bangladesh hosted a loan portfolio much greater than that of India, and was able "to reduce poverty at a significantly faster rate than other countries in south Asia – including India and Pakistan" (Johnson, 2006).

Having been the site of microfinance initiatives as a development movement, Bangladesh became saturated as a market, with little growth by 2012 given universal access to microfinance services (Chen, 2013). By this time "growth for individual loans to small businesses significantly outpaced traditional smaller microfinance lending to rural women in 2012...a sign of a saturated market and a push into new segments" (Chen, 2013). Moreover, strengthening regulations of microfinance institutions (MFIs) in the country, including capping interest rates to 10%, resulted in almost 50 MFIs losing their licenses (Syminvest, 2014).

More recently India has shifted its regulations, setting interest limits to 10 12% by 2012 in order to stabilize this industry (Chen, 2013). Prior to these regulations "MFIs were charging as high as 40%" (Syminvest, 2013a). Now that this market has stabilized "sky-high returns from the finance industry are history and so is the interest of the so-called venture investors and seed capital providers" (Syminvest, 2013a). The substantial investment in microfinance in India fits the trends toward privatization of financial services as well as communication industries in the country.

Unlike Bangladesh, India has been recognized as one of the fastest growing economies in the world, often referred to in the context of the BRICS, including Brazil, Russia, China, and South Africa (Westhead, 2009; Zakaria, 2008). Although not as strong in economic resources, Bangladesh "pioneered" the microfinance industry, replicated in India with projects offering entrepreneurship as a solution to poverty (Levin, 2007). Although government policy in India has done much to support economic liberalization and privatization toward integration into the global economy (Thomas, 2012a), poverty is still shockingly high, with almost half of the population considered as existing below acceptable living standards (Chakravartty, 2014).

While India and Bangladesh have more history with microfinance investment, Pakistan and Nepal have been more recent targets in the region. Pakistan particularly has been noted for its "staggering growth since 2008" in the microfinance sector (Syminvest, 2013b). Bank disbursements through MFIs, rural development programs and related interventions doubled in this five-year period, as the number of microfinance borrowers also grew from almost 1.6 million in 2008 to over 2.3 million in 2013 (Syminvest, 2013b). Part of Pakistan's attraction to the global investment industry was the establishment of branchless banking, implemented through commercial banking and communications services, "making Pakistan one of the most competitive and interesting markets in the world" (Chen, 2013).

Chen (2013) describes Nepal as a flourishing market for microfinance, recognizing that this country "rarely gets mentioned globally." MFIs here are not as well financed as those in Bangladesh, India, and Pakistan, but almost doubled between 2007 and 2011 from 12 to 21 banks (Syminvest, 2011). Regulations designed to structure loans to poor and rural communities have resulted in financial penalties and license revocations for many of these MFIs (Syminvest, 2011). Policies designed to guide these financial services toward development goals rather than institutional profit face pressures given these competing goals.

MFI investment, facilitated through global capitalist ventures, corresponds with exacerbating income inequities in the region (ADB, 2012). Government policies toward communications industries reflect this set of contradictions, in some cases attempting to promote public access to information resources yet in other cases privileging corporate agendas. These tensions can be seen in how public policies in the country have attempted to negotiate the distribution of public sector software (Thomas, 2012b) as well as other information and communication technologies (ICT) through supporting public–private partnerships.

Telecommunication services offer a significant illustration of the technological mandate to promote development that reaches the poor, constrained by public policies that privilege corporate interests. Related to these tensions, a current report is aptly titled: "Telecom: Enabling growth and serving the masses" (Deloitt, 2014). Chakravartty estimates that in 2007 about half of the nation's telecenters operated to produce profit for private industry, while the other half were administered through public–private partnerships (2012, p. 71). Throughout this decade, rural India experienced rapid growth in access to phone lines and mobile phones (IITM, 2005), with "companies battling to connect with its 300 million middle-class consumers" (Westhead, 2009), in pursuit of commercial enterprise, as well as nonprofit fundraising. But while the infrastructure was building potential for more access, people still needed to find ways to use these services. Development programs then were motivated by this interest in creating consumer demand for phones and other communication technologies, assuming that solving poverty and supporting profit might be compatible goals.

Development within the region of South Asia has been engaged in quite different ways not only across national governments, but also across transnational organizations, development agencies, and, relevant to this analysis, banks. How finance institutions structure loans as a solution to development is considered next.

Microenterprise as development

Microenterprise programs serve the agenda of MFIs, which offer people with fewer resources access to financial services that include loans and savings (de Gobbi, 2005). MFIs dominate economic approaches to development, although not all agree that this strategy works effectively to fight poverty (reviewed in Wilson, 2011). Microenterprise development more specifically targets clients willing to initiate small businesses, recruiting no more than five employees. These willing entrepreneurs are not only given access to credit, but are also typically trained in business skills such as marketing, management, and accounting (de Gobbi, 2005).

The narrative of microenterprise begins with the promise of 2006 Nobel Peace Prize winner Muhammad Yunus, proclaiming microlending as the solution to overwhelming poverty. Microenterprise programs illustrate a highly visible development approach, not only in the industry but also in global public discourse. Yunus becomes identified as the central character in this narrative, as heroically responding to the plight of women as victims of poverty. His initiative through the Grameen Bank relied on private-sector banking services to offer loans to defined groups for small-scale entrepreneurship. In his 2007 book on the subject, Yunus describes having distributed about 2.6 million loans, mostly to women (95%; p. 235), toward generating income, supporting housing, and funding education for the children of Grameen Bank borrowers. This approach fits a management perspective structuring mainstream development (Nederveen Pieterse, 2001; Roy, 2010).

Recent World Bank estimates claim that 30 million members of microfinance enterprises have received more than US$ 2 billion over the last 20 years (Khandker & Samad, 2014). Clearly commanding substantial global resources, microcredit became quite well known and popular within the development industry after the 1997 Microcredit Summit. Five years later, at the next Summit, Yunus (2007) estimated that 54 million families across the world had benefited from microcredit (pp. 256–260). And four years after that, professionals at the 2006 Global Microcredit Summit in Nova Scotia were even more enthusiastic (Sinclair, 2012, p. 129). Both advocates and heretics (as Sinclair calls himself) agree that microfinance has become institutionalized as a dominant development scheme (McAnany, 2012, p. 107).

Yunus' original conceptualization of microfinance asserted the rights of the poor to have access to credit, to enable their economic pursuits to improve their well-being. The Grameen Bank structured itself as "a private-sector self-help bank" with a "social consciousness" (p. 203). The social goals of the organization are at odds with the underlying structural foundation of the bank. On the one hand, Yunus recognizes that "[p]overty is not created by the poor. It is created by the structures of society and the policies pursued by society" (2007, p. 206). Critical of the World Bank, national governments, and other development agencies, Yunus declares his goals to be working to reduce poverty and to promote human rights. The prescription for this diagnosis though is to engage in a different style of banking, directed toward enabling loans to those with few resources, within the structure of a free-market economy. Along with this structural arrangement come resonating ideological themes, such as individual empowerment and self-reliance.

Self-reliance serves as an important refrain in the mantra of microlending, both at institutional and individual levels. Although the early years of the Grameen Bank (1977–1988) were supported by philanthropic organizations such as the Ford Foundation and the MacArthur Foundation, Yunus took pride in transitioning his work toward becoming an independent bank without external charitable support. Kristof and WuDunn agree that "markets and microlending are proving a powerful system to help people help themselves," as part of a "microcredit revolution sweeping the developing world" (2009, p. 187).

One adaptation to this model builds on the idea that the problem of poverty can be solved by market solutions, through a model of "creative capitalism" that sees the poor as a lucrative market (Roy, 2010). Finding ways to link "poor entrepreneurs in the global south" with the wealthy in the global North facilitates global capitalism by foregrounding the poor as a "frontier" new market (p. 30). Kristof and WuDunn (2009) assert that capitalism offers a foundation for women's empowerment:

> Microfinance has done more to bolster the status of women, and to protect them from abuse, than any laws could accommodate. Capitalism, it turns out, can achieve what charity and good intentions sometimes cannot. (p. 187)

Family dynamics that shift as women have more control over economic resources are possible, particularly when male partners "tolerate insubordination" from women in order to enjoy the benefits of profit.

In the pursuit of this new market, nonprofit programs were encouraged to "partner" with private industry, though this raised the specter of competing goals. The Grameen Bank "partnership" with the Monsanto corporation announced in the early years of this initiative (1998) contributed to the "disciplining" of farmers who managed their own seed storage rather than purchasing new seeds from Monsanto (Roy, 2010, p. 136). Vandana Shiva and others recognized the conflict between the interests of the corporation and those of these women, as the Grameen Bank subsequently cut its ties with Monsanto. This story ebbs and flows though over time as private institutions devoted to profit and those designed to promote public interest collaborate and compete in development intervention.

The solution of microenterprise to the problem of development is predicated on a foundation of a privatized development industry. Just as the heroism of celebrities in their visible contributions to and support of charity necessarily builds on wealth that accrues through profits in global communications industries, and exempted from public tax (see Chapter 4 on education strategies), Yunus, as a male hero, is celebrated for his emphasis on entrepreneurship in market economies and on individual empowerment of women. This approach exemplifies neoliberal approaches that build on the profits of global capitalism.

Privatization of the development industry more broadly resonates within the region of South Asia, particularly in terms of the privatization of communication industries. Thomas (2012a) and Chakravartty (2012) share concerns regarding the privatization of the public sector software and ICT industries in India, as limiting digital inclusion as well as civic participation. The prominence of private donors comes into play not only through the connection of development institutions with private corporations, but also through the individual contributions of donors to designated agencies. As one illustration, the KIVA program initiated in 2005 asks individuals to contribute money through its website toward loans, exhibiting photographs of loan applicants. In its first four years KIVA raised US$ 100 million through this strategy (McAnany, 2012). Individual donors might be attracted to this scheme, which appears to serve people more directly by avoiding costly intermediaries. Clear and accurate information on the actual processes of distribution, or on actual interest rates charged to clients, is not featured on these sites (Rosati, 2012; Sinclair, 2012).

This market model is structured not only to support the distribution of loans through microfinance, but also the sanctioned project of microenterprise, referring to the small business model based on operations with few staff (fewer than 5–10 paid employees depending on source) restricted to working in local areas. Although not all of these loans have been devoted to entrepreneurship (some are given for other resources, housing, and education), microenterprise has commanded most of the popular attention in development discourse. Moreover, not all entrepreneurial loans focus on goods and services related to communication technologies. However, their projected value in social change processes is worth exploring. Before considering the role of communication and the visibility of women in this discourse, it is worth recalling the criticisms made against microfinance.

Given the dominance of microfinance as a structuring approach to development, challenges to this mission are difficult to hear against the triumphant voices of the evangelical and converted. The very mission of microfinance elevates this approach to "paradigmatic" status, "of a new moment of development, one characterized by an interest in poverty alleviation and focused on ideas of self-help and empowerment" (Roy, 2010, pp. x–xi). Arguing against the mission of microfinance itself has become more difficult than raising remedial concerns with problems within the system.

Public discourse infrequently refers to the potential limitations of the Grameen banking model. When concerns with these programs are raised, attention is drawn to the high interest rates charged (24–36% according to Ved, 2011); the lack of mobility out of poverty for those taking loans; and the lack of replicability in other countries with different economies of scale.

One common refrain is that the idealism of the model is worth sanctifying, but its implementation by mere mortals is lacking. De Gobbi (2005) describes MFIs in her purview as poorly managed. Sinclair also raises concerns with implementation, given the physical distances and technological challenges involved in monitoring loans (2012, p. 11). John Hatch is referenced in this volume as well (Sinclair, 2012, p. 78) making a critical but not well known point that 90% of microloans finance consumption of goods such as televisions, rather than actual enterprise schemes. These small-scale businesses are also hard to sustain over time, as bigger corporations such as Walmart emerge and dominate local commerce. Part of the difficulty microenterprises face is the high interest rates incurred when attempting to leverage credit.

According to *New York Times* journalist Neil MacFarquhar (2010), while the global average interest rate on these types of loans was about 37%, loans in Mexico averaged about 70%, with Nigeria and others also being exceedingly high. And while interest rates for KIVA in the US may be under 10%, its interest rates in Southern Sudan, as an illustration, are up to 88% (Sinclair, 2012, p. 174). The appropriate boundary for interest rates on loans has become a serious point of contention in discussions of these interventions. Yunus himself describes his concern that microcredit should not enable banks to become reinvigorated loan sharks (Sinclair, 2012, p. 168), recognizing problems with profit motives taking over from altruistic intentions.

Moreover, actual interest rates are not reported to individual investors on websites such as KIVA and Microplace (MacFarquhar, 2010), meaning that people with good intentions would not know that their contributions may be contributing to exploitative practices. This concern leads to another identified problem in the industry: lack of transparency. Independent agencies can conduct valid assessments, but without regulation and accurate data their work is challenging. Some argue that further partnerships with corporations, particularly those with the ability to manage information, would improve this system toward transparency; others raise concerns that these very partnerships further the interests of global capital rather than improving the lives of the poor.

The overwhelming voice in this discourse is in support of this as a beneficial approach to development, even if it is faulty in terms of its implementation, with high interest rates, poor monitoring, and lack of transparency. As a solution to poverty, these voices raised in chorus applaud the work of a single man as a grand hero in this narrative, without recognition of the many people who work with him and participate in these programs, the economic systems that establish and sustain private banking services, or the political allegiances and national policies that structure aid and other financial exchanges.

Women's empowerment and gender roles

Women have visibly served as a central focus for development programs since the 1970s, when the Women in Development (WID) decade set out to bring attention to women's contributions to their communities. Along with recognition of women's challenges given gender dynamics, and the diversity of women's interests highlighted through global feminist critiques (see Chapter 1), women have remained visible in the development narrative, along with children, as vulnerable and as victims. What distinguishes microenterprise programs from other development approaches is that while most of the latter rely on objectified visions of women as passive recipients, there is potential within the former to conceptualize women as actively engaged in creating their own economic conditions, through owning, managing, and working in small businesses. In the microenterprise scheme, development programs assume, often explicitly, that women are more likely than men to spend their money efficiently, to allocate resources toward family interests, and to repay their loans. How this agency becomes articulated through this discourse is worth exploring, given this potential.

Women's conditions in South Asia are varied and complex, with notable women rising to the top of political hierarchies in national governments while gender violence and women's rights remain critical concerns. Within the region, some nations stipulate equal rights for women and men in their constitutions, but lack specific policies giving women the right to inherit property, and face physical and normative challenges when women and girls are raped and abused. The situations differ in these countries in terms of cultural and political histories, spiritual affiliations, and employment patterns within the region.

A celebrated advocate for girls' right to education, Malala Yousafzai, has brought more global attention to the region. Chapter 4, Communicating Gender in Education Development, highlights strategies on girls' education in Afghanistan as well as the African region through schools initiated by Oprah, Angelina, and Madonna, and discusses in more detail the advocacy of Malala, who is portrayed as both victim and celebrity in the Western media (Hegde, 2013). Her championing of girls' rights as a Pakistani teen has earned her nominations, such as the Nobel Peace Prize, as well as awards, such as the Sakharov Prize and the Clinton Global Citizens Award. While analysis in Chapter 4 focuses on girls' education as a development strategy, in this chapter I highlight interventions designed to improve women's economic conditions. While earning potential is related to literacy and educational attainment, development programs tend to isolate girls' education from women's employment. Still, the narratives that describe girls and women as victims of traditional culture are similar.

In contrast with the inability of the US thus far (by 2017) to elect a woman President, several women have achieved national leadership in South Asia. Indira and Sonia Ghandi, among other women, have led India, along with Prime Ministers Sheikh Hasina (who has not been a fan of microfinance for women) in Bangladesh, and Benazir Bhutto (who was assassinated in 2007) in Pakistan. Resonant with global conditions that restrict the wealthiest individuals to very few women, and that ensure that most of those who do reach the top echelons do so in terms of inherited or married wealth, it is notable that these women, remarkable in their own right, have been able to achieve their political status in part due to their family status and prestige. Apart from these national leaders, women have been elected to national parliament as well. The Inter-Parliamentary Union (IPU) charts that in 2013 one-third of national parliamentary positions were held by women in Nepal, one-fifth in Bangladesh and Pakistan, and only 11% to about one-tenth in India. While the rate of women reaching these positions of leadership is indeed notable, the broader conditions of women in the region must be recognized.

Descriptions of women's conditions in South Asia typically focus on patriarchal norms that contribute to domestic and sexual violence against women as well as their low political and social status and poor levels of health and education. Bhalla's (2011) essay on South Asian women for the Reuters news service squarely positions women's low status as a "plight" against the "mask" of "modernity," given that "many women live with the threat of appalling violence and without many basic rights." Among the conditions noted, she calls attention to gender norms that position women as "inferior," leading to "honor killings" in Pakistan, as well as "feticide in India and trafficking in Nepal." Bhalla cites studies by TrustLaw deeming Afghanistan, Pakistan, and India as among the "top five countries deemed most dangerous for women," as well as United Nations statistics documenting that "more women die in childbirth in South Asia…than any other place in the world except sub-Saharan Africa. And more than half the women in the region cannot read and write."

Patel's research (2006) on the status of women in South Asia confirms these trends, documenting UNDP statistics from 2003 showing women's relatively low participation in the labor force broadly and in industry specifically, as well as their much lower level of estimated earned income than men's. Literacy rates range from 25% in Nepal, 29% in Pakistan, and 31% in Bangladesh to a higher rate of 46% in India. More women are employed in the formal labor force in Bangladesh (42%) and Nepal

(41%) than in India (32%) and Pakistan (29%): in Nepal, women are more likely to be engaged in agriculture (91%) than in industry (1%) or services (8%). These trends are similar across other South Asian countries, though women are more likely to be involved in industry in India and Pakistan (11%) and in Bangladesh (8%) than in Nepal. Women's rights to inherit or own land are also limited in the region. According to Balasubramanian (2013):

> Land inheritance in the region has traditionally been patrilineal and estimates of women's land ownership are as low as 3 per cent in Pakistan and 11 per cent in Nepal (UNDP, 2010). Even when land redistribution programmes were carried out by governments in India, Pakistan and Bangladesh, they allocated land solely to males except when there was no adult male in the household. (p. 621)

Women tend to fare less well than men in South Asia in terms of employment overall and in ownership of firms. ILO data from 2012 (ILO, 2014) show a sharp disparity in terms of the percentage of women working in the formal sector compared with men in India (26% compared with 78%) and Pakistan (22% compared with 80%) particularly, with a slightly smaller disparity in Bangladesh (54% compared to 81%), and a much lesser one in Nepal (78% compared to 86%). The World Bank documents statistics on the percentage of firms with female participation in ownership through their Enterprise Surveys in Bangladesh (12.7%) and Nepal (21.8%), but not in India or Pakistan. Related to this context of labor it is important to note that UN studies of child labor estimate that 21.6 million of the 300 million children aged 5–14 are working: this includes about one-quarter of Nepalese children (27%), compared to 14% of those in Bangladesh, 8% in Pakistan and 5% in India (ILO, 2014). The market in child labor is related to poverty and lack of literacy. While domestic labor may be a culturally sanctioned practice for children, of more concern are the exploitative practices in slavery and trafficking documented by the ILO. Even though the overall percentages of children in India and Pakistan who are working are lower than those of their regional neighbors, these children are much more likely to be working in hazardous industries, harmful to their physical and cognitive maturation.

Women in South Asia, as in other regions, face challenges endemic to gendered dynamics limiting opportunities, through diverse circumstances and varied contexts. How gender channels roles for women and men in development narratives matters just as much to constructions of donors as recipients, as well as to the broader process of social change. Feminist concerns with representations of women in the narrative of social change question the degree of agency women are projected to possess. Within the microenterprise approach, women are described as being "empowered" through their experience as loan recipients. Although this is a dominant mode of development, there has been little evidence to document changes in women's conditions as a consequence of their collaboration with microenterprise schemes. This study then engages both with how women are framed within the broader narrative of development in this discourse, and how evaluations contribute to and limit our understanding of gender conditions as well as of strategic social change.

Constructions of women

Women serve as both targets and tools of development intervention, particularly as victims, thus justifying the heroic deeds of masculine banking executives. Women are frequently featured, in photographs as well as descriptions. According to Sinclair (2012) "their image helps justify the work of these agencies" (p. 160), even as the "savings of some of the poorest women of Africa were being stolen" (p. 157). Women's emergence as entrepreneurs within this portrayal may signal some agency, but this agency is restricted to small-scale businesses, which require neither the "physical skills" of men (World Bank, 2012) nor a capacity to manage or own larger or public organizations. Minor chords resonate with women's role as civic participants in social change. Their roles as victims, mothers, and entrepreneurs are much more dominant.

Overwhelmingly, the dominant theme in this discourse is the characterization of women as victims, without fail as "poor," or even, as the "poorest of the poor" (Anam, 2011). This articulation of poor emphasizes a lack of resources, making the case for targeting women in poverty, but also accentuating their vulnerability and therefore their need to be rescued. Along with this vulnerability comes the suggestion that women suffer from the constraints of traditional culture or "religious principles" (*Washington Post*, 1998), particularly when "poor women in rural areas . . . would not dare to even enter a regular bank" (Ved, 2011). Roy's exploration of microenterprise in South Asia (2010) relates targeted lending to poor married women, with an underlying motive to rescue victims of patriarchy from angry Arab and Muslim men (pp. 146–147). This approach fits a dominant trope in broader US perspectives of gender in Islam (see Chapter 3 on population programs).

Moving from the passivity of the vulnerable victim to the slightly enhanced agency of the family member, women are believed to be better targets for bank loans than men given their assumed dedication to family (such as in Kristof & WuDunn, 2009; Yunus, 2007). Explicit assumptions are made that women are better credit risks than men and are more likely to use profits to benefit children than men (US Department of State, 2004). Women's contributions tend to be defined in terms of familial roles, such as "send[ing] children to school" (Sappenfield & Trumbull, 2006) or improving "the living conditions for their children" (Hundley, 2006). Moreover, Yunus asserts that women who had borrowed from Grameen were more likely to use contraception and ultimately have lower birth rates (2007, p. 134). Grameen Bank programs target and fund women intentionally, with the assumption that women act responsibly on behalf of their families and require direct strategic attention. Women's role as mothers fits much of the broader development discourse on how women become visible (Wilkins, 1997).

More agency is accorded women as managing small businesses made possible through bank loans. In one scheme repeated frequently in the public press, women described as "phone ladies" by Yunus "buy specially designed cellphone kits costing about $150, each equipped with a long-lasting battery. They then set up shop as their village phone operator, charging a small commission for people to make and receive calls" (Corbett, 2008). These women are able to purchase telephones by taking out Grameen loans, which are repaid with interest. As Yunus explains, "[n]ow we have over 200,000 telephone ladies all over Bangladesh," who soon were able to add internet service to their entrepreneurial repertoire. "Those who argued these women would not know how to use the technology have been proven wrong" (Hundley, 2006). According to the *Washington Post* (1998), through this system

> [one] telephone lady in each village buys a phone set on credit and pays for it gradually by charging other villagers small sums for each use. Early experience has shown a sizable demand – to communicate with relatives working overseas, to announce family weddings, to check whether a strike in town has ended before bringing produce to market.

According to other reports: "On average, each of the nearly 200,000 Grameen telephone ladies earns a profit equivalent to twice the national average income" (Johnson, 2006). Women contribute then to development through their participation in local market economies.

While women may be portrayed in more active roles in this field, their agency tends to be defined in terms of borrowing money or running small businesses. The phrase repeated across narratives is that "most borrowers" are "women." Some but not most articles include attention to women as managing businesses, such as "starting cellphone businesses in poor villages in Bangladesh and elsewhere" (Hopkins, 2006). Sheikh Hasina, Bangladeshi Prime Minister, describes being

> so charmed when they told me that they will give cell phones to the rural poor women for doing business, and they will thus come out of extreme poverty ... [but I did] not see any phones in the hands of the poor women, [through] which they are supposed to earn money.
>
> (BBC, 2010)

Other economic roles for women include paid employment making saris in India (Mukherjee, 2013), and manufacturing "ready-made garments" in Bangladesh (Anam, 2011). Painted as "quaint," news of "brightly clad" women, moving through Northern Indian villages in "cameldrawn carts, tractors, ... carrying shallow bowls of fuel and food on their heads" (Timmons, 2007), highlights women though more as traditional caricatures than as active and intelligent workers. When engaging in business, women are commended for selling coffee, toothpaste, eye drops and other small sundries, particularly when "it is generally taboo for Indian women to travel outside of their communities alone" (Timmons, 2007).

Development discourse also has the potential to recognize women as actively engaged in their communities, as civic leaders, and participants. This portrait might refer to women's involvement in decision making that leads to voting or advocating for particular rights or policies. However, women were much less likely to be seen in this way in this discourse, apart from UN discussions, which did refer to women as having value by "leading the digital world and social movements" (UNDP, 2012). More integral to UN discourse but not repeated in public news sources, women's "full and equal participation in decision making" is seen as integral to sustainable development (UNEP, 2011).

Overwhelmingly, women are projected as objects of development, too vulnerable to enact their own rescue. For example, programs explicitly "target the poorest women through effective marketing strategies" (US Department of State, 2004), or implement bank schemes that "invest" in "girls and women" (UNDP, 2012). This approach is situated within the WID framework, targeting women but not addressing underlying gender dynamics.

While women are constructed as active agents in their local economies, this role is limited to that of small-scale entrepreneurship and to free-market participation. Understanding sustainability as "long-term productivity" (Arun et al., 2004), focusing development on short-term business plans loses sight of changing economic conditions. Moreover, contexts of access and regulation of communication technologies, particularly in terms of telephone and internet services, might limit entrepreneurial potential. And attributing value to women in terms of their familial roles draws attention away from their economic ambitions. Sustainability of these development strategies can be quite limited when focusing on loans to women for small business enterprise.

Avoiding the need for "physical skills" women are assumed not to possess, the World Bank (2012) encourages economic investment in women's abilities to use and sell small computers and mobile phones. Timmons (2007) observes the masculine spectacle of men and boys surrounding the traveling Nokia van as it travels through India, as "the latest sign of the communication blitz about to overtake rural India," which "has become the next frontier for the biggest players in the industry." These vans are not equipped to sell telephones, but rather to create desire for these devices, in order to compete with prominent players such as Motorola, the Indian service Reliance, and other service providers. This journalist's observation comes closer to a recognition of gendered dynamics in accessing phones than the interventions targeting women as victims, mothers, and entrepreneurs.

Constructions of men

Public discourse on the Grameen Bank approach sings the praises of the founding father as well as the promise of communication technologies in saving poor, rural women. Victims and solutions typically feature in the development narrative, particularly when authored by donor institutions and their allies. But in the microenterprise narrative, public discourse also attributes the heroism of development to Yunus, following the format of the Western idolized-great-man theory, in its gendered and individualist focus. The public attention granted to Yunus as a hero has been quite positive, focusing on his roles as pioneer, entrepreneur, and savior.

News coverage, particularly surrounding his 2006 Nobel Peace Prize, frequently referred to Yunus specifically as a "pioneer" of microfinance (such as Johnson, 2006 and Anam, 2011). As an example, an often referenced essay by MacFarquhar (2010) characterizes Yunus as the "darling of the development world," who "having pioneered the practice by lending small amounts to basket weavers in Bangladesh, was awarded a Nobel Peace Prize for it in 2006. The idea even got its very own United Nations year in 2005." Celebrating his role as a pioneer also became connected with Bangladesh as a nation, when he is described as aiding in "the newly independent nation of Bangladesh [which] was suffering a famine," creating a bank that "succeeded by reversing traditional banking rules" (Hundley, 2006). By going against "tradition," Yunus represents a "modern" "pioneer."

In addition to being a pioneer of a new nation, Yunus is celebrated as an economic success, particularly in his role as entrepreneur. This discourse celebrates the commercial success of the bank, by suggesting that the "world of finance is realizing Muhammad Yunus's idea is more than mere charity – it is good business" (Sappenfield & Trumbull, 2006). A few articles note Yunus' caution though that while "banks can make a profit...this is what loan sharks do" (Sappenfield & Trumbell, 2006). Overall though, the coverage offers resoundingly positive characterizations of Yunus as master of the economic agenda of banking systems as a tool for poverty alleviation. His success is considered in terms of his ability to sustain capitalist initiative.

What makes his characterization as a hero complete is the additional attribution of his being a "savior" to his political pioneering and capital entrepreneurship. His acts toward women tend to be characterized as "saving" "poor, self-employed women" from "dire poverty;" the *Washington Post* (1998) specifically states that "one third have escaped dire poverty" but no evidence is given, implying a mystical, magical beneficence. The microfinance industry radiated a halo of "saintly aura" (MacFarquhar, 2010), invoked by Kristof and WuDunn (2009) as a "revolution sweeping the developing world" (p. 187) with over US$ 60 billion in assets by 2010 (McAnany, 2012). Despite his concerns with the implementation, Sinclair agrees that professionals at the 2006 Global Microcredit Summit in Nova Scotia felt like "saviors" (2012, p. 129). David Korten's introduction to Sinclair's volume explains how difficult it can be to criticize this US$ 70 billion industry, given the dominant if naïve celebrations, hailing "microfinances as an almost sacred solution to global poverty" (p. 216). Roy describes how "the global microfinance industry has pursued microfinance with evangelical zeal" (p. 90), connecting Northern Christian norms of spirituality to concerns with debt and material assets (pp. 42–43). She agrees with Nederveen Pieterse (2001) that the missionary zeal frequently associated with modernization and development resonates with historical evangel-ical passions for reform. More recent coverage even implies a Christ-like quality to Yunus in current circumstances, as a "gentle man with a beatific smile," who is now a "broken man," living "in perpetual fear, afraid for his life" (Wilson, 2011).

Yet outside of this dominant public discourse this Grameen Bank pio-neer has faced some criticism both within and outside of Bangladesh, though rarely from the US. Yunus was forced to leave his position with the bank by the Bangladeshi Prime Minister in 2011 (Sinclair, 2012). A year later, the editorial board of the *New York Times* (2013) published a glowing review of Yunus and Grameen, accusing the Bangladeshi government of having little justification for

> nationalizing and breaking up the widely admired Grameen Bank, which pioneered the business of lending small amounts of money to poor women who want to start and grow businesses. Lawmakers should reject these destructive ideas and stop meddling in the affairs of this important financial institution, which serves 8.4 million rural women.

This current affirmation of faith underscores not only the portrayal of Yunus as entrepreneurial pioneer, but also as masculine savior of vulnerable women.

Articulation of gender

Women are visible in this discourse en masse, while the central-ity of the individual male, Yunus, contributes to his heroic status. If women are victims of poverty in South Asia, then microenterprise is proposed as the solution, structuring development intervention. As a development strategy, microenterprise works within a neoliberal frame-work privileging economic growth as a global development enterprise (Nederveen Pieterse, 2001; Sparks, 2011). Opening access to credit, microenterprise programs finance small-scale businesses among groups of women to build individual financial capital. Within this rubric of profitable enterprise, strategic programs are designed to alleviate poverty by offering loans to finance credit for proposed entrepreneurial plans. The group most frequently identified as a target and benefactor of these loans is women.

While microfinance as an industry can be seen as a structure enabling the management of poverty, this study focuses more specifically on how the industry manages women, as they become visible in the process of development (Roy, 2010, p. 33). Women's participation can be diversely understood within this rubric as ranging from ownership or management, to paid or volunteer labor, or as discussants of problems and solutions. The focus on women stems from concerns with gender inequalities that are believed to impede economic growth nationally and foster poverty locally. Gender equality is promoted through programs encouraging women to use ICT as tools in microenterprise (Arun et al., 2004). The intersection of women and communication technologies is evident in the ways women are assumed to work with ICTs through their microenterprise projects and value "modern" technologies such as computers and calculators over a "primitive abacus" (Roy, 2010, p. 72).

Communication

A dominant vision in this development narrative is that of a rural mother with a telephone. While women serve as the victims in need of rescue in this story, communications becomes the weapon that the development savior is able to bestow, bringing light to the darkness of poverty. Given that most of the women in this region who do receive loans do so to support agricultural businesses (de Gobbi, 2005), the focus on small businesses supporting telephones fits a Western vision of communications technologies as integral to modernity.

Communications broadly, and mediated technologies specifically, such as radio, television, phones, and computers with internet access, are seen as able to advance development goals, through raising awareness, inspiring mobilization, shifting norms, changing behavior, and advocating policy change. ICTs have played a central role in development discourse as instruments to promote commerce and citizenship. Much of the history of development communication focuses on the role of ICTs in enabling development goals (McAnany, 2012; see Chapter 1). Although digital media and other mediated channels also contribute to social change processes, the ICT literature privileges their economic and bureaucratic uses.

Television also becomes part of this glorified equation through which mediated communication multiplies the effects of strategic intervention toward development goals, whether through explicitly designed content, as in social marketing or entertainment education, or through the structure of its industry. Despite a lack of empirical evidence (see critiques noted by Hornik & McAnany, 2001), enthusiasts attribute lower fertility rates in Brazil and in India to the introduction of expanded television options in remote and rural communities (cited in Kristof & WuDunn, 2009, p. 245). Arguing a potential link between television options and birth rates, these advocates echo earlier hopes by Lerner (1958) that "changes occurred because TV brought new ideas into isolated villages that tended to be very conservative and traditional," more specifically such that "rural viewers came to recognize that the 'modern' way is for women to be treated as human beings" (Kristof & WuDunn, 2009, p. 245).

Expanding this view of the democratizing potential of ICTs while avoiding the possibility of hierarchical surveillance, Yunus suggests that:

> Information and communication technology gives us reason to hope that we are approaching a world free of power brokers and knowledge brokers. Individuals will be in command. There will be no screening authority on center stage. This is particularly exciting for all disadvantaged groups, voiceless groups, and minority groups. (2007, p. 253)

Communications as a tool toward decentralizing power and empowering individuals suits the conceptualization of ICTs and their role in development within a neoliberal framework, not only as a foundation for a modernization, but also for a globalization paradigm. For communications to work as a weapon against poverty, there needs to be a cast of characters ascribed victim and hero status, enacted through plots in a particular setting. The weapon of choice in this narrative is the telephone.

Although microfinance loans are used for many types of activities and microenterprise for various businesses, the Grameen model of development became most known in English-language public discourse for women purchasing telephones that they could then rent as a service to other customers (Gumucio Dagron, 2001). How telephones, as a part of communications technology more broadly, have come to be seen as a tool for social change can be characterized in terms of the economic value accrued through formal work setting up cellphone businesses, their potential as political tools for mobilization or surveillance, and their promotion of social connections with known family and friends.

Given the banking framework structuring this approach to development, not surprisingly, economic incentives dominate, in terms of individual profit as well as national economic growth. At the individual level, cell phone adoption is applauded in "low-income and poor communities, where the low cost of phones and the availability of cell networks even in remote areas has fueled the rapid growth;" the problem, in this framework, is not that people may not have a use for phones, which is assumed, but that "(p)olitical instability and dictatorships make it hard to work with telecom service providers, and some central banks are reluctant to cooperate with companies that could take away their control over their citizens' finances" (Kang, 2010). Within the national model of development, this assumption of instability and corruption within the governments of poor countries inhibits individuals' abilities to take advantage of telephones.

Accentuating the entrepreneurial potential of telephone sales in rural markets, the Grameen model justifies its value in terms of "having demolished the long-dominant stereotype of the poor as not creditworthy...Grameen has set its sights on the misguided view of the rural poor as inevitably isolated from the global economy" (*Washington Post*, 1998). This connection to global capitalism is key to this model of social change, particularly among those who focus on economic growth as a central goal. In some visions, this model is referred to as "inclusive capitalism," which encourages

> bottom-up economic development, a way of empowering individuals by encouraging entrepreneurship as opposed to more traditional top-down approaches in which aid money must filter through a bureaucratic chain before reaching its beneficiaries, who by virtue of the process are rendered passive recipients...For this reason, the cellphone has become a darling of the microfinance movement.
>
> (Corbett, 2008)

Women not only sell telephone services, but at times are taught to repair mobile phones (Monitor, 2007).

The cellphone not only features in small-scale entrepreneurship, but also as a product that unites national with corporate enterprise. The arm of Grameen that focuses on the phone "teamed with Norwegian telecom Telenor to create Bangladesh's largest mobile network, and to bring solar-powered phones to remote villages" (Sappenfield & Trumbull, 2006). Grameen and Telenor together were reported as having invested almost US$ 200 million, both to sell phones directly to urban residents as well as sponsoring service through loans to women in rural areas (Reed, 2002), resulting in "annual revenues of about $1 billion" (Corbett, 2008). This business model has been touted as having "revolutionized communications in Bangladesh" (Corbett, 2008), creating a "profitable business" (*Newsweek*, 1997) as well as a "microcredit movement" (Page, 2000).

Mostly the telephone is characterized as an economic resource or as a liberating force enabling social connection. Only one news article suggested that the telephone might also be a vehicle for surveillance. In a recent essay on Yunus, Wilson (2011) describes the hero as "afraid his phone calls [would be] tapped, recorded and played out in court, or worse, the court of public opinion."

Telephones, fitting the pattern of ICTs in development more broadly, become coded not only in terms of their potential economic function but also as emblematic of modernity, for the individual user as well as the nation. Bangladesh is described as "the country that has gone from famine to microcredit to mobile phones" (Anam, 2011), signifying a linear projection from tradition to modernity reminiscent of Lerner and Schramm. Technological progress is also associated with efficiency, an improvement achieved through telephones in much of this attention. For example, in one description of mobile phone services and development:

> Information and communications technology has a critical role to play in the recent and future growth of the microfinance sector. Automation of the microfinance process, which traditionally was done manually, has tremendous potential to increase efficiency as well as reduce the score for error and fraud among loan officers.
>
> (US, 2004)

In addition, microfinance allows "lower-cost services... delivered via mobile phones in point-of-sale devices, notably in Pakistan, Brazil... and Vodafone, Kenya" (Wilson, 2011).

Narratives articulating gendered roles in terms of heroes and victims, as well as problems and solutions chronicled in terms of communications technologies, tell stories of idealized social change, in these analyses in terms of microenterprise interventions in the setting of South Asia. Analyses thus have explored assumptions made about banking as an appropriate approach to development, communication technologies as valuable weapons against poverty, and gender in terms of agency within families, markets, and communities. Next, I explore conceptualizations, along with the nature of empirical evidence, of the success of these microenterprise programs as an entry into the subsequent discussion on accountability in Chapter 5.

Accountability and microenterprise

How success is defined tells us a great deal about how development interventions conceptualize the possibilities for social change. The underlying concern proposing microenterprise as a solution intends to resolve poverty as a development problem. The development approach underlying these more broadly conceived concerns assumes that women's empowerment is an intermediary step between poverty and economic health, and susceptible to development intervention. In this section, I consider the articulated goals of these interventions, reviewing evaluations of outcomes to assess the value of evidence that could contribute to understanding the merits or limitations of microenterprise as a development strategy. Overall, the central goal of microenterprise is to fight poverty through women's empowerment, which can be conceptualized as economic benefit through financial gain; a personal sense of confidence; social respect from others; or political gain in terms of rights and position. In this narrative, economic, political, social, and personal empowerment can be achieved through development interventions that increase access to, favorable attitudes toward, and use of communication technologies, as well as access to and use of formal banking services, according to published literature. Next I consider how development organizations construct their own success, given public literature on development programs that target women and use communications technologies in microenterprise projects in Bangladesh, India, Pakistan, and Nepal, implemented since 1995.

Economic empowerment

The microenterprise literature applauds access to information more broadly and to ICTs more specifically as "empowering." Yunus believes that selling telephone access not only gives women a way to earn income, but also forwards their "modernization" (2007, p. 228). He is not alone: the international donor community believes that microfinance has the ability to promote empowerment (de Gobbi, 2005). For example, the Small Enterprise Development (SEED) awards coordinated through UN Women prioritizes gender equality and women's empowerment (UNEP, 2011). The operationalization of empowerment most frequently invoked in this discourse calls for economic benefit.

More than any other intended consequence, these interventions highlight their strategies to promote women's economic empowerment, typically operationalized as generating income, through access to formal banking services offering credit and savings (de Gobbi, 2005). Linking digital media to entrepreneurship is integral to this model of economic empowerment. In descriptions of the Network of Entrepreneurship & Economic Development (NEED) program in India, groups of women work together (in "self-help groups") to market and sell their crafts through digital media. Targeted women are "primarily from poor, dispossessed, marginalised, or unreached sectors," becoming "empowered" through these sales (Singh, 2005).

A report from the Cherie Blair Foundation and International Center for Research on Women (Malhotra et al., 2012) shares this interest in having the "right technology in the hands of a woman entrepreneur (which) yields economic and social benefits for not just her, but her family, community and country." Their evaluations of four programs in India focus on how "mobile phones, the internet, and computers can increase women's ability to generate income." These case studies include a "franchised IT education center" training women entrepreneurs in banking, insurance, and other services; a "partnership" helping women to "manage ICT-based businesses (Citizens' Center Enterprises (CCEs)) that sell products and services to customers through computers, the internet, and mobile phones;" a cooperative bank training women in business skills and "enabling women to purchase mobile phones;" and "an interactive voice response mobile application that allows self-help groups" to access "web portals and marketing agencies to sell their products more efficiently and expand their businesses."

Emphasizing this entrepreneurial role, the Seelampur project in Northeast Delhi is one of several implemented through the Datamation Foundation Trust, funded through the World Bank and Microsoft, designed to teach poor women in this neighborhood vocational skills so they can market their embroidery, candles, and other handicrafts through ICTs. These technologies link buyers to producers, as well as offer venues for cataloging and marketing products and mechanisms for "quality control." A short video produced in 2005 by the United Nations Educational, Scientific and Cultural Organization (UNESCO, 2002) describes this infoDev project in Seelampur as a valuable ICT Learning Centre "in the hands of the poor," particularly women, who "benefit less from new educational and employment opportunities."

This characterization mostly relies on entrepreneurship, but an aligned role calls for women to have more ability to consume in the market, given their increased revenue. Consumption is described glowingly as part of the benefit of ICTs and business:

> ICTs...can catalyze women's economic advancement by promoting entrepreneurial activity, improving business practices, and breaking traditional gender barriers at home and in the marketplace. But the

private sector is only just beginning to see women as consumers; it has not yet realized the potential women entrepreneurs hold as a vibrant business market.

(Malhotra et al., 2012)

Yunus (2007), repeated by Kristof and WuDunn (2009), believes that women make better decisions on spending than men (D'Espallier et al., 2013).

In broader analyses of women's economic contribution to families across national boundaries, the ILO has documented Pakistan and Bangladesh as among the top ten recipients of migrant remittances (Herald, 2012). Women's economic empowerment may result in sharing resources within households and across national boundaries, and consuming more in the formal marketplace of cash exchange. Of more relevance, though, to these interventions would be documentation showing that participating in these loan schemes made a significant difference in terms of control over material resources.

Development institutions justify their appropriation of funds meant for the public good directed to private institutions by attributing poverty reduction to microenterprise intervention (US, 2004) through creating jobs and business ventures. Much of this attribution suffers from a lack of sound empirical evidence, relying on anecdotal reports or self-assessments by women participating in the loan schemes or working for these projects, with little comparative data. For example, the Seelampur program quoted project staff perceptions that women receiving loans had "developed self confidence" and client responses that they had earned money after receiving loans (though only by about one-fifth of them). More recently though there have been more rigorous evaluations assessing the economic impact of these interventions. Next I consider what we know based on evidence about the consequences of these interventions on economic conditions.

Critics of microfinance have pointed to the lack of evidence that poverty and inequities change substantially as a result of these services. Instead of improving the economic welfare of bank clients, their financial debts may become even more difficult to overcome. Some estimates suggest that 10–15% of borrowers leave such programs before paying back their debts (Roy, 2010, p. 107), thus suggesting the need to study not just current but also past participants. However, most studies sample current clients, such as De Gobbi's (2005) analysis of female client interviews in Nepal and Pakistan, as well as MFI records to assess impact on woman-owned enterprises, and on women's economic and social empowerment.

De Gobbi explains that women in Pakistan are more likely to work in the formal paid economy than women in Nepal. Financial services operate quite differently in everyday practices as well: in Nepal, MFIs were created to fit the image of Grameen services, along with small farmers' and credit and savings cooperatives; in Pakistan, people were more likely to borrow funds through informal means rather than through MFIs, which have been introduced more recently into the country than elsewhere in South Asia. The women receiving loans (de Gobbi, 2005) paid interest and principal on small sums, averaging US$ 125–156 over two-year periods. Their repayment rates according to MFI records were much lower than those recorded by Grameen in Bangladesh, at 75% in Pakistan and 84% in Nepal. De Gobbi (2005) attributes this to local perceptions of these loans as public sector initiatives rather than private ventures with strict sanctions if debts are not paid.

Roy (2010) remarks on the assumption in this rhetoric that women have inherent ability to manage money and be responsible entrepreneurs. Some comparative studies (such a D'Espallier et al., 2013) demonstrate that women are more likely to pay back loans than men, but at what cost? The cost to women may be high: Rankin's (2008) subsequent studies of female clients in Nepal describe women taking on multiple loans, swapping one to pay off another, and ultimately increasing their debt (p. 109). And the cost to MFIs offering loans may even out across services targeting men and women: D'Espallier et al. (2013) offer empirical evidence that while women indeed are more likely to repay loans than men, that reaching and working with women costs banks more, so that there is little cost advantage or disadvantage in working with women over men. Their study of 398 MFIs in 73 countries from 2001 to 2010 suggests that targeting women does not enhance the financial sustainability of MFIs. They also question the assumption that high repayment means that women's conditions improve, but instead raise concerns that falling into further debt can be a serious problem.

Although Sinclair does not challenge the foundation of microenterprise, he builds a case against the public relations effort that has established this as a dominant model of development with little documented evidence of its impact. Only recently has a more rigorous evaluation documented the consequences of microfinance interventions through panel survey data chronicling conditions at three points in time over

20 years in Bangladesh. Khandker and Samad's (2014) assessment suggests that microcredit programs do raise household welfare, particularly for female borrowers. They also document an industry that has increasingly introduced new microfinance institutions (MFI), mushrooming from just a few in 1992 to 576 registered institutions by 2011; and in that year, about one-third of all members of microfinance institutions participated in more than one program. The propensity to participate in these programs grew over time, from about one-quarter of studied households (26%) to about half (49%) of them in 1999 and over two-thirds (69%) of households in 2011. Their data also demonstrate that while Grameen targeted and reached mostly women (89% of its lending), BRAC (formerly the Bangladesh Rural Advancement Committee but now an NGO known as BRAC) has been more likely to work with men in recent years, although in 1999 it too collaborated almost entirely with women (95%, in 2011 down to 38%), placing more emphasis on small and medium-sized enterprises. Moving away from the attention of the 1995 Beijing Fourth World Conference on Women, targeting women seems to attract less recognition, as the dominant discourse has shifted from attention to women to tackling poverty.

By relying on panel data with households over time (and accounting for attrition), Khandker and Samad (2014) demonstrate that participation in group-based credit programs in Bangladesh, particularly among women, raises levels of individual consumption, as well as household net worth. They also note that most of the loans serviced are in the trade sector in Bangladesh, but that this industry has now become saturated with an abundance of loan opportunities, thus approaching an unsustainable market if micro-industry is further expanded. Increases in consumption contribute to the strength of capitalist markets, but may not be as relevant to other familial conditions, pertaining to health and human rights.

Loan repayment serves the interests of the banking industry, but does not address whether clients' conditions are better off than they would have been without participating in loan schemes. From the perspective of women interested in improving their circumstances, other indicators are far more important. Development institutions consider whether interventions have improved women's empowerment, conceived potentially in terms of economic, personal, social, or political characteristics. There is little evidence to document women's empowerment as a result of these interventions, but the public relations machine trumpets anecdotal stories (Sinclair, 2012).

Personal empowerment

Empowerment might mean more than money, when defined as a personal characteristic of self-confidence. Some reports attribute self-esteem to women's involvements in collective decision-making enforced through the mechanism needed to secure loans in groups, as well as to participation in political parties and women's associations (de Gobbi, 2005). Shari (1998) describes a central benefit for rural women participating in these programs as becoming more "confident" to expand their businesses.

Beyond a personal sense of efficacy, empowerment might also relate to one's perceived status within a social group. Social empowerment then refers to gaining "more respect and play[ing] a more active role in the family and community" (de Gobbi, 2005). Although this conceptualization is more sociological in nature than psychological, this condition tends to be operationalized within the individual perception of one's social status. Similarly, conceptualizing empowerment as physical mobility in public spaces offers a helpful, nuanced sense of capacity to negotiate a potentially male-dominated public sphere (Roy, 2010), but in operational terms again tends to rely on the self-reporting of individuals.

The problem with assessments of self-confidence is that these rely on self-reports among participating women (such as those taking part in the Seelampur project). For example, de Gobbi (2005) reports that in Nepal and Pakistan women report being more likely to gain in self-confidence and more likely to make financial decisions themselves. These interviews, though, occurred at one point in time, among existing clients, concerning their own perceptions of their change in status and control. Without comparison over time or with similar groups of women, we do not know if this warrants a condition connected with participation in group meetings or loan activity, being then even more susceptible to a validity concern with measurement, in that people participating in an institutional scheme may voice approval and agreement when questioned in order to please the researcher and the provider of needed services.

Although their intentions may be to privilege women in these funding schemes, monitoring done to demonstrate actual percentages given to female-only groups is rare (Sinclair, 2012, p. 142) apart from the recently reported World Bank study (Khandker & Samad, 2014). Moreover, it is difficult to document situations in which husbands send their wives to secure loans that men then use themselves. These programs do little to shift gender norms, when men profit from their wives' successful management of these loans.

Political empowerment

When conceptualizing empowerment, this discourse is dominated by economic attributes, with some attention to perceptions of self and status. Empowerment could also refer to a person's ability to be politically active and effective, whether in formal roles, as a voter or candidate, or informal ones, as a participant or leader. However, political empowerment seems absent.

Empowerment might be operationalized in terms of ability to make allocative decisions over how resources are used, within households or within businesses. Balasubramanian (2013) concludes that evidence of empowerment in South Asia remains "equivocal:" women may have more money to consume, but still lack the power to manage finances at home, or fend off domestic violence from husbands who feel threatened. Research evaluations need to consider whether power structures have changed, enabling women to manage their debts and finances (Roy, 2010 p. 108). Women may be more politically aware, but limited in their rights and challenged by gendered norms.

While the methodological approach of de Gobbi's study limits our ability to understand the impact of receiving loans, her comparison of Nepal to Pakistan does offer valuable lessons in the importance of context. She found that microenterprise was more beneficial to participating women in Nepal than in Pakistan, where gender discrimination was more limiting to women's decision making. Her analysis of broader conditions also points to helpful suggestions for future implementation: credit services are less useful in areas where women are not legally able to own or inherit property, which can be used as potential collateral against loans. Political structures and gendered norms structure the possibilities for individuals to engage in social change; more research situating these interventions within structural and normative contexts would contribute greatly to our understanding of social change and our ability to improve intervention.

Technology and empowerment

While empowerment is posited as an intermediary goal leading to poverty alleviation, promoting access to, favorable attitudes toward, and use of technologies is positioned as a necessary precursor to empowerment in this development model. For example, the Seelampur program promotes its success in that most (70%) of the women participating in the project had never before used computers, and based on self-reports were now doing so. Next I highlight some of the interventions that explicitly include ICT access, attitudes, and use within their strategies and assessments.

Many programs have been implemented with the goal of improving access to telecommunication services in rural India. These include NEED; the Swedish Program for ICT in Developing Regions (SPIDER); Global System for Mobile Communications (GSMA) Fund; and Seelampur. These projects share an approach that highlights entrepreneurship as a strategy for women to move themselves out of poverty. A 2003 publication describes NEED in India as a "non-profit organisation that creates and supports grassroots and networking initiatives designed to empower very poor people – especially women," particularly in rural regions in Uttar Pradesh. NEED is structured to support self-help groups of women to facilitate their access to credit for entrepreneurial activities, in agricultural and other projects that follow a model of microenterprise.

SPIDER has been working in several countries since 2004, funded through the Swedish Development Cooperation Agency (SIDA) and through Stockholm University, implemented through their Department of Computer and Systems Sciences. A 2012 report evaluates their collaborations from 2007 until 2011 in rural regions across the "global south," particularly in terms of impact on "women's lives." The goal of this program is to increase "access to ICTs" as a way to "promote sustainable socio-economic development." A report on the project implemented in India connects the "success of women-centered projects" with their ability "to demystify the technology," which needed to be "adapted to suit the women's reality." Women then are targeted because they "lag behind" in socio-economic development. An evaluation of this program assessed a self-help group training program including mostly female participants, who "gained access to group loans, extended their language skills by improving their English, and supported their husbands' fishing practices by buying fishing gear."

The National Information Infrastructure Testbed (NIIT), a global IT corporation, launched "an initiative intended to reach Indian women" to "help" them "play a more significant role in the emerging digital economy." Following a "mass IT literacy" campaign" initiated on "world computer literacy day" (2 December 2002), the Swift Jyoti program developed a course specifically designed to improve women's knowledge of computer use, teaching them how to access "women-oriented websites" on "entrepreneurship, financing, and parenting."

A recent study (2010) from the GSMA Development Fund, the Cherie Blair Foundation, and Vital Wave Consulting documents mobile phone use among women in low- and middle-income countries. They found that women are 21% less likely to own a mobile phone than their male counterparts, a figure that rises slightly in the Middle East and Africa and climbs to 37% in South Asia. Forecasting revenue opportunities for mobile companies, the study states that two-thirds of the remaining market population is female. Factors influencing ownership include household income, urban/rural location, age, occupation, and education level. Owning the mobile phone is limited by the cost of a handset and the monthly service; lack of family/spouse permission; and fear of the technology.

A study funded by the Australian Agency for International Development (AudAID) and the United States Agency for International Development (USAID) echoed this finding that technologies such as mobile phones and services must "meet the actual lived needs of women," but adds that this is to make them "commercially" viable. According to their research, women in Southern India find "pride" as well as value in having mobile phones, particularly when marrying and moving away from family with whom they wish to stay connected.

Although the suggestion that mediated communication serves market processes is common in this discourse, reports of the Seelampur project attribute even more to these technologies: not only will "marketing goods through skills-based ICT use...foster economic participation," but these ICTS also will allow women "to develop a 'voice' to meet their information and communication needs, and to express their creativity and independence." According to this research, women are using their access to digital media to learn English, take distance education courses, and learn more about health concerns. Women are also taught video and audio recording and editing techniques, so they have the ability to create, and not just see, content. It is assumed that content creation abilities will "enable community building, sharing development experiences, advancing the rights agenda and advocating against exploitation and oppression" as a way to advance women's empowerment. The connection of women's voices with advocacy against oppression could potentially challenge individual profit from capitalist entrepreneurship, but instead of being posed as a juxtaposition between collective resistance and individual gain, this relatively minor chord supporting women finding a "voice" harmonizes with the use of technology within free-market systems.

Most conceptualization of the goals driving this development work focuses on empowerment as economic gain through entrepreneurship in small businesses. Present yet less dominant are conceptualizations of empowerment as individual sense of self or perception of status and mobility within social groups and public spaces. Absent is a sense of political connection that would advocate toward improving policies that inhibit gender equity. The objectives of these development programs offer more specific intentions toward these more broadly conceived goals.

Limitations in evidence

The articulated goal to resolve poverty requires rigorous evaluation. One could begin by questioning the sampling, given that most microfinance clients are not among the extremely poor (Sinclair, 2012, p. 7). If the articulated goal is to solve poverty, then the interventions are targeting the wrong groups, and evaluations of these sampled communities offer little evidence that would help in understanding how best to structure a program designed for the groups at the lowest levels of poverty. Moreover, much of these data rely on self-reports from clients, with a vested interest, literally, in pleasing banking institutions that have the power to determine the fate of their financial future.

The evidence these evaluations offer is particularly limited by the lack of a comparison group, given that most studies focus on participating women only, without attention to a comparative group of participating men, of non-participating women, or even of participating women as individuals vs. those in collective groups. These research designs, even when based on correlational studies comparing participants to non-participants at a given point in time without random selection, offer little evidence that the program itself increases participants' household net worth, rather than simply suggesting that those who are able to receive credit and pay off loans are themselves somehow different and thus more able to earn wages than those not participating in microfinance schemes. Longitudinal data would help establish patterns over time, while ethnographic studies would help us understand power dynamics within families and communities. More research needs to be done to demonstrate strong empirical support for or rejection of this as an approach to fighting poverty. Monitoring information that guides the abilities of private banking services to offer loans that are repaid and to gain from high interest rates agreed upon by clients is there. The profit agendas of private industries appear to outweigh the need for rigorous evaluation among development agencies interested in the public good.

Moreover, an evaluation that would ascertain the economic shifts in women's conditions as part of gender dynamics would need to zoom out toward recognizing broader societal and political conditions. Advocacy that builds on social and political empowerment requires ongoing monitoring of existing policies and their consequences. Accountability is necessary for improving intervention (McAnany, 2012, pp. 114–115), but research questions need to address not only single projects, but programs more broadly, in terms of structures of funding and policies as well as normative climates. Moreover, not only should the intended objectives be assessed, but also the unintended consequences, in order to address social problems in their complexities.

Unanticipated consequences

Next I consider trends over time in key indicators for Bangladesh, the initial site of microfinance; India, the wealthiest of these countries ensconced in privatization; Pakistan, more recently attracting these investments with more digital banking services, and Nepal, rarely discussed but also active in microfinance.

If these interventions were able to help women find employment, as one manifestation of economic empowerment, then we would see their employment rates growing over time. But since 1997, women's formal employment rates have not improved, but have fallen slightly, from 55% in 1997 to 54% in 2012; the gap between women and men has not changed, with men's employment in the country falling as well, from 84% in 1997 to 81% in 2012. Trends in India, also with substantial private investment, follow similar patterns, with women's employment at 33% in 1997, 2002, and 2007, falling to 26% in 2012 (as men's also fell from 80% to 78%). Employment patterns in Nepal are similar in terms of trends over time, but women in this country are much more likely to be employed (78% in 1997 and 2012), and the difference between men's and women's employment rates is much smaller (men's employment rates were 87% in 1997 and 85% in 2012). While Nepal marks the highest employment rate for women in this sample, Pakistan has the lowest, at just 12% in 1997; however, Pakistan is the only country witnessing a substantial change for women's employment, from 12% to 22% by 2012, while men's employment remained constant at 80% over time.

In the narrative positing economic empowerment as a goal, telephones feature as tool for facilitating these entrepreneurial activities, as a commodity, a service, and a business tool, as well as a symbol of modernity. According to statistics from the International Telecommunication Union (2014), over time phone subscriptions have grown dramatically in Bangladesh (from 0.02% in 1997 to 63% in 2012), where this technology has featured prominently in the narrative if not in resource allocation. The upward trends in subscriptions to these services also grew in India and Pakistan between 1997 (0.1% for both) and 2012 (70% for the former and 67% the latter). Nepal's patterns establish the emergence of this consumer later over time (0% in 1997), and it was almost at Bangladesh's figures by 2012 (60%).

Unanticipated consequences require careful observation, outside of the direct scope of intervention. For example, Acaroglu (2013) writes of the women and children in India tasked with extracting slivers of gold from old phones, exposing themselves to serious health risks. This recycling is made possible by the extravagant waste of wealthy consumers (in 2010, 150 million phones were sent to trash in the US alone), and the resistance of manufacturers to adapting their production systems to make phones easier and safer to dismantle.

In addition to the environmental consequences of communications technologies (Maxwell & Miller, 2012), programs may affect people beyond those directly targeted. These interventions target married women, typically as vehicles to family dynamics, which means familial relationships should be considered as well as individual women in program assessment. Buried in the details of a recent report, the researchers find that as average female borrowing increases at the village level, girls' enrollment in school decreases (Khandker & Samad, 2014, p. 23). This may be due to shifting household responsibilities if mothers are spending more time outside the home earning incomes through formal market structures. The potential exacerbation of gender gaps in schooling given women's participation in the formal economy requires further research and consideration.

How interventions define success structures their implementation, as well as possibilities for donors and recipients to engage in intervention. The long-range goal is to fight poverty, with intermediary stages leading to women's empowerment, as well as their access to, receptivity toward and use of communications technologies, contingent upon their participation in microenterprise programs. Women's empowerment is conceptualized in diverse ways, from economic and political characteristics to social conditions such as self-confidence and perceived respect from others. Some of the evaluations reviewed also document women's access, attitudes and use of communications technologies as a precursor to empowerment. The projected ability of women's connection to communications technologies to be empowering is contingent upon their engagement with credit services offered through formal banking institutions. This narrative resonates with a neoliberal approach to global development.

Communicating neoliberal development

Development interventions designed to solve the problem of poverty have transitioned "from modernisation to microcredit," according to Rosati (2012, p. 97). Modernization, at least in the former dominant paradigm, operated at the level of nation-state in theory, yet in practice necessarily meant being positioned within a global system of loans and aid, imports and exports, migration and immigration. Nederveen Pieterse (2001) posits modernization as a "secular version of the Christian perspective" (p. 25) as a "neocolonial discourse" of universalism (p. 28). Global capitalism has emerged as a foundation through which development is conceived, implemented, and assessed. Roy (2010) refers to this as the "post-WWII transnational capitalist project of development (which)... has unified the world – so-called developed and developing nations alike – in a total subservience to the market, to capital, to the products of our own work" (p. 107). Neoliberal ideals serve the interests of the elite in promoting microcredit as an appropriate path to development rather than public services.

Indicative of this broader concern, Roy (2010) describes how microfinance serves to facilitate the control of capital and of knowledge about poverty. Through the rules and norms imposed through microfinance, these programs "emphasize profits rather than human development" (p. 5). Roy's careful historical analysis of multilateral and nonprofit institutions demonstrates how an approach that had originated in the global South became transformed as powerful development institutions in the global North began to pay attention and coopt these strategies. The Washington Consensus, privileging economic privatization and policy deregulation, revised this development approach to work within a global free market model, constructing "geographies shaped by neoliberalism... celebrated as places of progress rather than of devastation" (p. 20). These programs need to be understood within increasing private investment in the region in communications technologies, and in private foundations (such as Gates and Dell) with wealth based in the global communications industries.

This analysis illustrates ways in which this discourse contributes to neoliberal triumphs at the expense of sustainability and of gender equity. These programs assume rather than question the benefits of privatized bank services, reducing women's roles to those of bank borrowers and small-scale entrepreneurs who contribute to free-market systems. While this discourse benefits global industry, there are serious latent implications ignored by the celebration of the bank's success.

In the quest for poverty alleviation, not only does this goal remain elusive, but unintended consequences of these interventions may also cause more harm than good for children, women, and men. Unregulated systems of production offer more opportunities for child labor and exploitation. Women, as the majority group working in garment factories, are killed and injured when avoidable fires and building collapses trap them (AP, 2013). Bangladesh has been the site of several recent tragic fires, one incident of which alone killed over 1,000 people, despite rhetorical proclamations by global clothing companies that they would improve working conditions in the country's US$ 20 billion per year garment industry exporting mostly to European and US markets (AP, 2013). Garment workers, mostly women (1300 of these 1600 striking) initiated a hunger strike protesting their pay being withheld, incurring beating and spraying by local police; the 4 million Bangladeshi workers in this industry, again, mostly women, still receive poor wages and work in unsafe conditions (Hammadi, 2014). And in India, in response to sudden growth of the microfinance industry (US$ 460 million allocated in 2005, up from US$ 30 million in 2002), male farmers committed suicide while women were forced into prostitution (Sinclair, 2012, p. 203). Health and safety, either in the family or in the workplace, do not feature in this glamorization of small-scale entrepreneurship.

The development industry is faced with increasing attention to accountability and rigorous assessment of programs (McAnany, 2012). Critical scholarship can offer more comprehensive frameworks contributing to accountability, that positions research in terms of understanding how best to solve social problems, and not just assessments of whether donor interests are being met. Situating discourse analysis within the political-economic conditions of global capitalism informs our understanding of development in ways that should contribute to improved praxis. Attention to sustainability demands that we consider accountability over time, in our quest to address critical concerns with global poverty.

References

Acaroglu, L. (2013). Where do old cellphones go to die? *International Herald Tribune,* 6 May, p. 8.

Anam, T. (2011). Bangladesh at the crossroads. *Financial Times*, 19 May, p. 21.

Arun, S., Heeks, R. & Morgan, S. (2004). *Researching ICT-Based Enterprise for Women in Development Countries: A Livelihoods Perspective*. University of Manchester, UK: IDPM.

Asian Development Bank (ADB). (2012). *Asian Development Outlook 2012: Confronting Rising Inequality in Asia*. Retrieved from http://www.adb.org/publications/asian-development-outlook-2012-confronting-rising-inequality-asia. May 2012.

Associated Press (AP). (2013). Bangladesh garment factory fire kills 10 people. Retrieved from http://abcnews.go.com/International/wireStory/bangladesh-garment-factory-fire-kills-20506935, 8 October 2013.

Balasubramanian, S. (2013). Why micro-credit may leave women worse off: Non-cooperative bargaining and the marriage game in South Asia. *The Journal of Development Studies*, *49*(5), pp. 609–623, DOI: 10.1080/00220388.2012.709618. 21 July 2014.

Bhalla, N. (2011). South Asia's growing modernity masks women's plight. *Reuters*. Retrieved from http://www.reuters.com/article/2011/06/15/us-women-danger-south-asia-idUSTRE75E0CI20110615, 4 June 2011.

British Broadcasting Corporation (BBC). (2010). Bangladesh PM pledges probe into alleged graft by Grameen Bank. *BBC Monitoring South Asia*, December 6.

Chakravartty, P. (2012). Rebranding development communications in emergent India. Nordicom 33. *Communication, Media and Development: Problems and Perspectives, Special Issue*, pp. 65–76.

Chakravartty, P. (2014). Anti-politics and information societies in the south. In K. G. Wilkins, J. D. Straubhaar & S. Kumar (Eds.), *Global Communication: New Agendas in Communication* (pp. 163–182). New York: Routledge.

Chen, G. (2013). Financial inclusion in 2012: South Asian highlights. Retrieved from http://www.cgap.org/blog/financial-inclusion-2012-south-asian-highlights. 26 March.

Corbett, S. (2008). Can the Cellphone Help end Global Poverty? *New York Times*. April 13. MM, p. 34.

Deloitte/Confederation of Indian Industry. (2014). *Telecom: Enabling Growth and Serving the Masses*. Retrieved from http://www2.deloitte.com/content/dam/Deloitte/in/Documents/technology-media-telecommunications/in-tmt-telecom-enabling-growth-and-serving-the-masses-noexp.pdf.

D'Espallier, B., Guerin, I. & Mersland., R. (2013). Focus on women in microfinance institutions. *The Journal of Development Studies, 49*(5), pp. 589–608.

de Gobbi, M. S. (2005). *Nepal and Pakistan: Micro-Finance and Microenterprise Development: Their Contribution to the Economic Empowerment of Women*. Geneva: ILO.

Devarajan, S. & Nabi, I. (2006). *Economic Growth in South Asia: Promising, Un-equalizing, Sustainable?* World Bank: DC.

GSMA. (2010). Striving and surviving: Exploring the lives of women at the base of the pyramid. Retrieved from http://www.gsma.com/mobilefordevelopment/wp-content/uploads/2013/01/GSMA_mWomen_Striving_and_Surviving-Exploring_the_Lives_of_BOP_Women.pdf. 5 November 2013.

Gumucio Dagron, A. (2001). *Making Waves: Stories of Participatory Communication for Social Change*. New York: Rockefeller Foundation.

Hammadi, S. (2014). Bangladeshi workers receive overdue pay after police break hunger strike. Retrieved from http://www.theguardian.com/global-develop ment/2014/aug/11/bangladeshi-garment-workers-receive-overdue-pay. 11 August 2014.

Hegde, R. S. (2013). Gender, Media and trans/national spaces. in C. Carter, L. Steiner and L. McLaughlin (Eds.), *The Routledge Companion to Media and Gender* (pp. 92–102). London: Routledge.

The Herald. (2012). Zimbabwe; Money transfers by migrant workers up 8 percent. *Africa News,* 12 July.

Hopkins, J. (2006). Giving your business what it needs to fly; three successful entrepreneurs share what they learned that put their firms on path to prosperity. *USA Today.* October 26. p. 1E.

Hornik, R. & McAnany, E. (2001). Theories and evidence: Mass media effects and fertility. *Communication Theory Special Issue, 11*(4), pp. 208–227.

Hundley, K. (2006). A success story. *St. Petersburg Times,* May 5. p. 1D

India Institute of Technology Madras (IITM) (2005). Annenberg Research network on International Communication (ARNIC) presentation, University of Southern California. October. Retrieved from http://www.comminit.com/global/node/243350. 5 November 2013.

International Labor Organization (ILO). 2014. Child labor. Retrieved from http://www.ilo.org/legacy/english/regions/asro/newdelhi/ipec/responses/. 21 July 2014.

International Telecommunications Union (ITU). (2014). Statistics. Retrieved from http://www.itu.int/en/ITU-D/Statistics/Pages/stat/default.aspx. 21 July 2014.

Johnson, J. (2006). Give the man credit in creating the concept of "micro-loans", the campaigning banker Muhammad Yunus transformed the lives of millions of Bangladeshis and earned himself a Nobel prize. *Financial Times,* 9 December, p. 14.

Kang, C. (2010). For the Poor, cellphones can offer lifeline. *Washington Post,* 8 September, p. A16.

Khandker, S. R. & Samad, H. A. (2014). *Dynamic Effects of Microcredit in Bangladesh. World Bank Development Research Group Agriculture and Development Team.* Policy Research Working Paper 6821. March 2014.

Kristof, N. D. & WuDunn, S. (2009). *Half the Sky: Turning Oppression into Opportunity for Women Worldwide.* New York: Vintage Books.

Lerner, D. (1958). *The Passing of Traditional Society: Modernizing the Middle East.* Glencoe, IL: The Free Press.

Levin, D. (2007). Cheap glasses bring hope, and wages, to poor villagers. *International Herald Tribune,* p. 1.

MacFarquhar, N. (2010). Banks making big profits from tiny loans. *New York Times.* Retrieved from http://www.nytimes.com/2010/04/14/world/14microfinance.html?pagewanted=all&_r=0. 13 April 2010.

Malhotra, A., Kanesathasan, A. & Patel, P. (2012). Connectivity: How mobile phones, computers and the internet can catalyze women's entrepreneurship. *ICRW and Cherie Blair Foundation for Women.* Retrieved from: http://www.icrw.org/files/publications/Connectivity-how-mobile-phones-computers-and-the-internet-can-catalyze-womens-entrepreneurship.pdf.

Maxwell, R. & Miller, T. (2012). *Greening the Media.* New York: Oxford University Press.

McAnany, E. (2012). *Saving the World: A Brief History of Communication for Development and Social Change.* Urbana: University of Illinois Press.

Mukherjee, K. (2013). Lighting up hope; Social entrepreneurs start new energy model to bring light, power to rural India. *Straits Times.* 25 February.

Nederveen Pieterse, J. (2001). *Development Theory: Deconstructions / Reconstructions.* London: Sage Publications.

New York Times Editorial Board. (2013). Bangladesh takes aim at Grameen Bank. *New York Times.* Retrieved from http://www.nytimes.com/2013/08/07/opinion/bangladesh-takes-aim-at-grameen-bank.html?ref= muhammadyunus. 6 August 2013.

Newsweek. 1997. Big Bang for a small buck. *Newsweek.* 17 February, p. 58.

Page, S. (2000). Clinton praises bank's battle against poverty Bangladeshi villagers bused to meet president following security threat. *New York Times,* 21 March, p. 6A.

Patel, V. (2006). Economics: Labor and health. Retrieved from ///Users/kwilkins/Downloads/Economics_Labour__Health_EWIC__Vibhuti_Patel-libre.pdf. EWIC 4_f6_1-29. 20 April 206 5:24 PM Page 15.

Rankin, K. (2008). Manufacturing rural finance in Asia: institutional assemblages, market societies, entrepreneurial subjects. *Geoforum,* 39, pp. 1965–1977.

Reed, S. (2002). Private Sector; Helping the Poor, Phone by Phone. *New York Times,* 26 May, p. 2.

Rosati, C. (2012). Media and the democratisation of privation: Towards new communicative geographies of anti-poverty. In S. Melkote (Ed.), *Development Communication in Directed Social Change: A Reappraisal of Theory and Practice* (pp. 95–126). Singapore: AMIC.

Roy, A. (2010). *Poverty Capital: Microfinance and the Making of Development.* New York: Routledge.

Sappenfield, M. & Trumbull, M. (2006). Big banks find little loans a Nobel winner, too. *Christian Science Monitor,* 16 October, p. 1.

Schramm, W. (1964). *Mass Media and National Development.* Stanford: Stanford University Press.

Shari, I. H. (1998). Siti Hasmah: Our success due to proper organisation. *New Straits Times (Malaysia),* 14 October.

Sinclair, H. (2012). *Confessions of a Microfinance Heretic: How Microlending Lost its Way and Betrayed the Poor.* San Francisco: Berrett-Koehler.

Singh, A. (2005). Network of Entrepreneurship and Development (NEED) in India. Retrieved from http://www.comminit.com/global/content/network-entrepreneurship-economic-development-need-india. 5 November 2013.

Sparks, C. (2007, reprinted 2011) *Globalization, Development and the Mass Media.* London: Sage.

Swedish International Development Agency (SIDA). (2012). Swedish Program for ICT in Developing Regions (SPIDER). Retrieved from http://www.comminit.com/global/content/connectivity-how-mobile-phones-computers-and-internet-can-catalyze-womens-entrepreneursh. 5 November 2013.

Syminvest. (2011). Nepal: Microfinance institutions double in five years. Retrieved from http://www.syminvest.com/news/nepal-microfinance-institutions-double-in-five-years/2011/11/27/2989. 18 February 2014.

Syminvest. (2013a). India: Microfinance institutions get a boost from development funds. Retrieved from http://www.syminvest.com/news/india-micro finance-institutions-get-a-boost-from-development-funds/2013/7/10/3817.

Syminvest. (2013b). Pakistan: Microfinance sector: survival of the fittest. Retrieved from http://www.syminvest.com/news/pakistan-microfinance-sector–survival-of-the-fittest/2013/7/8/3813.

Syminvest. (2014). Bangladesh: 50 Micro-lenders lose licences. Retrieved from http://www.syminvest.com/news/bangladesh-50-microlenders-lose-licenses/2014/7/23/4460.

The Monitor. (2007). Uganda; Working together to improve lives. *Africa News.* 6 June.

Thomas, P. (2012a). *Digital India: Understanding Information, Communication and Social Change.* Los Angeles, CA: Sage Publications.

Thomas, P. (2012b). Public sector software, participatory communications and social change. *Nordicom, 33,* Special Issue, pp. 77–90.

Timmons, H. (2007). For the rural poor, cellphones come calling; Wireless. *The International Herald Tribune,* p. 11.

Todhunter, C. (2012). Poverty and rising social inequality in India. *Global Research.* Retrieved from www.globalresearch.ca/poverty-and-rising-social-inequality-in-india/5303105, 30 September 2012.

United Nations Educational, Scientific, and Cultural Organization (UNESCO). (2002). *Putting ICT in the Hands of the Poor.* Asia Pacific Bureau: UNESCO.

United Nations Development Programme (UNDP). (2012). ICT and Telecom: Summit Sparks Record-Setting Global Conversation on Power of Tech, Social Media. *Africa News,* 25 September.

United Nations Environment Program (Nairobi). (2011). Africa; UN announces seed award winners 2011 with focus on entrepreneurs. *Africa News.* Retrieved from: http://www.unep.org/newscentre/Default.aspx?DocumentID=2661&ArticleID=8991. 8 October 2013.

US Department of State. (2004). PanAfrica; Women-run businesses best credit risks, Foundation head says. *Africa News,* 5 February.

Ved, M. (2011.) Why Grameen Bank needs a closer look. *New Straits Times* (Malaysia), 11 April, p. 19.

Wahid, M. R. & Hannah, J. (2014). Return of the basket case. *Foreign Policy,* 3 January. Retrieved from http://www.foreignpolicy.com/articles/2014/01/03/return_of_the_basket_case_bangladesh. 13 February 2015.

Washington Post. (1998). A different Asian bank. Editorial. *The Washington Post,* 6 February, p. A24.

Wilkins, K. (1997). Gender, Power and Development. *Journal of International Communication, 4*(2), pp. 102–120.

Westhead, R. (2009). India's new charity begins at the doorstep; Economic growth finds global charity fundraisers now recognizing nation's expanding potential. *Toronto Star,* 2 July, p. A8.

Wilson, E. (2011). Asia: Politics pulls down the microfinance pioneer. *Euromoney.* June. Retrieved from http://www.euromoney.com/Article/2842235/BackIssue/82455/Asia-Politics-pulls-down-the-microfinance-pioneer.html.

World Bank. (2012). *Gender Equality and Development.* Washington DC: World Bank.

World Bank. (2014). *South Asia.* Retrieved from http://data.worldbank.org/region/SAS. 21 July 2014.

Yunus, M. (2007). *Banker to the Poor: Micro-Lending and the Battle Against World Poverty.* New York: Public Affairs.

Zakaria, F. (2008). *The Post-American World.* New York: W.W. Norton and Company.

3
Communicating Gender in Population Development

Feminist critiques of global development raise concerns with the lack of agency in women's roles as well as the limited recognition of gender as necessarily connected to normative and structural conditions of power. Population programs particularly focus attention on women as reproductive agents, valuing women in terms of their attribution as potential and actual mothers. There is potential for population programs to situate interventions with an understanding of gender dynamics or even to reinforce women's leadership rather than targeting women specifically in more passive and limited roles. This chapter explores how development discourse articulates the construction of gender, articulated in institutional documentation describing programs and evaluations, as well as through public discourse. Within this narrative I also explore constructions of development problems and solutions, situating communication as a tool within this narrative, but also as a way of structuring our critique of gendered representation and of social change frameworks.

This chapter builds on feminist critiques concerning the nature of development, the role of communication, and the construction of women and gender, referencing the possibilities as well as limitations of global development discourse on population issues within Egypt. The development industry has attended to women's and gender issues in quite disparate ways over time, after ignoring women's contributions as active agents in communities for decades prior to the Decade for Women beginning in the 1970s (Wilkins, 2005). The 1994 UN International Conference on Population and Development (ICPD) in Cairo, along with the 1995 Fourth World Conference for Women in Beijing, marked opportunities for women to perform leadership roles in determining strategies for improving gender equality. Egypt offers a particularly important case study for this analysis, given the attention population programs have received in international development, its hosting of an important global conference on the subject, and its positioning within regional and global power dynamics.

Given the strategic importance of Egypt to the US, and the prominence of population issues as a serious matter for development, this study focuses on public discourse about women and development issues in Egypt, with additional attention to the privileging of media and communication technologies anthropomorphized as active agents themselves. Understanding these as complex concerns, I explore how population becomes articulated as a development concern; how women and gender come to be understood in the process of political and social change; and how communication technologies are referenced within this process.

Population programs may be conceptualized and implemented in quite different ways and with diverse justifications. Understanding population intervention begins with a construction of the development problem, which might be seen as a concern for individual women's access to and use of contraception, women's reproductive rights, demographic planning, or global environmental concerns. Modernization approaches to development, tending toward supporting national interventions, rely on bureaucratic and managerial approaches to planning, requiring census and other demographic data. Neoliberal approaches to development, which do not preclude modernization approaches, target individuals for social change, rather than consider the structural conditions that contribute to health status. Communication campaigns on population rely on the premise that information and communication technologies ICTs have the capacity to promote beneficial change. Part of the development narrative explored includes attention to the role of communication in the process of strategic development intervention.

In this chapter, I consider the institutional and public narrative of development population programs in terms of the articulation of women and potential for recognizing gender dynamics, as well as the constructions of communication in social change. This analysis focuses on Egypt specifically, as a case study that illustrates a potential tension in gender representation, as well as particular power dynamics. On the one hand, population programs tend to focus on women as passive targets, with the added weight of a global elite objectifying and denigrating women in the global South, particularly when considering women in Islamic countries. However, since the 1994 UN ICPD was hosted in Cairo, there is potential for public attention to women in

Egypt to recognize their capacity for leadership and active engagement. These global development conferences and programs are created and funded by institutions with their own missions and interests working within global power dynamics. Power can be considered from various angles, from taking patriarchy and Orientalism as ideological lens, to focusing on political-economic global connections and trends toward privatization in the development industry. How the limited discourse on women and gender becomes manifest in public discussions of development needs to be situated within contexts of national development, regional conditions, and global dynamics.

Development in Egypt

In this section, I characterize relevant contexts in situating analyses of development programs in Egypt. These include political and economic contexts structuring Egypt's position within global and regional dynamics, as well as national programs. Orientalism and patriarchy also contribute to ideological contexts that help explain the dynamics between Western development agencies and Egyptian programs, as well as assumptions guiding attention to population as a key issue for development intervention. Following this review of contextual considerations I review key concerns for development intervention in Egypt guiding population programs.

Political-economic context

Political and economic conditions structure development work through global, regional, and national economic conditions as well as hegemonic processes asserting political power. Relevant to this analysis are the global economic conditions of the development industry more broadly, as well as the relative positioning of Egypt within the region and in relation to US politics and development funding. It is important to understand the global conditions structuring development as not simply North vs. South dynamics, but rather as a manifestation of a development "geometry" (Shah & Wilkins, 2004) through which differences in access to resources matter more than territorial positioning.

Within the region, Egyptian leadership has mobilized Arab support from some nations while antagonizing others at various historical stages, projecting itself as a regional leader, even if other nations see themselves as competing for that role. The Arab region itself hosts a complex set of power dynamics within the Middle East, including the wealth of Saudi Arabia and other Gulf countries, tensions with and within Israel, cultural and linguistic differences with Turkey and Iran, media dominance of Lebanon, Qatar, and Egypt, support for Palestinian sovereignty, military intervention and violent conflicts in Iraq, Syria, and the Levant, and emerging resistance against longstanding regimes. The US assumption that Egypt should be a critical ally in the region makes this a particularly important nation from the perspective of US foreign policy (Wright, 2014), translating into substantial US funding for Egyptian development.

Recent trends in development funding overall demonstrate that while bilateral and multilateral agencies still dominate in terms of overall development funding, private funding sources are gaining in visibility and emerging proportionately as donors (see Chapter 1). Funding for maternal mortality specifically resonates with this trend, though it is combined with programs addressing children in global development assistance for maternal and child health (MCH). Financing directly attributed to maternal and reproductive health is difficult to disentangle from the broader category combining newborn and child health with that of the mother (MNCH). Some estimates document global funding for MNCH increasing on a global scale until 2010, at US\$ 6.48 billion, more than 2.5 times the amount recorded in 2003 (Hsu et al., 2012), declining in more recent years since 2010, with little relationship between bilateral expenditures and actual rates of mortality (Hsu et al., 2012; Requejo et al., 2014). The Partnership for Maternal, Newborn & Child Health, administered by the World Health Organization (WHO) and funded by a network of bilateral and multilateral agencies as well as private foundations, estimates higher figures, with US\$ 8 billion being spent in 2010, increasing to US\$ 8.7 billion in 2012 (OECD/CRS in PMNCH, 2014).

Overall, maternal health specifically has been underfunded by bilateral and multilateral agencies (Hogan et al., 2010; Kristof & WuDunn, 2009), which have decreased their funding dramatically since 1990 (UN agencies from 32 to 14% in 2007; bilateral funding from 47 to 27% in 2007; Ravishankar et al., 2009). A major increase in funding for health from private sources, from 19% in 1998 to 27% in 2007, can be explained in part by the initiation of the Gates Foundation into development work and by the expansion of drug and equipment donations from corporations (Ravishankar et al., 2009), as well as an emerging privatization of global development (Wilkins & Enghel, 2013). When the US Agency for International Development (USAID) decided to consider finding additional resources to contribute to global maternal and child health, the agency invited "corporate executives and millionaire philanthropists" to find "inefficiencies" in order to redirect funds (Cha, 2014).

Reflecting its "partnership" with corporate industry through Coca-Cola, USAID planned to invest "$21 million in a program that will expand the use of the beverage maker's delivery system to transport critical medicine and supplies such as oral rehydration packets, zinc and malaria treatments to rural communities in Africa" (Cha, 2014, para. 16). Although private and corporate donors are becoming increasingly visible in the development landscape, most of the total funding (76% of all ODA) allocated for maternal and child health and for reproductive health still originates through bilateral agencies.

Concerned that initial MDGs devoted to reducing maternal and child mortality will not be met, Oxfam America argues that it is partnerships at the local level that matter in working to improve maternal and child health, not just at the level of donors, referencing USAID connections with the WHO (Lentfer, 2014). USAID conceives of population and reproductive health within the broader domain of health, structured within its Bureau for Global Health, which also includes offices devoted to HIV/AIDS, health systems, and other health issues, infectious diseases (such as malaria and tuberculosis), and nutrition. Although the Office of Population and Reproductive Health formally falls within the Bureau for Global Health, and is structurally separate from the Gender Equality and Women's Empowerment Office, gender advisers work with this as well as other more established units within USAID. USAID has been a dominant bilateral agency working broadly in the field of population and maternal health, and within the case study considered here is part of a broader foreign aid package to Egypt.

Given Egypt's status as a key ally to the US within regional politics, national leaders have negotiated economic support cautiously over time, attempting to maintain this bilateral relationship while sensitive to national politics both within Egypt and within the US. Relative to most other countries targeted for aid, US government funding to Egypt has been high, averaging about US$ 2 billion a year since 1979, only surpassed by the amount of aid devoted to Israel, Afghanistan, Pakistan, and Iraq (Meyer, 2013).

Although US military assistance to Egypt has remained relatively stable with a slight decline since 2003 (at US$ 1599.7 million then and US$ 1301.4 million in 2012), even with dramatic changes in the Egyptian government, economic assistance has been quite variable over time, and has significantly reduced since 2010 (from US$ 505.8 million in 2003 to US$ 102.6 million in 2012). Most of this US economic assistance is channeled to the country through USAID for economic support and security support, with much less funding devoted to development, child survival, and agriculture. For example in 2012, of the total US$ 102.6 million spent on economic assistance, most of it (88%) went to USAID for economic and security support (86%), with only 2% for development and other issues; the remaining allocations supported State Department (7%) interventions on refugees, anti-terrorism, and narcotics control, or Department of Defense and other US grant programs (5%). US support is but one of many forms of assistance that Egypt receives from several sources. As a prominent political leader in the region, Egypt's national alliances with the US and other global actors have shifted dramatically over time, as has its internal leadership. These political and economic dynamics structure the possibilities for development funding, and are further justified and reinforced through the ideological prisms of Orientalism and patriarchy.

Orientalism in context

Another relevant condition of power in this context is that of Orientalism. This manifestation of ideological hegemony allows global elites to justify their dominance in economic and military strength through the assertion that some cultural communities are superior to others, in this case structured through Northern, Western perspectives on what become configured as "Orientalist" cultures (Said, 1971). The ideological structuring of Orientalism conflates several prejudices, against Eastern (from a Western point of view), Arab, and Islamic communities (Paik & Wilkins, 2005; Wilkins, 1995). The overly generalized and simplistic characterizations of these communities in Western discourse become manifest in unjust and harmful narratives foregrounding violence and building on problematic assumptions about gender. Working through ideological dominance, Orientalism becomes manifest in institutional decisions with political and economic consequences.

Constructions of women are problematic when women in Islamic communities are portrayed as victims, used to justify military and development intervention. Abu-Lughod (2013) raises this concern in her recent book connecting Western mediated representations of "Muslim women" to "a mission to rescue them from their own cultures" (p. 6). Military intervention corresponds with development agendas when their projects are justified as necessary and inevitable rescue missions. This homogenizing discourse serves to depoliticize serious global concerns that contribute to inequities as well as to distance women's suffering from donor communities. Hollywood narratives pervade these rescue fantasies differentiating heroes from victims also through eth-nicity, gender, nationality, and class, contributing to the privilege and prejudice that divide transnational communities (Mohanty, 1991).

Shirazi's research on Muslim women and their representation docu-ments and appreciates their collective movements to promote women's rights (2009), an active contribution largely ignored in Western media coverage (Shirazi, 2010; Wilkins, 1995). Relying on Orientalist stereo-types, public attention to Islam accentuates and generalizes the violence of a few, victimizing the plight of women. This stereotyping contributes to privileging of Muslim women as being considered necessary targets for development intervention (Shirazi, 2010).

While identification with Islam indicates religious beliefs and cul-tural practices, Western discourse mistakenly conflates this affiliation with Arab communities and Middle Eastern territories. Roy (2010) notes that while celebrities tend to be drawn to Africa (see Chapter 4 on education), "Brangelina to Namibia, Madonna to Malawi – another geography arouses imperial anxiety: the Middle East" (p. 21). Conceptu-alization of the Middle East in development "complicates the narrative of millennial development" (p. 148), whereby women are characterized as victims, best rescued through entrepreneurial missions, such as the Citygroup Foundation conference described by Roy (2010, p. 149) or the USAID program in 2001 focusing on empowering poor Arab women through first bilateral and then commercial funding (pp. 152–153). Constructions of women in development narratives need to take into account the particular ideological assertions rooted in political dynam-ics across groups with power and those attempting to gain access to those resources.

Patriarchy in context

Like Orientalism, patriarchy refers to an ideological dynamic that asserts one group as naturally and inevitably more powerful than another, with material consequences for those struggling for recognition and jus-tice. Gender dynamics are highlighted through attention to patriarchy more generally, but are necessarily connected to Orientalist ideologies in the development work described in this chapter. Development dis-course more broadly brings in assumptions about gendered roles in narratives of maternal and reproductive health, and in specific stories of girls and women in Egyptian intervention. While global and regional conditions of patriarchy contribute to the broader global development discourse, conditions specific to Egypt matter as well. Gender conditions in Egypt need to be understood in their particular context, which is in no way generalizable to other Arab or Islamic nations where concepts of women as national political leaders and having political rights are in stark contrast across these regional communities.

Past UNDP reports from 2004 have ranked Egypt low on gender empowerment scales, at 75th out of 78 countries on this index, but even worse on a gender-related development index (GDI). These low rankings are attributable to women's low participation in paid employment and in formal governance, pronounced gender gaps in literacy and education, and frequency of gender-based violence. At a national level, the Egyptian government has made public statements in support of gender equality. Moreover, some of the noted conditions have improved over time, particularly in terms of women's educational and literacy attainment. Recent estimates contrast 43% of women over 25 having secondary education with 59% of men, and two-thirds of women being literate compared with 82% of men (UNICEF, 2014).

However, men still dominate the documented labor force (75% are employed, compared to only 24% of women in 2014), with women's economic participation being fairly consistent over time even with more girls being more educated and literate (varying from 28% in 1990, 21% in 2000, and 26% in 2012) (Ministry of Health, Arab Republic of Egypt, 2014). Comparatively, women are much less likely to have economic opportunities than men in Egypt, not only within global parameters (Egypt ranked 124th out of 132 countries in the World Economic Forum gender gap index, 2012) but also within the region (it is 7th among 15 countries in the Middle East; ECWR, 2014). Political participation though is even more restricted, with fewer than 3% of elected parliamentary seats held by women in 2013 and very low political engagement more broadly (Klugman et al., 2014, p. 164).

Despite formal policies in support of women's rights, social norms continue to support discrimination against women. Sexual harassment, widely documented in the country (ECWR, 2014), can be difficult to challenge. According to a 2005 Demographic and Health Survey (DHS), one-third of Egyptian women reported experience with domestic violence, rising to 41% among the poorest group (Monazea & Khalek, 2010). While national agencies formulate policies on behalf of women, social norms restrict women's everyday experiences.

An established index of gender inequality combines indicators of employment, political participation and education with those of reproductive health, such as maternal mortality and adolescent fertility. A recent *Human Development Report* (2014) notes improvement across these measures in Egypt, with a 0.67 rate on this index in 1995 improving slightly with a drop to 0.58 by 2013; this trend is similar in other Arab countries though it has been more dramatically reduced in Kuwait (from 0.59 to 0.29) and Tunisia (from 0.42 to 0.27). These trends toward improvement correspond with the global development and national objectives established in the 1994 ICPD to promote gender equality, not only through improving women's conditions, but also through motivating men to take responsibility for sexual health and family life (Natividad et al., 2014).

While patriarchal preferences for men's dominance in political, economic, and social realms continue to contribute to problematic conditions for women, there appears to be documented movement toward gender equality. These trends may be in part a result of broader conditions facilitating girls in formal education and women in the labor market, but may also be promoted through strategic intervention. The development industry relies on the assumption that specific intervention has the capacity to contribute in meaningful ways to improving conditions such as maternal and reproductive health. The health of people is contingent upon the overall conditions that provide resources and services in local communities and supported through government programs and policies for the public good.

Development in Egypt

In terms of its national development, Egypt is currently categorized as a middle-income country and in the "medium human development" ranking (at 112th out of 187 ranked countries in the Human Development index, 2012), having improved over time in measures of life expectancy, literacy, and income. Life expectancy at birth has been most recently documented to be 71 years of age for men and 76 for women (Egyptian profile, 2014). Prior to recent transitions in leadership, the Egyptian government agreed at a 2000 UN meeting to focus its development interventions on reducing extreme poverty, promoting universal primary education for all children, combating maternal and child mortality, and addressing environmental sustainability.

Although the Egyptian government has reported its commitment to investing in health services, access to physicians remains challenging, with about 2.83 physicians available for every 1000 people in the country (Index Mundi, 2014). According to the WHO global health expenditure database, Egypt has been spending proportionately less of its GDP on health, from 5.4% in 2000 down to 4.7% by 2010; by comparison Tunisia (to 6.2%), Kuwait (to 2.6%), and Yemen (to 5.2%) have all increased their proportional spending on health care during this time period. The most serious infectious diseases documented in Egypt include bacterial diarrhea, hepatitis A, typhoid fever, and schistosomiasis. What attracts health funding though is not just a matter of incidence but also a matter of political significance, subject to the perceived inevitabilities of conventional wisdom as well as the negotiations across competing communities.

The very articulation of development status can be seen as part of a broader ideological narrative. Mitchell's classic critiques of conventional development discourse highlight the problematic presumption taken when constructing Egypt's problems as a product of too many people with too little arable land (1991). His work has inspired subsequent scholarship chronicling how the development industry constructs problems as apolitical conditions that require technical solutions through managerial processes (Escobar, 1995). Mitchell questions who benefits from the assumption that Egypt suffers from overpopulation, offering counter arguments concerning calorie consumption and nutritional benefits. It appears that at the time of his analysis, although Egyptians consumed high levels of calories on average, the wealthy were eating quite a bit more meat, while the poor were suffering from malnutrition. He attributes emerging Egyptian dependence on the US for grain imports as less a product of overpopulation and more a result of increased meat consumption (1999). Quite relevant to this analysis is the concern that development programs tend to be justified in ways that appear natural and necessary, obscuring attention to power.

Considering Egyptian development in the 1990s, Mitchell (1999) observes "neoliberalism" as a "triumph of the political imagination." Conventional narratives of this era suggest that Egypt was in economic crisis early in this decade, but purportedly improved through deregulation and privatization, exacerbating economic inequalities and strengthening in local elite wealth. US aid supports private enterprise within Egypt, and when considering public agencies within the country focuses on the Egyptian military (Mitchell, 1991). Despite temporary suspension of US military aid to Egypt in 2013 over concern with the way al-Sisi came to power, the military within Egypt is recognized as having been stable and strong throughout changes in leadership, though at the expense of civic participation (Kirkpatrick, 2014). Absent from the broad discourse on development in Egypt is attention to the military, particularly important given the substantial proportion of US funding dedicated to this industry, as well as the tested stability of the Egyptian military, even with dramatic changes in leadership since 2011. The rise of General al-Sisi to national leadership is a testament to the enduring power of the Egyptian military (Kirkpatrick, 2014). That some forms of development become more visible, such as economic growth (Escobar, 1995), over others, such as the growth of the military industry, illustrates the political nature of these narratives.

Research approach

Within development narratives of population concerns, the recognition of particular frames of problems and the justifications for their institutional solutions reinforce dominant assumptions about the nature of social change, the potential of communication, and roles attributed to gender. To explore public discourse I rely on public sources documenting program missions and descriptions and evaluations of population interventions, funded through foreign agencies and implemented in Egypt. I also include attention to news sources as another manifestation of public discourse on the topic. This analysis builds on elite news published since the year of the ICPD conference. Search terms included "gender" or "women," and "development" in "Egypt" or "Cairo" on news sources available in English-language publications from 1994 to 2014 identified through the LexisNexis database. Focusing on English-language sources necessarily limits this sample from being more comprehensive, but foregrounds global elite discussions of these issues. Within these parameters there are 185 relevant articles, published through sources in North America (31%), Asia (10%), Western Europe (18%), Egypt and other Arab countries (35%), and Sub-Saharan Africa (5%).

Population and development

Within development work, substantial resources have been devoted to population control when justifying programs in terms of their perceived benefit to women (Staudt, 1997). Population programs have been critiqued for valuing women in terms of their breeding and feeding potential, as passive targets rather than as active subjects of social change (Wilkins, 2005). While much of the development discourse has indeed limited women's agency to these narrow roles, public attention to UN conferences and historical junctures (such as the 1995 Beijing conference and the Decade for Women 1976–1985) have offered the potential for women to be recognized as leaders, actively engaged in contributing to policies and programs. Health programs do not necessarily need to be focused on women exclusively, but can follow "gender transformative" approaches (Kraft et al., 2014). Population in development can be seen as more than merely an intervention to promote individual behavior change (such as increasing contraception use), but also as connected with sustainability, poverty reduction, and women's reproductive rights.

The fifth of the MDGs aims to reduce maternal mortality dramatically, defined as the "death of women during pregnancy, childbirth, or in the 42 days after delivery" (Hogan et al., 2010, p. 1), through achieving universal access to reproductive health. Of all the MDGs, this outcome is among the least likely to achieve success. The original timetable for this objective will not be met. Kristof and WuDunn (2009) note that although child mortality has been reduced, maternal deaths are still prevalent, particularly in the global South, and, importantly, they are preventable. Hogan et al. (2010) document that almost 300,000 women died from preventable causes related to pregnancy and childbirth in 2013, with this rate being 14 times higher in poor compared to wealthier countries (p. 29). A UN report published in 2014 documents a 45% drop from 1990 to 2013. Most of these deaths, one-third of which occurred in India and Nigeria, would have been preventable with access to better health services. Strategic interventions to strengthen movement toward reducing maternal mortality call for women's active engagement and decision-making in political governance as well as within family and reproductive health decisions, and for raising the age of first marriage for girls (UN Women, 2015).

Population as a development issue includes varied concerns justified by quite different arguments. As a subject of intervention, population programs can attempt to improve access to and service delivery of family planning techniques and contraception, reproductive rights, gender dynamics contributing to sexual and fertility decisions, maternal health services and policies, along with the many relevant economic, normative and political dimensions contributing to women's and men's sexual health, reproductive potential, and demographic patterns. Development planning itself depends on demographic assessments, with tools such as the census (Wilkins, 2004a). Population programs themselves are justified at the level of individual rights and choices as well as social obligations and circumstances in relation to environmental pressures, and at times, at odds with political pressures for communities to sustain their numbers to show strength in times of conflict.

Strategic intervention in the development industry takes shape in the form of programs with missions articulating population as a central character in the development landscape, manifest in funded projects implemented through donor allocations in countries with fewer resources. Another form of strategic intervention, though perhaps less often seen as such, emerges with the convening of global conventions, attracting recognition for particular development themes, such as women, poverty, or sustainable development. These conferences are strategic in their organized attempts to frame global problems and to privilege institutional solutions. The 1994 ICPD conference in Cairo maintains a central position in the history of global population discourse. At this UN-hosted event, delegates:

> reached a consensus that the equality and empowerment of women is a global priority. It approached this not only from the perspective of universal human rights, but also as an essential step towards eradicating poverty and stabilizing population growth. A woman's ability to access reproductive health and rights is [a] cornerstone of her empowerment. It is also the key to sustainable development.
>
> (UNFPA, 2014a)

According to Ali, the ICPD in 1994

> pressured international family planning programs to be more sensitive to the issue of reproductive rights based on ideas of gender equality, equity, and the empowerment of women. The move paralleled a shift from a model of service delivery, based primarily on targets and incentives strategy, to one that integrated information, education, and communication.
>
> (2002, p. 374)

Current reviews of this conference describe the event as contributing a major paradigmatic shift, which "marked a historic global consensus on sexual and reproductive health and rights, at a time that also saw the international resurgence and consolidation of conservative sexual and reproductive politics and movements" (Natividad et al., 2014, p. 594). In the same volume of *Global Public Health*, contributors also advocate pushing a gender- and rights-based approach even further in support of sexual and reproductive health and rights (SRHR; Gruskin & Sundari Ravindran, 2014; Sen, 2014). The 1994 event signifies a significant challenge to privatizing trends in social service financing of public programs in health and family planning, as well as to previous global conferences on population and development that "had been defined by (neo-)colonial concerns regarding overpopulation and the need to curb the population growth rates of poor countries in order for the 'developing world' to achieve economic progress" (Natividad et al.,

2014, p. 594). This conference initiated public articulation of gender as a central feature in understanding women's health.

How has development been conceptualized in discussions of women and gender in Egypt subsequent to the ICPD conference in 1994? Development concerns could conceivably be addressing a variety of issues such as gender inequities in resources or rights, women's political interests, population and maternal health, education, or gender-based violence. How women's interests become categorized in relation to development goals is explored next.

A dominant concern attracting attention in this sample was that of economic gain, particularly through microenterprise (21%). This is an important context in which to understand how attention to population (12%) and maternal health (11%) issues are situated within broader attention to women and gender in development. News focused on population as a development concern might cover issues such as fertility rates, family planning, reproductive rights, or sustainable development. Maternal health coverage considers mortality as well as access to services and contraception that contribute to women's reproductive health. Some of the articles reviewed also considered women's education (16%), political participation (14%), policy issues concerning national programs and responsibilities (14%), as well as domestic (4%), and other manifestations of violence (8%).

Attention to development also focuses on women's participation in formal economic and political systems, as well as educational systems. Among these potential connections education was the most dominant theme (16%). Typically these discussions approach educational issues as apolitical ways to approach gender equity in literacy skills and school enrollment, often as a way to delay marriage by keeping girls in school longer. Stories also emphasized advancing economic empowerment and resources (21%), as a "smart investment" that contributes to lower fertility rates. Political engagement was the least likely of these three spheres to be addressed (5%), highlighting how few women were in elected positions of power or holding leadership positions. This broad trend reflects Egypt's more beneficial effort at improving girls' education but relatively lesser progress in improving women's economic position or political status.

Violence is an important feature in these discussions, in part because of the tendency for coverage to focus on women as victims. Close to 12% of the articles assessed included attention to gender-based violence, with most of these specifically considering domestic violence such as marital rape and abuse, bride burning, and honor killing. Other forms of violence described included instances in war, sex trafficking, and sexual harassment. Many of these descriptions considered violence against women as problematic for society as a whole. Some discussed potential reasons behind the prevalence of sexual harassment in Egypt, as a product of urban crowding, lack of privacy, or men feeling "threatened by an increasingly active female labour force, with conservatives laying the blame for harassment on women's dress and behaviour" (Toronto Star, 2009, para. 14). While some attention to violence may be promoting a passive stance for women when emphasizing their roles as victims, the connection of gender-based violence to health and other social outcomes allows gender differences to be understood as critical contextual factors.

Public attention to development issues might cover broad trends in society, such as education, literacy, or poverty levels, or strategic interventions more specifically. The development enterprise depends on problems being articulated in ways that justify institutional intervention. On a global scale, this means legitimating the actions of donor agencies in creating development programs.

About one-quarter (26%) of the reviewed articles explicitly mentioned donor interventions in their consideration of development issues. Among the donors listed, the groups receiving the most attention were USAID specifically along with UN agencies combined, followed by the World Bank; the Gates Foundation was the next most central actor, with much more celebration in recent years given its recent initiation into the development industry. In 2014, the Khalifa Fund for Enterprise Development, which distributed US$ 200 million in loans from the UAE to Egypt, attracted a great deal of attention. Another private foundation mentioned is the Ford Foundation, and commercial firms specifically noted include Microsoft, Nike, Pepsi, Google, and Mastercard, among others. Next I consider how gender and women figure within these broader narratives of development.

Gender

Current attention to women's issues and gender concerns is integral in global discourse promoted by dominant development institutions, through their assertion of the MDGs (UN, 2014). Among other concerns, the MDGs focus on reducing maternal mortality and achieving universal access to reproductive health services, relevant to women's health and population issues. While attention to women in development is valuable, recognition of gender highlights potential concerns with the ways in which programs articulate problematic assumptions about women and men in society. Feminist critiques of mainstream development enterprises underscore the patriarchal nature of discourse that privileges men's roles over those of women, valuing women in terms of their reproductive potential (Wilkins, 2007).

The initial year of news analysis is intentionally chosen to be 1994, a year marking the potential for women to be constructed as active leaders engaged in global development. This year signifies a pivotal moment in the history of gender and development, when prominent leaders convened to create a collective declaration on behalf of women's reproductive health rights, as a significant issue in global development. This 1994 conference is notable not only for the significant attention given to reproductive rights in public discourse, but also for the leadership of many women from diverse backgrounds, countries, and organizations. As leaders of these varied constituencies, their collective rhetoric and actions can be seen as enacting agency within global development discourse.

How, then, are women articulated in global attention to gender dynamics in Egypt subsequent to this 1994 event? How often is this strategic enactment of collective voice referenced in the news? In the 20 years since ICPD, out of the 185 news stories discussing "women" or "gender" in "Egypt" in English-language digital news, over half (59%) specifically referenced this conference. Positive coverage followed the few years following the ICPD conference, citing globally known women in leadership positions and articulating the strengths of women and of collective movements. Women in the Arab region were commended for "making progress at all levels of society" (Eid, 1994).

Some of these sources (though not many at 6%) explicitly identified women as active global leaders. Often noted Hillary Clinton made news as the "honorary head of the delegation" (PR Newswire, 1999), while other articles cited Dr. Nasif Sadik, head of the United Nations Population Fund (UNFPA), as hoping to expand attention to HIV/AIDS as a critical concern since the 1994 event (Deutsch, 1999). In connection with the International Steering Committee Meeting on the Economic Advancement of Rural Women held in 1996, Jordan's Queen Noor was celebrated by press in Malaysia and Lebanon. Almost two decades later, local news coverage in Egypt described this as a high-status conference that "brought together world leaders, government officials, rights campaigners, and representatives of civil society and the media from 179 countries to discuss developmental challenges, linking these with human rights issues, especially women's issues," commending the group for including discussion of female genital mutilation (Amin, 2012).

References to the ICPD more than a decade later raised concerns with the established goals not being met. Noeleen Heyzer, leading the UN Economic and Social Commission for Asia and the Pacific (ESCAP), finds that the ICP goals "remain out of reach for too many countries and too many groups of people in Asia and the Pacific" (States News Service, 2009). According to the *Guardian*, "As the UN looks to mark the 20th anniversary of the Cairo agreement this year, women's rights organisations are, more and more, having to concern themselves with fighting reactionary policies that seek to chip away at hard-won rights" (Ford, 2014, para. 4). Jordanian coverage leading up to and including a 20-year review of the 1994 ICPD describes the Cairo conference as one of several regional events organized through various UN institutions as well as the African Union and the Arab League, to review the "challenges facing the region's population over the next several years and their effects on women and gender equality" (*The Jordan Times*, 2013), in an attempt "to influence the future of global population and development" (Malkawi, 2013). While the first Arab Women's Conference held in Cairo was applauded by a Nuha Mahmoud Al Ma'ayata, a woman running for office in the Jordanian parliament, she worried that the current "absence of women in Egyptian political life is tragic," attributed in part to a "rise in religious conservatism" (Sweis, 2012, para. 35).

How did coverage of development issues vary by region? North American news sources (44%) were more likely to cover population concerns than those from other regions, while Arab (57%) and Sub-Saharan (88%) news sources devoted the largest percentage of their coverage to economic issues. Asian news sources tended to cover issues related to political participation (44%), as did Western European sources (44%).

The emphasis on economic development presented in Asian (40%) and Arab news sources (44%) might be interpreted as relevant responses to high rates of unemployment and concerns over economic insecurity. On the other hand, both regions focused much less on political participation, with 8% of Asian news sources and 25% of Arab news sources addressing the political participation of women. Such patterns may indicate the reluctance of these countries to address political structures preventing women's political participation. Arab news sources paid relatively less attention to issues of population (10%) and maternal health (11%), in comparison to North American media, where the ICPD appears to have been a more significant issue.

How did attention to development concerns shift over time? The sharp increase in highlighting of women's political participation (57%) more recently (from 2010 to 2014; compared with 9% from 1994 to 1999; 23% from 2000 to 2004; and 11% from 2005 to 2009) corresponds with well-publicized political protests that included women as active participants. During this time, attention not only to political participation, but also policy, education, and economic issues increased from previous years, reflecting the greater movement towards accelerated social change in the region. Attention to economic development issues also increased over time, reflecting increasing attention to national economies and to corporate programs facilitating development goals.

While a large number of news articles reviewed were published between 1990 and 1994, there were no publications from Arab news sources during the first decade observed; the proportional increase to one-fifth and then in the more recent era to three-quarters of the publications analyzed may be a product of a growing news industry publishing in the English language, intentionally producing texts meant for elite consumption. Although ICPD is considered to be a milestone event (included in over half of the articles reviewed), during the early years the conference was covered mostly by Western news, mainly in North American (55%) and West European (30%) news sources; in later years the ICPD did gain the interest of Arab news sources (63% of articles reviewed from the Arab news sources mention ICPD) as the news industry publishing in English began to grow.

This analysis demonstrates the potential for women to be understood as leaders and as politically engaged, while the broader patterns also highlight women's political as well as economic contributions to their societies. Next, how women's roles are constructed overall, and the types of empowerment privileged, are considered.

Women's empowerment

How do women come to be featured in these stories as subjects of development, and then more specifically, which version of empowerment is promoted? Overall, global attention to women in the context of Egypt highlights women's roles as "women" generically (30%), but also more specifically as political citizens (24%), mothers (12%), students (9%), small-scale entrepreneurs (20%), or victims of violence (5%).

Although political engagement was not highlighted as a prominent development theme, women's political status and rights as citizens did feature in one-quarter of these articles. These political rights related to policies such as inheritance rights, divorce laws, and age of legal

marriage initially, but women's active participation in protests referenced their role as citizens. Women's potential as entrepreneurs or
as active earners in formal labor markets brought attention to economic opportunities and employment, often discussed in terms of
microfinance programs.

Some stories (12%) reviewed emphasized women's roles as mothers,
specifically as central caretakers of children. In this portrait, women
appear to have value to society through their potential to give birth
and to act on behalf of the family. Slightly fewer (9%) concentrated
on women and girls as students, promoting educational approaches to
development. Some attention (5%) was also given to women as victims
of domestic and other forms of violence.

News sources from North America were more likely to frame
women's role as simply "women" (54%) and as citizens (42%) than as
entrepreneurs (23%). News sources from Western Europe also more or
less represented women equally as women (44%) or as citizens (41%).
News sources from Asian (33%), Arab (48%), and African regions (50%)
more frequently portrayed women as playing the role of entrepreneur in
development. This finding may be interpreted as indicative of a prioriti-
zation of economic growth in news sources originating from developing
countries. The focus on women's economic contributions might also
represent a way to avoid addressing the political and social barriers
women face by focusing on their individual economic potential (mostly
limited to small-scale economic activities).

Despite the focus on reproductive rights through the 1994 conference,
this early time period was more likely to focus on "women" without
connection to active economic, political, or social agency or affiliation. Portraying women's role in development as "women" recognizes
the agency and independence of women free from other relational ties
(e.g. mother, wife, daughter) in making decisions over issues such as
birth control, family planning, and female genital mutilation. This also
reflects the message of ICPD that population issues and maternal health
need to be conceptualized as human and women's rights.

The Egyptian Initiative for Personal Rights (EIPR) produced its own
report, *Reclaiming & Redefining Rights: ICPD+20: Status of Sexual and
Reproductive Health and Rights in the Middle East and North Africa* (2013),
doing just that. Instead of seeing 2014 as an end to the mandates
proposed in 1994, they suggest extending the Program of Action "indef-
initely" (p. 4). Reproductive rights are seen as a way to ensure that
women have "autonomy over their bodies," both in protecting health
and in preventing violence. This mandate has a clear gender framework,

acknowledging the challenges of patriarchal culture and the importance of civic inclusion, arguing not just for reproductive health, but also for reproductive justice.

The framing of women as entrepreneurs intensified over time (by 8% from 1994 to 1999 and 5% from 2000 to 2004, up to 29% from 2005 to 2009 and increasing to 59% from 2010 to 2014), resonant with trends toward privatization within the development industry. There is a similar pattern of fluctuation in citizen frames over the four time periods, with a rapid rise in the "women as citizens" frame from 2005–2009 (13%) to 2010–2014 (58%). This is most likely due to the salience of women's roles as political activists in political protests.

Among the news articles reviewed, close to half (44%) explicitly refer to "women's" "empowerment" as a central issue. These articles were published from news services in the Arab region (37%) as well as those from North America (32%), Europe (11%), Asia (12%), and Africa (7%). There is a dramatic fluctuation in the appearance of the word "empowerment" over time (21% from 1994 to 1999; 12% from 2000 to 2004; 15% from 2005 to 2009; and 52% from 2010 to 2014), in line with similar emerging attention to women's active political and economic roles.

What becomes articulated as empowerment is explored next, whether conceptualized as an individual attribute promoting choices and behaviors, as geared toward economic gain or political agency, or as a collective movement toward improving social status. Among articles focusing on women's empowerment, slightly more than half emphasize economic empowerment (55%), followed by social (48%) and political (30%) empowerment.

Articles that consider empowerment in terms of social conditions raise concerns with contexts of violence, of marriage, and of divorce. In the earlier time period, social empowerment was conceived as women's right to use contraception and to plan families, resonant with the ICPD agenda. To illustrate this dominant theme, one article defines "women's empowerment" as an ability to choose a "smaller family size ... [so that women] have 'the freedom to decide if, when and how often' to reproduce" (Stackhouse, 1994, para. 4). This same article quotes Gita Sen, a prominent Indian academic and feminist, applauding this connection of empowerment with broader population issues: "If somebody had said five years ago that population policy would be concerned with reproductive health and women's empowerment, they would have been laughed at" (para. 17). If ICPD is seen to set the definition of social empowerment as exercising control over reproductive rights, international attention to the sexual harassment of women highlights the social empowerment of women as enabling them to protect themselves in the fight against sexual violence (41%).

> Informal youth-based initiatives that have sought to transform the streets of Cairo, Egypt, into harassment-free spaces for women, point to strong evidence that they can contribute to positive social and political change. They do not speak of "gender empowerment," but their catchy slogans – "Don't harass: the street is yours and hers" and "Look me in the eye" – have been widely circulated online, by people in the street carrying messages for passersby to read and in the media. The powerful graffiti images associated with these campaigns speak volumes. Groups of men in vests inscribed with "against harassment" have roamed the squares and streets, seeking to prevent women from being assaulted and establishing new models of masculinity. These young men are leaders, organisers and innovators in challenging patriarchy in ways that strike a chord with a public.
>
> (Tadros, 2014, para. 5–7)

Siddiqui (2002) recognizes the collective rights of women in Egypt, as well as social norms of patriarchy, in an article at first announcing that "Arab women [are] the least empowered," but elaborating further that:

> Patriarchy is anchored not just in religion – and particularly in its more conservative interpretations – but culture, tradition, economics and politics. Variance in the treatment of women across the Middle East attests to it. The UN report, for example, praises Jordan and Egypt for giving women the right to initiate divorce.
>
> (para. 11)

Social conditions tend to be the target of women's empowerment in these discussions, but occasionally surface as inhibiting factors. News reports challenge social and religious practices that are seen as undermining gender equality, such as child marriage, female genital mutilation, and the wearing of the chadar (*The Scotsman*, 1995; *This Day*, 2014), putting wardrobe choices somehow on equal footing with physical surgery and legal partnership. While this concern with women's clothing characterizes much of the problematic representation of women as suffering from static "traditions," cultural practices can also be understood as dynamic; a former director of the UNFPA builds on this assumption that cultural contexts have the ability to support rather than merely constrain transition (*Daily News Egypt*, 2009d). Siddiqui (2002) contributes to this understanding of culture as complex, citing Esposito who contends that: "Those wearing the hijab are not passive victims of male-imposed mores but active agents for change. They regard veiling as an authentic practice that preserves their dignity and freedom, enabling them to act and to be treated as persons rather than sex objects" (para. 21). In contrast to envisioning social conditions in more monolithically negative tones, some sources articulate women as proactive agents of change in their societies.

While this conceptualization of women as a group highlights women's capacities and rights, other statements suggest empowerment of women is connected with familial obligations. For example, coverage of the ICPD suggests that "empowering women and girls is key to ensuring the well-being of individuals, families, nations and our world" (*The Statesman*, 2014). While women may indeed be central in the lives of families, there is a potential risk of relying on problematic gendered stereotypes.

Many fewer articles discuss women's political empowerment, but those that do describe gender rankings that concern the particularly low political involvement of women in the Egyptian government. However, this assertion of women as active agents is limited when their participation is circumscribed to a formal venue of governance, and when the voices of these movements are dominated by the wives of political leaders.

Voice, as one critical manifestation of political participation, tends to be dominated by women whose status results from their marriages rather than their personal merits. Former first lady of Egypt Suzanne Mubarak was quoted across national news sources calling for "Arab women" to "be empowered to play a more active role" (Associated Press International, 2001, para. 3) and to be actively involved "in decision-making, to improve their role in media and non-governmental organizations and to develop financial capabilities" (Gavlak, 2000, para. 2; also referenced in Xinhua General News Service, 2000a; Xinhua General News Service, 2000b). Another former political leader's wife, Leila Ben Ali of Tunisia, is also commended for her work with NGOs, such as the Arab Women's Organization, noted as promoting "women's 'empowerment,' [and as] a favorite of leaders' spouses. It was founded at the behest of Suzanne Mubarak" (Rosenberg, 2011, para. 20).

One theme of the Cairo conference was "empowering women" through "increased education and awareness of their reproductive rights" (Eid, 1994, para. 1). A Canadian news source marks this shift as moving attention from "women's development" to "female empowerment," particularly women's rights "to control their reproductive capacity as well as to adequate health care," making the Cairo conference a critical "forum on social justice" (Stackhouse, 1994, para. 17). Notable in this narrative are the voices of Gita Sen, well-known Indian feminist and scholar (Stackhouse, 1994), and Sameera Al-Tuwaijri, UN Director (States News Service, 2014), rather than the wives of national leaders. Along these lines, another news source appreciates the work of "an increasingly vibrant array of local and international women activists and NGOs (for) setting especially effective agendas that meet the needs of women in their own countries" (*Daily News Egypt*, 2010b, para. 4).

According to the United Nations Arab Human Development Report (2005), Arab women are the least "empowered" women anywhere in the world. Using Egypt as their example, they explain that "[w]hen women applied to be judges in the State Council, Egypt's highest administrative court, the council's general assembly voted against it, arguing that women's emotional disposition and maternal duties rendered them unfit (Al-Naggar, 2010, para. 15)." Although the decision was later overruled, no women have been appointed (Arabic Network for Human Rights Information, 2013; Sweis, 2012). Although the recent Arab uprisings gave women much credit for their significant role, "they were labeled unpatriotic when they put forward the gender agenda before the new political class" (*This Day*, 2014, para. 11). More recent attention to women in politics describes their active participation in public protests against the regime (*This Day*, 2014). But when articulated as participation in formal political structures, empowerment is typically coupled with formal economic participation in a paid workforce.

Former US Secretary of State Hillary Clinton asserts this economic articulation as part of US policy, suggesting "that the US government will 'more strongly embed family planning in our health agenda, because we also think it's an economic issue, and it's an empowerment issue, and it's an issue that cuts across much of what we do in development work'" (*Right Vision News*, 2011). The World Bank maxim that "gender equality is smart economics" appears to be referenced frequently as a justification for empowering women (*Daily the Pak Banker*, 2011a, 2011b, 2011c).

Women may be empowered so that "their talents and skills can boost countries' competitiveness and support growth in an uncertain global economy" (*Daily the Pak Banker*, 2011a, para. 16). It is critical to note that supporting reproductive health is justified as a way to promote women's economic empowerment, not only to benefit national economic growth but also specifically to "keep many families afloat" (*Daily the Pak Banker*, 2011a, para. 17). The intersection of population as rights to reproductive services and fertility control with individual, familial, and national economic benefit situates women's health as a necessary human right as well as a necessary condition for sustainable economic development.

Economic empowerment becomes clearly articulated as a development goal, institutionalized through bilateral and multilateral intervention as well as events such as the Global Summit of Women, branded as "Davos for Women" (Hugin, 2006, para. 2). Organizations such as the Egyptian Business Women's Association, along with the African Alliance for Women's Empowerment, have organized meetings, similar to many other nongovernmental organizations globally, to explore "economic empowerment" specifically in "support of Small and Medium Enterprises to Meet the Millennium Development Goals (MDGs) and the Post 2015 Development Agenda" (PR Newswire, 2013, para. 3). When USAID collaborated with the Egyptian government on the New Horizons Program in the 1990s, they linked "economic empowerment" through microenterprise with "ensuring access to safe, high quality family planning services and health care" (The White House, 1999, para. 23). Programs through the Middle East Partnership Initiative (MEPI) connect economic empowerment with political and educational development goals as well.

While economic skills might be applied in the world of public sector planning or nonprofit service, it is business entrepreneurship that is privileged, particularly when applied to small- and medium-sized enterprises. Development goals are designed "to empower Arab women and youth to keep pace with the cutting edge of development, economic management and planning" (Jordanian News Agency, 2010, para. 7), or to increase "the acceptance of women in business" (Middle East Company News Wire, 2012, para. 7).

Linking this economic benefit to women's emergence as "social entrepreneurs," development programs such as the Vital Voices Global Partnership are "enabling them to create a better world for us all" (PR Newswire, 2008). Another article quoting "Leila Farah El-Mokaddem, the African Development Bank's new Resident Representative in Egypt," agrees that through "expanding income generation to both women and men, families are collectively better off, while the economy is more productive resulting in an overall win–win situation" (African Development Bank, 2014, para. 1).

Resonant with the themes raised in discussions of microenterprise as a viable channel toward empowering women, economic gains can be partnered with technology. A US news source emphasizes this link when describing the TechWomen Program, as "[c]hampioning two distinct but equally key themes of President Obama's June 2009 Cairo speech, TechWomen both supports development in the field of technology and empowers women" (US Federal News, 2010, para. 3). These articulations of empowerment highlight the status of women: yet women's potential needs to be understood as conditioned through the context of gender.

Articulation of gender

Development interventions that target women do so with attention to women's health and rights specifically, often without attention to broader gender dynamics, which can be articulated explicitly or implied indirectly through attention to both women and men. In public discourse concerning population programs, male partners' perceptions and actions have the potential to become part of the story, in conjunction with women's, but these gender dynamics are less typically articulated than attention to women alone. Men do not become visible without women in discussions focused on gender. In the news sources, only about one-third (31%) of the articles included attention to gender. Discussions of political protests and activist campaigns did address women and men as actively engaged, and at times specifically recognized sexual harassment and gender equality concerns.

Health program frameworks or narratives that consider gender transformative potential are rarer. A campaign called "He for She" (*The New Zealand Herald*, 2014) or the "White Ribbon Campaign" (US Official News, 2014) are examples of such gender narratives that recognize gender equality as being implicated not only in the actions of women but also in the involvement of "men as fathers, sons, husbands and brothers" (*The New Zealand Herald*, 2014, para. 14). Neither are men particularly nor gender dynamics more broadly considered in this narrative. The focus of development, like that of the intervention descriptions, targets women for change. Next I consider how media and communication technologies figure in this public discourse.

Communication

Communication for development builds on the idea that mediated technologies and communication processes have the potential to facilitate the goals of social change interventions. Considering the discourse of how communication might work within this context allows us to expand our vision to critical analyses of communication about how mediated technologies and processes are expected to work.

Among other strategies, population programs consider communication campaigns as strategies to inform and educate women to change their behavior in alignment with use of contraception devices. A great deal of social marketing research analyzes the potential for mediated campaigns to raise the knowledge, attitudes, and behaviors of women targeted through development intervention. In addition to a straightforward psychological model of individual social change, another conceptual model suggests that information, skills, and social support enhance strategic life choices, such as the timing and circumstances of marriage. Communication is seen as broadening people's senses of possibility and agency. In the case of girls and women's rights, choice might not only be considered in terms of the right to choose the timing and partner of marriage, but also in terms of the right to divorce, the right to inherit, and the right to consent to sexual activity, whether within or outside the confines of marriage.

A somewhat odd assumption that watching television could contribute to women's empowerment has been studied with conflicting results: while women in Egypt are not necessarily more or less "empowered" given their media habits, Kabeer (2011a) suggests that women in Bangladesh who watch talk shows demonstrate more tendencies toward empowerment than those who do not; this finding though does not allow us to do more than establish correlations without potential attribution to underlying factors such as socio-economic status. Moreover, some of these studies illustrate broader trends, whereas evaluations analyze the effects of strategic interventions.

While development interventions appear to favor communication as a strategy to build knowledge and skills among girls, communication as technology is privileged as a tool to promote economic skills, particularly in the private sphere. Not yet in Egypt but in neighboring Jordan, along with Chile and India, the Intel Teach education program is designed "to prepare young people to thrive in today's digital world" (Glinski et al., 2013, p. 3), through teaching skills and confidence in using new technologies. The story highlighted in a program description applauds a female math teacher in Jordan for teaching her 9th grade students about the stock market, exemplifying the value placed on free-market economics. Another example of a development program promoting computer skill training as a way to help women find jobs in the private sector was implemented in Egypt and Jordan, along with Lebanon. This training program for female as well as male students was administered through the UNDP and national governments, along with Cisco Systems (Gill et al., 2010). The implied framework of change centers on individuals learning digital media skills and mathematical competencies that allow them to engage in particular market activities.

News attention to the role of communication as a technology facilitating social change was not nearly as prominent as in the narratives depicting microenterprise development schemes, more closely connected with global capitalism and privatized communication industries. But when Information and Communication Technologies are included in these discussions, they are more likely to appear within US publications than those distributed by other nations.

US sources were the most likely to include explicit discussion of media and communications (38%). Comparatively fewer articles from the Arab (34%), European (19%), and Asian (9%) regions discussed media or communication technologies.

Moreover, media and communication technologies were more likely to be featured as integral to women and development issues over time. In the earlier years observed (1994–1999), just over one-tenth (12%) of the articles recognized media, slightly increasing to 18% in subsequent years (2000–2004). Resonant with the rise in attention to digital media and the dominance of IT in development, in the most recent period 40% of news articles included media in some aspect of their coverage. The way media are constructed within these discussions is explored next.

Several of the articles (13% of those discussing the media) articulated the media as a problem, concerned with problematic representations of women, in popular culture as well as the news. Media representations have the potential to reinforce gender stereotypes but at the same time, the potential to promote more equitable gender norms. One article published in the US raises concerns with problematic US portrayals of Iran as a country, but itself relies on a problematic conflation of women's dress with modernity/tradition dichotomization (Wilkins, 1995): describing an urban, prosperous environment, the author declares that "modernity is everywhere," filled with young Iranian women who are "pushing the fashion envelope with tiny and colorful head scarves that barely hide streaked and carefully arranged hair" (Inhorn, 2006, para. 3). Other articles raised concerns with problematic stereotypes as a topic for inclusion in development conferences.

When not framed as a problem, the media might be constructed as a vehicle to promote beneficial change. Almost half (40%) of these articles focus on media and popular culture as strategic venues to promote social change. Those conceptualizing the media's role as campaign intervention are intended to promote awareness of women's rights, through the work of British and Arab NGOs (*Al Jazeera*, 2010; Holmes, 1994; *St. Louis Dispatch*, 1999). For Arab youth with little access to information on reproductive health from parents or schools, global media serve as an alternate source of awareness to traditional sources of information (*Yemen Times*, 2008). Global media sources like CNN are also used to promote transnational awareness and government accountability: CNN footage of a young girl undergoing female genital mutilation "sent shockwaves across Egypt and the rest of the world" and "embarrassed the Egyptian government which until then had turned a blind eye to the practice" (Amin, 2012, para. 4).

Another article describes "the girl effect" program in Nigeria as a:

> movement... making girls visible and changing their social and economic dynamics by providing them with specific, powerful and relevant resources. Girl Effect University was established by the Nike Foundation in collaboration with the NoVo Foundation, United Nations Foundation and Coalition for Adolescent Girls. The girl effect is fuelled by hundreds of thousands of girl champions who recognise the untapped potential of adolescent girls living in poverty. The Population Council has been working in Nigeria and establishing a network of Safe Space Youth Clubs for vulnerable girls in northern Nigeria to promote social networking, knowledge transfer, and skills acquisition that is socially, religiously, and culturally acceptable. It has organised and produced radio shows to encourage young girls to stay in school and delay marriage.
>
> (Bilkisu, 2013, para. 6)

This development program is worth citing given the partnership of private and commercial agencies with multilateral agencies, with the illustration of the assumption that radio content has the potential to change girls' decisions on whether to stay in school and when to marry. This social change model relies on the social marketing framework that assumes individuals may change their knowledge, attitudes and behaviors if exposed to the right mediated information. This model focuses on mediated content, whereas other development strategies emphasize mediated technologies as channels for communication.

Digital media serve in this narrative as a central feature enabling women and girls to be active as civic and political agents in their society (32%), particularly within the Egyptian community (for example, see *Daily News Egypt*, 2010a). This civic engagement, however, is not just about political participation, but connected clearly with participation in free-market economies. The Mama Keba program rewards an app developed in a local African context that "helps low-income pregnant women to budget and prepay for prenatal care and the cost of delivery" (Clinton, 2010, para. 15); similar programs funding app development, including Apps 4 Africa and Mobile Justice, operationalize women's empowerment in their society as owning cell phones (*Right Vision News*, 2010). The World Bank reports working with the Affiliated Networks for Social Accountability in the Arab world to encourage mobile phone use to report on public services (Dumbuya, 2010). The central casting of private corporations in the development narrative promoting digital media technologies is part of the "South–South partnership" story (The Middle East, 2013).

In addition to enabling economic gain through technological skills, digital media may be of political value, as a platform for voice, as a space for debate, and as a mobilizing agent for protests and political advocacy (15%). Digital media are seen as ways for women to organize "to create positive change in the world" (*Islamic Finance News*, 2012b, para. 3), offering a "bold Arab voice at the forefront of the global women's movement [that] would be a magnet for Arab media, which have been slow to amplify messages of women's equality, as well as a galvanizing force for the next generation of local civil society activists" (*Daily News Egypt*, 2010b, para. 7). Beyond this amplification role, media also offer a space for political debate, as by an Egyptian student, who claims that "she has become more politically aware in post-Mubarak Egypt: 'Since the revolution, I've been watching news and analyzing news. We were never encouraged to have political views before'" (*Daily News Egypt*, 2012, para. 14).

More recent coverage, across countries, has articulated the role of the media in facilitating political protests in Egypt, as well as political engagement more broadly on behalf of women. *US News* explains:

> Women helped organize the initial protests through social media and marched in the uprising with men as equal partners. Images of these predominately Muslim Arab women were captured and broadcast around the world, showing they were not the helpless and diffident people they are often mistaken to be, but vital and valuable instruments in the cause for change.
>
> (Choate-Nielsen, 2012)

Networks across women's organizations enable participants across many countries "to share strategies on utilizing social media" (Taylor, 2012, para. 5). A Facebook page devoted to "Women of Egypt" is "set up to collect photos of rebel women taking part in the revolutions [and] shows grandmothers, schoolgirls, women wearing the niqab and others with their heads completely uncovered" (Banyard, 2011, para. 7). Being in control of content, "25-year-old activist Hadil El-Khouly [claims] these women defied expectations. 'They are breaking many stereotypes of what it means to be Arab and means to be Muslim. Arab women are not victimised women waiting for the West or men to liberate them'" (Banyard, 2011, para. 7).

While earlier attention to communication technologies focused on enhancing microenterprise, more recent attention to digital media corresponds with women's participation in protest, confirming this conceptualization of communication as a channel. This discourse also attends to communication as context when promoting campaigns with particular messages designed to educate women and girls, or when raising concerns over gendered stereotypes. Next, I consider how these strategies have conceptualized and documented their outcomes.

Accountability

The ultimate goals of population programs can take on various manifestations, from conceptualizing success in terms of individual behavior change, toward shifting normative assumptions about gender roles in society and concerns over gender-based violence, to creating policies that enforce equitable conditions and ensure safety. Next I explore conceptualizations and measures of success through evaluations of population programs in Egypt, in light of relevant conditions and trends.

Prior to the ICPD conference in 1994, the most widely used form of contraception among women in Egypt was the pill. Subsequent methods, including the Intrauterine Device (IUD) and Norplant), were subsidized through USAID programs to promote methods they believed to be more easily used. Current estimates suggest that almost two-thirds (60%) of Egyptian women with current sexual partners use some form of contraception. Most of these methods are manufactured and distributed directly by the pharmaceutical and health industries, with the most popular forms being the IUD (60% of all contraception users), the pill (20%), and injectables (12%), with very few using condoms (1%) or being sterilized (2%; Egypt Demographic and Health Survey, 2014). Unmet need for contraception dropped from 16% in 1995 to 9% in 2008.

Ali offers an insightful analysis of family planning programs implemented in Egypt, based on his ethnography of a USAID program in the early 1990s (Ali, 2002). Through his research he observes how population control as an intervention privileges individual choice and responsibility as a persuasive approach, encouraging women to see themselves as individuals. As such, this family planning program's focus on individuality is "situated within the global political economy that recognizes markets and labor relations" (p. 370). Development schemes in Egypt encouraged the national government to privatize health care and other industries as part of this emerging global capitalism (Ali, 2002; Mitchell, 1999).

Similar to other countries in the Arab region, Egypt's maternal mortality rates (MMRs) have been dramatically reduced since 1995. Documented maternal deaths per 100,000 live births have declined from 150 in 1995, to 100 in 2000, 78 in 2005, and 66 in 2010 (WHO, 2014). Tunisia and Yemen have witnessed similar dramatic declines, from 110 in 1995 to 56 in 2010 for the former and 520 in 1995 to 200 by 2010 in the latter. In this regard, Egypt has met ICPD targets by reducing lifetime risk of maternal death.

Maternal health builds on access to health care, which has been steadily increasing in the country, as well as overall fertility and contraception use, along with critical foundations in economic resources, supportive social norms, and political engagement. Development and national programs have worked to slow population growth and to improve access to contraception. The Total Fertility Rate (TFR) has been declining gradually over time, from 4.4 in 1988 to about 2.9 in 2014. In conjunction with the TFR, the Contraceptive Prevalence Rate (CPR) has been consistently documented at about 60% (in 2008 and 2014), up slightly from 48% in 1991.

It is worth noting not only which women's health issues are prominent, but also which are not. Although cervical cancer is the second most prevalent cancer among women in developing countries as a whole, due to their lack of access to screening and early detection, this is not a central health issue in Egypt (where the prevalence rate of 514 is far less than that of Turkey, which stands at 1443) or in the region more broadly. Researchers attribute this relatively low incidence rate to women in Egypt being older at initiation of intercourse, and having a restricted number of sexual partners. Moreover, HIV prevalence in the Middle East and North African (MENA) regions is comparatively much lower than in other global regions. Adult HIV prevalence in the MENA region is estimated at 0.2%, excluding areas in Somalia and the Sudan.

A central health concern for women and girls in Egypt remains that of female genital mutilation (FGM), referring to the cutting of female external genitalia. Despite government policies prohibiting this practice (which was criminalized in national law in 2008), along with Islamic and Christian authorities in Egypt condemning it, many doctors still conduct this surgery on Muslim and Christian girls in the country. Recent UNICEF records (2013) confirm that FGM is widely practiced still, and had been performed on 91% of women aged 15–49 in Egypt; among younger women aged 15–17 years this rate dropped to 74%, supporting anecdotal evidence that social norms and expectations are changing (El-Ikhwa, 2014;). The UN and other development agencies consider this an unnecessary practice with potential for serious health complications, such as bleeding, problems urinating, infections, infertility, complications in childbirth, and risk to infant health.

Women's health is impacted on both directly and indirectly by the prevalence of gender-based violence. Domestic violence not only has the capacity to injure and kill women, but also increases their risk of problematic or unwanted pregnancies, sexually transmitted diseases, and harm to infants and children, documented in Egypt and in other national trends (Monazea & Khalek, 2010). Violence, along with institutional and normative excuses for its occurrence, clearly challenges women's chances to live healthy lives. These patriarchal conditions are part of the context through which development interventions attempt to reach more narrowly focused objectives.

National development interventions, funded through bilateral and other development agencies, attempt to improve maternal and repro ductive health through a variety of programs. US development interventions in Egypt resonate historically with modernization and neoliberal approaches (Mitchell, 1999; Wilkins, 2004b). Bilateral modernization approaches may be somewhat diminished with the emergence of transnational social movements (Escobar, 2000), but how these political and social movements contribute to social change varies substantially across context. Ali (1996) reminds us of the need to be careful in assuming that social movements serve similar goals, describing tensions between Islamist political groups and the Egyptian state in the 1990s.

Population programs can be seen as both attempting to control women's bodies through fertility regulation and technologies as well as enhancing women's control through enabling choices in contraception, sexual health, and family size. The central issue of control is relevant across gender dynamics, including conditions that lead to gender-based violence and female genital mutilation. Maternal mortality may be only one manifestation of population interventions, but clearly connects to development goals. One predictor of maternal mortality is age of first marriage: thus some interventions attempt to encourage girls to marry later in life, assuming this means that they will engage in sexual intercourse when older and thus be less at risk for complications in pregnancy and childbirth.

Development interventions discouraging child marriage do so with the understanding that girls and women deserve to have control over their bodies, consonant with reproductive rights and violence prevention. The conceptual framework for these interventions, outlined in publications from the International Center for Research on Women (ICRW; Warner et al., 2014) places the focus on individual girls within broader contexts of households, within institutions and community norms, and then within social norms and structures. These concentric circles target girls through offering opportunities and alternatives toward self-transformation, self-awareness, self-efficacy, and aspirations; their ultimate goal is to motivate girls' mobility, visibility, and voice. In terms of power dynamics, these goals function at an individual level of persuasion, but less so in terms of an ability to change the rules of the game, through shifting structures and norms (Wilkins, 2000).

The global development industry, through declarations such as the UN Convention on the Rights of the Child (2000) and the ICPD, describes child marriage, when pronounced prior to 18 years of age, as a human rights violation, as well as a "hindrance to key development outcomes" (Malhotra et al., 2012, p. 2). Child marriage is associated with earlier ages of childbearing, higher maternal mortality and morbidity, higher infant mortality rates, lower educational status, risk of HIV infection, and risk of violence.

Although the legal age for marriage in Egypt is 18 for both women and men, the median age for marriage among women is about 21 years old, comparatively younger than women in Kuwait and Tunisia (where the median age for marriage is 25–27) but similar to women in Yemen, whose legal age for marriage, however, is much younger, at 15 (El-Zanaty & Way, 2009; UN Statistics Division, 2008). In a UN survey of Egyptian women in their early 20s in the years 2004–2008, 17% reported that they had been married before they were 18 years old. Funded through the WHO, ICRW conducted a comprehensive analysis of interventions addressing child marriage (ICRW, 2013; Klugman et al., 2014; Malhotra et al., 2012). Two of their case studies focused on projects implemented in Egypt. The ISHRAQ program, funded through a consortium of donors including Save the Children, Caritas, CEDPA, Population Council, the

Ministry of Youth, and the National Council of Childhood and Motherhood, targeted 12–15 year old girls not enrolled in school. The program encouraged them to get back into school through attending community courses in literacy, numeracy, health and life skills, finances, and sports, all in "girl-friendly spaces," and through sponsoring community discussions about alternatives to child marriage. Evaluators' assessment of these 2001–2004 results suggests that the more involved girls were in this program, the more likely they were to state that they would prefer to marry when older, as well as to choose their partners.

New Horizons, an earlier program (1999–2002) sponsored by CEDPA, North South Consultants Exchange, and USAID, attempted to reach a much larger group of girls than did the later program reviewed above (15,000–30,000 compared to ISHRAQ's fewer than 5000). Similar to the program above, though, New Horizons focused on strategies to improve empowerment, through teaching skills and building supportive networks and communities. Across evaluated programs, those that integrated community mobilization with individual attention to girls appeared to have the most effect on individual changes in knowledge, attitudes, and behavior.

Evaluations of what has worked to reduce maternal mortality point to the importance of education for girls and women as a way to improve economic opportunities as well as to sustain health, evidenced in Bangladesh's trend toward 40% MMR improvement (Prasad, 2014). A Gates funded comprehensive evaluation of trends in 181 countries from 1980 until 2008 determined that overall global maternal mortality has been decreasing by about 1–3% per year, with more than half of these preventable deaths in India, Nigeria, Pakistan, Afghanistan, Ethiopia, and the Democratic Republic of the Congo in 2008 (Hogan et al., 2010). They single Egypt out, along with China, Ecuador and Bolivia, as working more quickly than others to achieve this development goal to reduce maternal mortality. Egypt's MMR of 352 in 1980 dropped dramatically to 43 by 2008 (by comparison the rate in 2008 in the US was 17), declining about twice as quickly as that of Turkey, which then had a higher rate of maternal mortality (58; Hogan et al., 2010).

Whereas most information, education, and communication (IEC) campaigns in health demonstrate a hierarchy of effects, with knowledge being more likely to change than attitudes, this evaluation determined that attitudes were more resistant to change than behavior (Malhotra et al., 2012). These findings may need to be reviewed with caution though, given that of all the interventions ICRW identified that addressed child marriage, only 10% had been evaluated, and even fewer with rigorous designs enabling documentation of strategic contribution to individual change.

Some of the interventions in reproductive and maternal health recognize "empowerment" as a corresponding goal, tending toward conceptualizations that favor voice and decision making in the home and in local politics. Recent research on empowerment interventions in Egypt found significant correlations across these indicators, similar to the results established in assessments of programs in Bangladesh and Ghana (Klugman et al., 2014). Kabeer's (2013) study of women's empowerment across several countries includes Egypt as one of her case studies: her analyses demonstrate that women are more likely to make use of reproductive services when facilities are clean, staff are friendly, and wait times are short. But beyond these predictable conditions leading to service use, the more concerning challenge of public mobility also inhibits many women from seeking formal health care. Women are more likely to do so when employed, which enables public mobility. Kabeer (2013) notes the "consistently significant effect of location in predicting women's empowerment" (p. 34), meaning that women in the Southern part of the country living in more socially conservative communities were less likely to vote, be employed, have ease of mobility, or feel control over their own lives.

On the 20th anniversary of the ICPD, UNFPA published a report chronicling trends in population, maternal health, poverty, education, and human rights, and projecting future proposals for further intervention (UNFPA, 2014b). When trends are reported though in terms of averages across individuals in countries, the visibility of the social and political exclusion of women, along with other marginalized groups, becomes lost (Kabeer, 2011b). The documentation of women's conditions is important, but needs to be understood within broader differences in gender as well.

The recently instituted "Rights-Oriented Research and Education (RORE) Network for Sexual and Reproductive Health" argues for evaluations to look beyond singular health outcomes to include attention to conditions of gender equality within a framework of human rights. In order to understand why "well-intentioned programs fail to achieve desired results," which is a serious concern, these scholars advocate "exploring structural factors that create and/or exacerbate inequalities that limit the enjoyment of fundamental human rights and, consequently, of sexual and reproductive rights for some people" (Gruskin & Sundari Ravindran, 2014, p. 649).

How evaluations can be improved to promote a social-justice orientation will be explored in more depth in the final chapter. In relation to this particular focus on population programs, it is critical to understand the politics of framing this as a development concern, in less controversial approaches focusing on health and education, or in more controversial arenas pertaining to safe abortions, adolescent sexual health, and comprehensive sexuality education and rights (Girard, 2014, p. 607). Girard (2014) remains concerned that future agendas should be more cognizant of the need to provide safe abortion services and prevent homophobic violence, particularly given that these topics were not fully recognized during the 1994 ICPD event. As Sen (2014) argues, the accountability of policies and programs needs to have a broader vision that concerns quality and equity.

The development discourse underlying these program and evaluation descriptions privileges girls and women as individuals, as central agents of change, with community mobilization and social support serving more as supporting characters. Communication plays a central role in providing content designed to encourage girls to marry later, and women to use contraception. When visible as a technology, girls and women are taught skills in order to engage them in free-market economies. Narratives in public discourse and guiding intervention and assessment can be understood as part of a neoliberal narrative of development.

Communicating neoliberal development

Narratives of development, articulations of gender, and attention to communication technologies can be understood within the broader parameters of neoliberal agendas, in this case connecting population programs within a particular context of Egyptian political-economic dynamics as well as broader global conditions of Orientalism and patriarchy.

Feminist critiques of the development industry question the construction of women, the articulation of gender, and the allocation of resources to issues that emphasize women's role as mothers rather than as active political and economic agents. Population and maternal health programs particularly suffer from this trap, highlighting women as individual agents responsible for decisions over when and how to marry, as well as how to plan and prepare for bearing children. While it is imperative to understand women as having control over their bodies and futures, targeting women as individuals ignores the powerful forces within relationships and families, and conditions that structure health resources and gender differences. The power dynamics that contribute to exacerbating material differences as well as inhibiting human rights challenge the potential for development programs to be gender transformative, shifting rather than perpetuating norms. Attention to gender would mean recognizing men's roles in sexual health and fertility through the conceptual models that guide intervention. Hegemonic assertion of gendered assumptions, rooted in patriarchal ideologies, is further complicated within the particular Orientalist context of Western perspectives of Arab and Muslim cultures.

To add more depth to previous research concerning the limited, passive portrayal of women as objects of development intervention, this study considers the potential for women to be constructed as active agents of social change. Resonant with broader development discourses focusing on privatization and microenterprise, women's roles as economic agents and as political participants have become more visible in more recent news coverage. Women's "empowerment" becomes more clearly present in this vocabulary over time, though what is meant by this term varies distinctly, from economic and political capabilities to social and individual competencies. The North American narratives are much more likely than those from other regions to focus on entrepreneurial approaches, and to explicate communication technologies in direct connection with "empowerment," whereas the Arab and South Asian discussions are more likely to consider the media as a problem than as a solution.

The year 1994 marked a critical juncture in global development, with global recognition of reproductive rights as a central development concern, broadening attention from population issues being seen as restricted to behavior-change interventions. The Cairo conference in this year engaged women as leaders and participants, actively contributing to dialogue and policy. During these years, and 20 years later with reviews of progress made (and not made) toward development goals, women as leaders could be featured in these narratives.

However, largely absent from this discourse is an understanding of gender. Although images of women are constructed more broadly and with more agency, their connections with men, in cultural, political and economic contexts, is missing. Without the visibility of the implications of lack of political rights, of access to health care, of equal pay and material resources, and of supportive norms, we are presented with depoliticized discourse that claims women may be best "empowered" when partnering with external, Western agencies through their use of communications technologies in commercial ventures and in democratic political reform. While this narrative may serve the ideological interests and capital accumulation of the global elite, it does not do justice to the collective efforts of communities of women and other marginalized groups struggling against their oppression.

Sen (2014) argues that women's reproductive and sexual health would be better served by understanding health system reform policies as well as human rights approaches. This would mean understanding health as not just a consequence of individual choice, but as conditioned: "The drive for sexual and reproductive rights represents an inclusive trend towards human rights to health that goes beyond the right to health services, directing attention to girls' and women's rights to bodily autonomy, integrity and choice in relation to sexuality and reproduction" (Sen, 2014, p. 599).

However, maternal health, particularly as articulated through the MDGs, tends to be conceptualized more in terms of individual decisions over contraception rather than reproductive rights, and when women's concerns do become referenced with gender equality, economic relevance is privileged. Interventions to promote gender equality, according to the 2012 *World Development Report*, represent "smart economics." This repeated connection of economics with intelligence, reinforced through development discourse as situated within particular neoliberal market conditions, elevates numeracy as a skill for private-sector employment and free-market growth. Numeracy as a skill to promote critical thinking and strategic action for the public good is absent from this narrative.

In their assessment of global gender gaps, some trends in educational access and employment suggest movement toward more equitable conditions. But although women tend to live longer than men, girls and women are much more likely to suffer preventable deaths than boys and men, particularly in low- and middle-income countries (World Bank, 2012). The authors of this report declare that "globalization can help" to keep more women alive longer: they argue that liberal economic conditions, such as open trade, and cheaper communications technologies allowing women to connect to markets, contribute to better health services, which improves maternal care. One recent approach to preventing child marriage offers cash incentives to families with daughters who delay marriage: this approach to intervention monetizes this choice, reinforcing the commodification of girls. Some nongovernmental organization professionals have reported (in personal confidential communication) that their attempts to pursue more gender transformative strategies have been challenged by Gates Foundation staff, who prefer focusing on access to and use of contraception. Others believe that the best way to convince public agencies to fund maternal health intervention is through documenting the financial costs of domestic violence, of child marriage, and of maternal mortality. These models emphasize economic concerns and individual-level change.

Highlighting individuals as agents of social change, justified in terms of potential financial loss, resonates with a neoliberal model of development. While development within Egypt can be seen as historically fitting a modernization approach, this analysis confirms Mitchell's (1999) assertion that neoliberalism dominates development discourse in and about Egypt, relying on bureaucratic frameworks at the expense of promoting political and human rights. While the Egyptian regime may itself be restricting more participatory political processes, it is its political-economic context within the region as a political leader and within the world as a US friend with economic benefits that serves as the foundation for this neoliberal emphasis.

The role for communication within this neoliberal framework for development privileges content as a tool to promote behavior change, and skills to use computer technologies as a way to integrate into the labor market and the global market economy. Neoliberal narratives of development encourage the idea that target populations will grant consent to being managed for the public good given the right communication campaign. Using "modern" contraception resonates with this broader conceptualization of development as a regime toward social control, particularly of women (Ali, 2002).

The neoliberal emphasis on individuals as agents for social change, in this case individual women learning skills and making decisions that affect their reproductive health, ignores the structures that limit how education can be used and how decisions can, and should, be challenged. Understanding the structures of choice, in order to contribute more directly to interventions that can be gender transformative, is critical if we are to promote gender equality as a matter of social justice.

References

Abu-Lughod, L. (2013). *Do Muslim Women Need Saving?* Cambridge: Harvard University Press.

African Development Bank. (2014). Banking and Insurance: North African women and SMEs – an opportunity hiding in plain view. *Africa News.* 28 March, Retrieved from *LexisNexis Academic* Database.

Al Jazeera. (2010). Plea to refocus UN millennium goals. *Al Jazeera.* 20 September, Retrieved from *LexisNexis Academic* Database.

Ali, K. A. (1996). Politics for family planning in Egypt. *Anthropology Today, 12*(5), pp. 14–19.

Ali, K. A. (2002). Faculty deployments: Persuading women and constructing choice in Egypt. *Society for the Comparative Study of Society and History, 44*(2), pp. 370–394.

Al-Naggar, M. (2010). In Egypt, women have burdens but no privileges. *New York Times.* 13 July, Retrieved from *LexisNexis Academic* Database.

Amin, S. (2012). The battle against female genital mutilation. *Daily News Egypt.* 15 November, Retrieved from *LexisNexis Academic* Database.

Arabic Network for Human Rights Information. (2013). Legal assistant unit at Cairo center for development and human rights getting nine judicial rulings for battered women. *Africa News.* 12 December, Retrieved from *LexisNexis Academic* Database.

Associated Press International. (2001). Arab first ladies and activists demand more power for Arab women, support for Palestinian women. *Associated Press.* 11 November. Accessed 31 August 2014.

Banyard, K. (2011). Women are key activists in this revolution. Women are creating slogans, women are at the front and defending protesters ... They are not waiting for the West or men to liberate them. *The Times* (London). 16 February, Retrieved from *LexisNexis Academic* Database.

Bilkisu, H. (2013). Girl Effect University. *Daily Trust* (Abuja). 7 March, Retrieved from *LexisNexis Academic* Database.

Cha, A. E. (2014). With help of private industry, USAID review finds $2.9 billion for maternal, child health. *The Washington Post,* Retrieved from http://www.washingtonpost.com/national/health-science/with-help-of-private-industry-usaid-review-finds-29-billion-for-maternal-child-health/2014/06/24/4dec87e4-fae7-11e3-8176-f2c941cf35f1_story.html. 20 March 2015.

Choate-Nielsen, A. (2012). Writing history: Muslim women reshape their destiny with newfound freedom. *Deseret Morning News,* Retrieved from *LexisNexis Academic* Database.

Clinton, H. R. (2010). Remarks at the TEDWomen Conference. 8 December, Retrieved from http://www.state.gov/secretary/20092013clinton/rm/2010/12/152670.htm.

Daily News Egypt. (2008a). Egypt celebrates third annual campaign for MDGs. *Daily News Egypt.* 28 October, Retrieved from *LexisNexis Academic* Database.

Daily News Egypt. (2008b). USAID project aims at empowering underprivileged women. *Daily News Egypt.* 8 October, Retrieved from *LexisNexis Academic* Database.

Daily News Egypt. (2009a). Women were stronger 30 years ago, says panel. *Daily News Egypt.* 27 December, Retrieved from *LexisNexis Academic* Database.

Daily News Egypt. (2009b). Conference discusses women's rights in MENA region. *Daily News Egypt.* 18 December, Retrieved from *LexisNexis Academic* Database.

Daily News Egypt. (2009c). Women complete first ever management program in Egypt. *Daily News Egypt.* 4 November, Retrieved from *LexisNexis Academic* Database.

Daily News Egypt. (2009d). New development program for women in Egypt. *Daily News Egypt.* 4 October, Retrieved from *LexisNexis Academic* Database.

Daily News Egypt. (2010a). UN official highlights challenges in achieving MDGs in Arab world. *Daily News Egypt.* 2 December, Retrieved from *LexisNexis Academic* Database.

Daily News Egypt. (2010b). Arab women to head UN's new gender program? *Daily News Egypt.* 1 April, Retrieved from *LexisNexis Academic* Database.

Daily News Egypt. (2011). UN women's first report notes progress and remaining inequalities for Egyptian women. *Daily News Egypt.* 7 July, Retrieved from *LexisNexis Academic* Database.

Daily News Egypt. (2012). The rise of the debate culture in Egypt. *Daily News Egypt.* 15 February, Retrieved from *LexisNexis Academic* Database.

Daily News Egypt. (2013). Arab women feature in Ana Hunna by Hadel Hegazy. *Daily News Egypt.* 29 September, Retrieved from *LexisNexis Academic* Database.

Daily the Pak Banker. (2011a). Op-Ed: Empowering women powers nations. *Daily The Pak Banker.* 21 September, Retrieved from *LexisNexis Academic* Database.

Daily the Pak Banker. (2011b). The Middle East and North Africa: A new social contract for development. *Daily The Pak Banker.* 7 April, Retrieved from *LexisNexis Academic* Database.

Daily the Pak Banker. (2011c). Centennial celebration of International Women's Day. *Daily the Pak Banker.* 10 March, Retrieved from *LexisNexis Academic* Database.

Deutsch, A. (1999). AP photo AMS101. *Associated Press International.* 8 February, Retrieved from *LexisNexis Academic* Database.

Dumbuya, I. K. (2010). Nation needs to tackle more challenges on the MDGs. *Concord Times (Freetown).* 5 October, Retrieved from *LexisNexis Academic* Database.

Egypt Demographic and Health Survey. (2014). *Egypt Demographic and Health Survey 2014: Main Findings,* Retrieved from http://www.dhsprogram.com/pubs/pdf/PR54/PR54.pdf. 20 March 2015.

Egyptian Center for Women's Rights (ECWR). (2012). *Report on Egyptian Women's Conditions in 2012: Women Get Out to the Streets,* Retrieved from http://ecwronline.org/pdf/reports/2013/egyptian_women_conditions_in2012.pdf. 6 January 2014.

ECWR. (2014). *2014: The Year of Unfulfilled Promises for Women: Women's Status Report 2014 Summary,* Retrieved from http://ecwronline.org/upload/annual_report/2014%20report.summerypdf.pdf. 20 March 2015.

Egyptian Initiative for Personal Rights (EIPR). (2013). *Reclaiming and Redefining Rights. ICPD+20: Status of Sexual and Reproductive Health and Rights in the Middle East and North Africa.* September. Cairo: EIPR.

Eid, L. (1994). Queen Noor discusses women's issues. *United Press International.* 11 October, Retrieved from *LexisNexis Academic* Database.

El-Ikhwa, M. (2014). Egypt making slow progress on genital mutilation. *Middle East Institute.* 19 November, Retrieved from http://www.mei.edu/content/news/egypt-making-slow-progress-genital-mutilation. 6 January 2014.

El-Zanaty, F. & Way, A. (2009). *Egypt Demographic and Health Survey 2008,* Retrieved from http://dhsprogram.com/pubs/pdf/fr220/fr220.pdf. 20 March 2015.

Emirates News Agency. (2007). UN honours Sheika Fatima. *Emirates News Agency.* 22 April, Retrieved from *LexisNexis Academic* Database.

Emirates News Agency. (2008). AWO hail Sheika Fatima's support to women's issues. *Emirates News Agency*. 5 January, Retrieved from *LexisNexis Academic* Database.

Escobar, A. (1995). *Encountering Development: The Making and Unmaking of the Third World*. Princeton: Princeton University Press.

Escobar, A. (2000). Place, power, and networks in globalization and postdevelopment. In K. Wilkins (Ed.), *Redeveloping Communication for Social Change. Theory, Practice and Power* (pp. 163–173). Lanham, MD: Rowman & Littlefield.

Ford, L. (2014). 2014 is a key year for women's rights and gender equality. *The Guardian*, Retrieved from *LexisNexis Academic* Database.

Gavlak, D. (2000). Arab women discuss raising status. *United Press International*. 21 November, Retrieved from *LexisNexis Academic* Database.

Gill, K., Brooks, K., McDougall, J., Patel, P. & Kes, A. (2010). *Bridging the Gender Divide: How Technology can Advance Women Economically*. Washington, DC: ICRW.

Girard, F. (2014). Taking ICPD beyond 2015: Negotiating sexual and reproductive rights in the next development agenda. *Global Public Health: An International Journal for Research, Policy and Practice, 9*(6), pp. 607–619.

Glinski, A. M., Weiss, E., Shett, A. & Gaynair, G. (2013). *Preparing Girls and Women for 21st Century Success: Intel® Teach Findings*. Washington DC: ICRW.

Gruskin, S. & Sundari Ravindran, T. K. (2014). Realising the ICPD 20 years later: Shifting the paradigms for research and education. *Global Public Health: An International Journal for Research, Policy and Practice, 9*(6), pp. 647–652.

Hogan, M. C., Foreman, K. J., Naghavi, M., Ahn, S. Y., Wang, M., Makela, S. M., Lopez, A. D., Lozano, R. & Murray, C. J. (12 April 2010). Maternal mortality for 181 countries, 1980–2008: A systematic analysis of progress towards Millennium Development Goal 5. *The Lancet, 380*(9850), pp. 2053–2260, DOI:10.1016/S0140-6736(10)60518-1.

Holmes, C. (1994). World population conference: Grim statistics, grimmer reality Cairo slums pack ample evidence of growing crisis. *The Atlanta Journal and Constitution*. 12 September, Retrieved from *LexisNexis Academic* Database.

Hsu, J., Pitt, C., Greco, G., Berman, P. & Mills, A. (2012). Countdown to 2015: Changes in official development assistance to maternal, newborn, and child health in 2009–10, and assessment of progress since 2003. *The Lancet, 380*(9848), pp. 1157–1168.

Hugin. (2006). IBM to send international delegation to 2006 Global Summit of Women. *Hugin*. 6 June, Retrieved from *LexisNexis Academic* Database.

Index Mundi (2014). Egypt demographic profile, Retrieved from http://www.indexmundi.com/egypt/demographics_profile.html. 6 January 2015.

Inhorn, M. C. (2006). A more open mind toward Iran. *The Chronicle of Higher Education*, Retrieved from *LexisNexis Academic* Database.

Islamic Finance News. (2012a). Nevine Loutfy wins best woman in the corporate sector award across the MENA region by the American Chamber of Commerce Annual MENA "Women in Business" award program. *Islamic Finance News*. 18 May, Retrieved from *LexisNexis Academic* Database.

Islamic Finance News. (2012b). Yahoo! Business and human rights program and Yahoo! Maktoob host women leaders from Middle East and North Africa for "Change Your World! Cairo" Summit on Social/Digital Media. *Islamic Finance News*. 20 January, Retrieved from *LexisNexis Academic* Database.

Jordan Times. (2012). Combining secular and religious views. *The Jordan Times.* 13 February, Retrieved from *LexisNexis Academic* Database.

Jordan Times. (2013). Regional conference on population to be held in Cairo. *The Jordan Times,* Retrieved from *LexisNexis Academic* Database.

Jordanian News Agency. (2010). API organizes a conference on women and youth in Arab development. *Jordanian News Agency.* 17 February, Retrieved from *LexisNexis Academic* Database.

Kabeer, N. (2011a). *Contextualising the Economic Pathways of Women's Empowerment: Findings from a Multi-Country Programme.* Pathways Policy Paper. October. Brighton: Pathways of Women's Empowerment RPC.

Kabeer, N. (2011b). *Policy Brief: MDGs, Social Justice, and the Challenge of Intersecting Inequalities.* No. 3. March. London: Centre for Development Policy and Research.

Kabeer, N. (2013). *Paid Work, Women's Empowerment, and Inclusive Growth: Transforming the Structures of Constraint.* New York: UN Women.

Kaiser Family Foundation. (2013). The US Government and global maternal, newborn & child health. *The Henry J. Kaiser Family Foundation,* Retrieved from http://kff.org/global-health-policy/fact-sheet/the-u-s-government-and-global-maternal-newborn-and-child-health/. 20 March 2015.

Khanna, P. (9 November 2008). Arab women's body to discuss empowerment. *Indo-Asian News Service,* 7 October, Retrieved from *LexisNexis Academic* Database.

Kirkpatrick, D. (2014). As Egyptians grasp for stability, Sisi fortifies his presidency. *New York Times,* Retrieved from http://www.nytimes.com/2014/10/08/world/as-egyptians-grasp-for-stability-sisi-fortifies-his-presidency.html?_r= 0. 23 January 2015.

Klugman, J., Hanmer, L., Twigg, S., Hasan, T., McCleary-Sills, J. & Santamaria, J. (2014). *Voice and Agency: Empowering Women and Girls for Shared Prosperity.* Washington DC: World Bank Publications.

Kraft, J., Wilkins, K., Morales, G., Widyono, M. & Middlestadt, S. (2014). An evidence review of gender-integrated interventions in reproductive and maternal-child health. *Journal of Health Communication, 19*(1), pp. 122–141.

Kristof, N. D. & WuDunn, S. (2009). *Half the Sky: Turning Oppression into Opportunity for Women Worldwide.* New York: Vintage Books.

Kuwait Times. (2011). Gender equality facilitates development, productivity. *Kuwait Times.* 15 September, Retrieved from *LexisNexis Academic* Database.

Lentfer, J. (2014). All eyes on maternal and child health: Ideas, money and know-how not enough. *Politics of Poverty.* 1 July. Boston: Oxfam America.

Malaysia General News. (2008). Arab Women Organization conference ends on successful note. *Malaysia General News.* 14 November, Retrieved from *LexisNexis Academic* Database of general news.

Malaysian Government News. (2013). More OIC member states sign women development statute. *Malaysian Government News.* 6 February, Retrieved from *LexisNexis Academic* Database.

Malhotra, A., Kanesathasan, A. & Patel, P. (2012). Connectivity: How mobile phones, computers and the internet can catalyze women's entrepreneurship. ICRW and Cherie Blair Foundation for Women.

Malik, K. (2013). *Human Development Report 2013. The Rise of the South: Human Progress in a Diverse World,* Retrieved from http://hdr.undp.org/sites/default/files/reports/14/hdr2013_en_complete.pdf. 20 March 2015.

Malik, K. (2014). *Human Development Report 2014. Sustaining Human Progress: Reducing Vulnerabilities and Building Resilience*, Retrieved from http://hdr.undp.org/en/content/human-development-report-2014. 20 March 2015.

Malkawi, K. (2013). Regional conference on population to be held in Cairo. *Jordan Times*. 18 June, Retrieved from *LexisNexis Academic* Database.

Meyer, T. (2013). FAQ on US aid to Egypt: Where does the money go, and how is it spent? *Propublica*. 9 October, Retrieved from http://www.propublica.org/blog/item/f.a.q.-on-u.s.-aid-to-egypt-where-does-the-money-go-who-decides-how-spent.

Middle East Company News Wire. (2012). Arab International Women's Forum holds 'Young Arab Women Leaders – The Voice of the Future' conference. *Middle East Company News Wire*. 10 December, Retrieved from *LexisNexis Academic* Database.

Ministry of Health, Arab Republic of Egypt. (2014). *Success Factors in Women's and Children's Health: Mapping Pathways to Progress, Egypt*, Retrieved from http://www.who.int/pmnch/knowledge/publications/egypt_country_report.pdf.

Mitchell, T. (1991). *Colonizing Egypt*. Berkeley, CA: University of California Press.

Mitchell, T. (1999). No factories, no problems: The logic of neo-liberalism in Egypt. *Review of African Political Economy, 26*(82), pp. 455–468.

Mohanty, C. T. (1991). Cartographies of struggle: Third world women and the politics of feminism. In C. T. Mohanty, A. Russo & L. Torres (Eds.), *Third World Women and the Politics of Feminism* (pp. 1–50). Bloomington: Indiana University Press.

Monazea, E. M. & Khalek, M. A. (2010). Domestic Violence High in Egypt, Affecting Women's Reproductive Health, Retrieved from http://www.prb.org/Publications/Articles/2010/domesticviolence-egypt.aspx. 6 January 2015.

Natividad, M. D., Kolundzija, A. & Parker, R. (2014). ICPD both before and beyond 2014: The challenges of population and development in the twenty-first century. *Global Public Health: An International Journal for Research, Policy and Practice, 9*(6), pp. 594–598.

The New Zealand Herald. (2014). Hillary Clinton urges equality for women and girls. *The New Zealand Herald*, 8 March 2014.

Park, J. & Wilkins, K. (2005). Re-orienting the orientalist gaze. *Global Media Journal, 4*(6), Article 2, Retrieved from http://lass.calumet.purdue.edu/cca/gmj/oldsitebackup/submitteddocuments/spring2005/referreed/parksp05.htm. 20 March 2015.

Prasad, R. (2014). More education among women helps reduce maternal and child mortality in Bangladesh. *The Hindu*. June 30.

PR Newswire. (1999). Planned Parenthood president Gloria Feldt appointed to US delegation to the Hague International Forum Feb. 8–12. *PR Newswire*. 2 February, Retrieved from *LexisNexis Academic* Database.

PR Newswire. (2008). Leading US & Egyptian women executives to discuss development of philanthropic sector in Egypt in Cairo, Egypt, 22–23 November 2008. *PR Newswire*. 20 November, Retrieved from *LexisNexis Academic* Database.

PR Newswire. (2012). British Council conference to raise awareness on women's rights in Middle East and North Africa. *PR Newswire*. 1 March, Retrieved from *LexisNexis Academic* Database.

PR Newswire. (2013). AUC Chairperson calls for coordinated efforts for empowerment of the African women to play their role in African development. *PR Newswire Africa.* 24 April, Retrieved from *LexisNexis Academic* Database.

PR Newswire Europe. (2012). British Council conference to raise awareness on women's rights in Middle East and North Africa. *PR Newswire Europe.* 1 March, Retrieved from *LexisNexis Academic* Database.

Ravishankar, N., Gubbins, P., Cooley, R. J., Leach-Kemon, K., Michaud, C. M., Jamison, D. T. & Murray, C. J. L. (2009). Financing of global health: Tracking development assistance for health from 1990 to 2007. *The Lancet, 373*(9681), pp. 2113–2124.

Requejo, J., Bryce, J. & Victora, C. (2014). *Countdown to 2015: Decade Report (2000–2010) with Country Profiles. Taking Stock of Maternal Newborn and Child Survival,* Retrieved from http://whqlibdoc.who.int/publications/2010/9789241599573_eng.pdf.

Right Vision News. (2009). Turkey: Arab women on the move. *Right Vision News.* 24 November, Retrieved from *LexisNexis Academic* Database.

Right Vision News. (2010). USA: Secretary Clinton's remarks at the TEDWomen Conference. *Right Vision News.* 14 December, Retrieved from *LexisNexis Academic* Database.

Right Vision News. (2011). USA: Achieving the ICPD agenda by 2014 and the MDGs by 2015: Advancing family planning and reproductive health. *Right Vision News.* 19 April, Retrieved from *LexisNexis Academic* Database.

Rosenberg, D. (2011). As Middle East erupts, wives of leaders become targets of rage. Regarded as glamorous and progressive in the West, their image backfires at home. *Jerusalem Post.* 17 February, Retrieved from *LexisNexis Academic* Database.

Roy, A. (2010). *Poverty Capital: Microfinance and the Making of Development.* New York: Routledge.

Said, E. (1971). *Orientalism.* New York: Vintage.

Sen, A. (1995). Human rights and capabilities. *Journal of Human Development, 6*(2), pp. 151–166.

Sen, G. (2014). Sexual and reproductive health and rights in the post-2015 development agenda. *Global Public Health: An International Journal for Research, Policy and Practice, 9*(6), pp. 599–606.

Shah, H. & Wilkins, K. G. (2004). Reconsidering geometries of development. *Perspectives on Global Development and Technology, 3*(4), pp. 395–416.

Shirazi, F. (2009). *Velvet Jihad: Muslim Women's Quiet Resistance to Islamic Fundamentalism.* Gainesville: University of Florida Press.

Shirazi, F. (2010). *Muslim Women in War and Crisis.* Austin, TX: University of Texas Press.

Siddiqui, H. (2002). Arab women the least empowered. *Toronto Star.* 14 July, Retrieved from *LexisNexis Academic* Database.

St. Louis Dispatch. (1999). The fewer, the merrier. *St. Louis Dispatch.* 9 July, Retrieved from *LexisNexis Academic* Database.

Stackhouse, J. (1994). A victory for women's rights: Cairo/The population and development conference has felt the growing influence of a global network that is effecting profound change in the international arena. *The Globe and Mail.* 12 September, Retrieved from *LexisNexis Academic* Database.

States News Service. (2005a). US provide skills training to Middle East women. *States News Service.* 17 February, Retrieved from *LexisNexis Academic* Database.

States News Service. (2005b). US commitment to women in Middle East. *States News Service.* 17 February, Retrieved from *LexisNexis Academic* Database.

States News Service. (2005c). US supports advancement of women in the Middle East. *States News Service.* 6 September, Retrieved from *LexisNexis Academic* Database.

States News Service. (2009). Treaty linking women's rights and development still vital after 15 years – UN. *States News Service.* 17 September, Retrieved from *LexisNexis Academic* Database.

States News Service. (2013). Through film and life, rural women address poverty and early marriage in Egypt. *States News Service.* 10 January, Retrieved from *LexisNexis Academic* Database.

States News Service. (2014). UN Women Arab States office launches Arabic version of the UN Women "One Woman" song. *States News Service.* 13 March, Retrieved from *LexisNexis Academic* Database.

Staudt, K. (1997). *Women, International Development, and Politics: The Bureaucratic Mire.* Philadelphia: Temple University Press.

Sweis, R. (2012). Women's rights are at a standstill in Jordan: They are largely left out of leadership spots even as change sweeps region. *The International Herald Tribune.* 8 November, Retrieved from *LexisNexis Academic* Database.

Tabbara, A. (2003). Arab women have more to say in politics but still suffer discrimination. *Agence France Presse.* 7 March, Retrieved from *LexisNexis Academic* Database.

Tadros, M. (2014). Rethinking feminism. *Addis Fortune.* 30 March, Retrieved from *LexisNexis Academic* Database.

Taylor, A. (2012). Arab women gather together to discuss activism amid popular upheavals. *The Daily Star,* Retrieved from *LexisNexis Academic* Database.

The Middle East. (2013). Human development: Job opportunities key to sustained economic development. *The Middle East.* 17 April, Retrieved from *LexisNexis Academic* Database.

The Scotsman. (1995). China calling. *The Scotsman.* 31 August, Retrieved from *LexisNexis Academic* Database.

The Statesman. (2014). Rich countries advance women, poorest don't: UN. *The Statesman.* 14 February, Retrieved from *LexisNexis Academic* Database.

This Day (Lagos). (2014). Post-2015 agenda – Addressing the inadequacies in women's rights. *This Day (Lagos).* 5 June, Retrieved from *LexisNexis Academic* Database.

Toronto Star. (2009). Women in Arab world driven inside by sexual harassment, says 1st regional conference on topic. *Toronto Star.* 15 December, Retrieved from *LexisNexis Academic* Database.

UN Arab Human Development Report. (2005). The Arab Human Development Report 2005: Towards the rise of women in the Arab world, Retrieved from http://www.arab-hdr.org/publications/other/ahdr/ahdr2005e.pdf. 20 March 2015.

UN Statistics Division. (2008). *UN Data Gender Info,* Retrieved from http://unstats.un.org/unsd/gender/default.html. 20 March 2015.

UN Women (2015). Progress towards meeting MDGs for women and girls. Retrieved from http://www.unwomen.org/en/news/in-focus/mdg-momentum#sthash.NPuv7vKC.dpuf. 6 January.

UNFPA (2014a). *ICPD Overview,* Retrieved from http://www.unfpa.org/public/icpd. 22 October 2014.

UNFPA (2014b). *Framework for Actions for the Follow-up to the Programme of Action of the International Conference on Population and Development: Report of the Secretary General,* Retrieved from http://icpdbeyond2014.org/uploads/browser/files/93632_unfpa_eng_web.pdf. 15 January 2015.

UNICEF (2014). *Information by Country: Egypt Statistics,* Retrieved from http://www.unicef.org/infobycountry/egypt_statistics.html. 6 January 2015.

United Nations. (2014). *The Millennium Development Goals Report 2014,* Retrieved from http://www.un.org/millenniumgoals/2014%20MDG%20report/MDG%202014%20English%20web.pdf. 20 March 2015.

US Federal News. (2010). Secretary Clinton announces techwomen program at presidential summit on entrepreneurship. *US Federal News.* 29 April, Retrieved from *LexisNexis Academic* Database.

US Official News. (2014). Human rights council holds annual full-day discussion on women's rights. *US Official News.* 18 June, Retrieved from *LexisNexis Academic* Database.

Warner, A. Stoebenau, K. & Glinski, A. M. (2014). *More Power to Her: How Empowering Girls Can Help End Child Marriage.* Washington DC: ICRW.

White House. (1999). Morocco: Press schedule for the first lady's trip to Morocco. *Africa News.* 29 March, Retrieved from *LexisNexis Academic* Database.

Wilkins, K. (1995). Middle Eastern women in Western eyes: A study of US press photographs of Middle Eastern women. In Y. Kamalipour (Ed.), *The US Media and the Middle East: Image and Perception* (pp. 50–61). Westport, CT: Greenwood Press.

Wilkins, K. (2004a). The civil Intifada: Power and politics of the Palestinian census. *Development & Change, 35*(5), pp. 891–908.

Wilkins, K. (2004b). Communication and transition in the Middle East: A critical analysis of US intervention and academic literature. *Gazette: The International Journal for Communication Studies, 66*(6), pp. 483–496.

Wilkins, K. (2005). Out of focus: Gender visibilities in development. In O. Hemer & T. Tufte (Eds.), *Media and Glocal Change – Rethinking Communication for Development* (pp. 261–270). University of Göteborg: NORDICOM.

Wilkins, K. (2007). Confronting the missionary position: The mission of development/the position of women. *Communication for Development and Social Change: A Global Journal, 1*(2), pp. 111–125.

Wilkins, K. & Enghel, F. (2013). The privatization of development through global communication industries: Living proof? *Media, Culture and Society, 35*(2), pp. 165–181.

Wright, L. (2014). *Thirteen Days in September: Carter, Begin, and Sadat at Camp Davis.* New York: Alfred A. Knopf.

World Bank. (2012). *World Development Report: Gender Equality and Development,* Retrieved from http://siteresources.worldbank.org/INTWDR2012/Resources/7778105-1299699968583/7786210-1315936222006/Complete-Report.pdf. 20 March 2015.

World Health Organization (WHO). (2014). Trends in maternal mortality: 1990 to 2013. Estimates by WHO, UNICEF, UNFPA, The World Bank and the United Nations Population Division, Retrieved from http://apps.who.

int/iris/bitstream/10665/112682/2/9789241507226_eng.pdf?ua= 1. 20 March 2015.

Xinhua General News Service. (2000a). First Arab Women Summit concludes in Cairo. *Xinhua General News Service.* 20 November, Retrieved from *LexisNexis Academic* Database.

Xinhua General News Service. (2000b). Participants in first Arab Women Summit arrive in Cairo. *Xinhua General News Service.* 17 November, Retrieved from *LexisNexis Academic* Database.

Wilkins, K. (2000). Accounting for Power in Development Communication. In K. Wilkins (Ed.) *Redeveloping Communication for Social Change: Theory, Practice & Power* (pp. 197–210). Boulder, CO: Rowman & Littlefield Publishers, Inc.

Yemen Times. (2008). Social stigmas and the adolescent experience of Yemeni youths. *Yemen Times.* 14 December, Retrieved from *LexisNexis Academic* Database.

4
Communicating Gender in Education Development

While women's access to education and health services has been improving in most countries, clear disparities between women and men remain, particularly in terms of poverty and political rights. Although women are estimated to constitute 40% of the global workforce, women earn far less than men for the same positions, and are much less likely to be among the global political and economic elite. When women do accrue their wealth separately from familial networks, typically they do so through fame enabled by their commodification in global media industries. But for the vast majority not privileged with fame or fortune, gender inequities in education remain, along with the resulting loss of subsequent social, cultural, and financial capitals.

The second MDG promotes "universal primary education," for all boys and girls by 2015, something that is seen as critical in contributing to "gender equality" and "empowering women," which is the third goal of this multilateral initiative. Many bilateral, multilateral, and nongovernmental programs have been created and funded in support of these goals, including the UN Girls' Education Initiative designed to assist national governments in these efforts (UNGEI, 2013a). Girls' education has been justified in a variety of ways, as a matter of justice and fairness, as necessary for economic development, as correlated with critical health practices that affect families and children, and even as a potential deterrent to sexual slavery and terrorist acts (Kristof & WuDunn, 2009). Girls' education also becomes celebrated when schools are built, funded by global celebrities.

This chapter focuses on the work of three female celebrities, Oprah Winfrey, Madonna, and Angelina Jolie, who are engaged in global development, particularly in the field of girls' education. Situating celebrity participation within broader trends of privatizing global development, this niche represents a particular manifestation of political-economic capital created through the profits of media industries in global capitalism. Focusing on female celebrities allows us to consider the complex ways in which women's interests become articulated in the construction of donors as well as recipients in the process of strategic social change. With reference to these particular programs, construction of even these women as donors highlights their maternal roles, without referencing gender dynamics that contribute to inequities in economic resources, political rights, and social responsibilities. This analysis is situated within the particular cases of girls' education programs in South Africa, Malawi, and Afghanistan.

Girls' education in South Africa, Malawi, and Afghanistan

The articulation of girls' needs is explored in discussions of educational interventions advocated by three female celebrities. Oprah, Madonna, and Angelina have contributed to building girls' schools and educational programs in South Africa, Malawi, and Afghanistan. While each of these countries suffers from populations in poverty and women dying in childbirth, their structural circumstances and gender dynamics differ.

Within the field of girls' education, Afghanistan appears to be the most challenging of these three, with one of the highest proportions of children not in school in the world (about 20%), and stark disparity between the proportion of girls and boys attending primary school (46% of girls and 63% of boys) and secondary school (21% of girls and 43% of boys, 2008–2012), along with literacy levels (18% of females aged 15–24 compared with 50% of males in that age group; UNGEI, 2013a; UNICEF, 2013a). UN documentation attributes the problem of girls not attending primary school in this country to lack of accessibility and security; not enough female instructors; poverty and unemployment; and child marriage. Finding ways for girls to attend school may be constrained by broader social norms, perpetuated by there being high fertility rates (5.1; World Bank, 2012), few (20%) women in the formal labor force, with little change in this over the past decade, and stark differences in literacy rates.

While poverty appears to be a central concern (with as many as 72% living on less than US$ 1.25 a day in 2010) for girls' enrollment and attendance at primary schools in Malawi, along with the added impact of HIV/AIDS (10% of adults aged 15–49; UNAIDS, 2013), gender differences in this country are not all that dire comparatively: youth literacy rates are similar across boys and girls at 87%, and girls are slightly more likely than boys to attend primary school (86% of girls and 84% of boys, 2008–2012) and have similar attendance levels at secondary school (10% of girls and 10% of boys, 2008–2012; UNGEI, 2013b; UNICEF, 2013b), although this rate is quite low. Gender dynamics differ dramatically from those in Afghanistan, with more women in the labor force (85%) than men (81%) in 2013, though women's fertility at 5.5 in 2012 is slightly higher in Malawi, with a higher maternal mortality rate, at 510 per 100,000 live births, than the fertility rate in Afghanistan (5.1) in 2012 (World Bank, 2012).

Similar to Malawi, education in South Africa appears to be on more equitable terms: literacy rates are high across both genders (97% for boys and 98% for girls), along with primary school enrollment (90% of boys and 91% of girls, 2008–2012), with more girls (48%) than boys (41%, 2008–2011) attending secondary school (UNGEI, 2013c; UNICEF, 2013c). The percentage of residents in poverty is much lower (9%) in South Africa than in Malawi, as is the maternal mortality rate (140 in 2013) and women's fertility rate (2.4; World Bank, 2012). Whereas women are proportionately more likely to be employed formally than men in Malawi, though, in South Africa we see the opposite trend, with the ratio of three women to every four men in the labor force

While globally girls are not attending formal schools or achieving literacy according to UN standards at the same levels as boys, in these three cases gender differences in education seem much more pronounced in Afghanistan than in South Africa or Malawi. Relative need in a particular context, then, does not appear to be a guiding criterion for investment in girls' education in these particular African countries. The significance when funding girls' schools appears to be placed more on how this will play in donor communities than on maximizing development resources.

Research approach

Consonant with the other analyses considered in this book, I explore constructions of women and gender in development discourse, in this case considering women as donors of development. With each of these cases, there is potential for women to be considered as more actively engaged than the passive stance critiqued in feminist scholarship: whether as leaders of international events or as entrepreneurs of small-scale businesses. In this example, women actively fund these programs as donors in girls' education. How their representation fits within broader gendered norms is explored in public discourse about these specific programs. In this chapter, my attention to development focuses on these female celebrity donors, considering the ways they engage in development broadly as well as more specifically in the field of girls' education. Instead of considering only how communication is seen as facilitating development goals or as contributing to discursive explanations of development, in this chapter communication is considered also as a global industry, enabling the acquisition of wealth and fame that allows select individuals to participate in development as donors.

The analyses here are based on reviews of development reports and assessments, including foundation mission statements, as well as news published in the English language in North American, Asian, and African publications. I explore how these three women become cast as donors, not only in academic literature, but also in public discourse published in news services from the beginning of 2008 until the end of 2014. The news sources were retrieved from LexisNexis, using search terms focusing on their individual names, in connection with "girls' school" or "foundation" in the designated countries where their schools were built. Because Angelina's school in Afghanistan was built more recently, attention in the earlier sampled years includes her work as a donor through her foundation in the African and Asian regions. Of the 133 news articles included in this sample, most of the attention recognized the schools funded by Oprah (53%) and Madonna (49%), with several stories including attention to both Madonna and Oprah. Only 8% of this sample described the work of Angelina as a donor. Oprah's earlier establishment of a girls' school in South Africa contributed to more coverage in the earlier years reviewed, mostly (61%) in 2008–2009, steadily falling each year since. Madonna's subsequent initiation of a girls' school project, along with controversy over her adoptions, contributed to the most frequent coverage during the years 2009–2011 (66%). Angelina's coverage intensified a year later, with most attention in 2010–2011 (46%) and again in 2013 (36%). Although fewer articles recognized Angelina as a donor, when they did so the articles were considerably longer (median=659 words). While almost as many articles were published about Madonna as a donor as those devoted to Oprah, the former attracted shorter news stories (median=383 words, compared with Oprah's median=536 words).

Similar to the diversity of her development portfolio, news sources in English highlighting Angelina as a donor were more diverse geographically, with roughly a third coming from African, a third from Asian (including Middle Eastern), and a third from North American sources. Given that Madonna and Oprah focus their development programs on more targeted countries in the African region, it is not surprising that their news coverage is much less prominent in the Asian region (3% for Oprah and 8% for Madonna). Oprah has attracted a substantial amount of news both within South Africa and in the African region (41%), whereas Madonna's controversies and programs were included by African sources in 26% of the articles noted, with much more attention from North American news (66%).

Geographical region matters not only in terms of source of publication, but also as subject within news content. Almost all of the news (97%) about Oprah concerned her school in South Africa, a dominant reference point as well in about one out of five news stories on Madonna (17%) and Angelina (18%). Most of Madonna's geographical references were to Malawi (95%), whereas Angelina's work in Afghanistan, initiated more recently, was covered in about half (45%) of the articles about her work as a development donor. These results are contingent upon the structuring of search terms particularly asking for articles about these celebrities' work in girls' education and children's welfare.

Although this is a limited selection of print news sources, as a collection these narratives allow comparative analyses of female celebrity philanthropist representations within elite global news circulation. Their ability to attract attention in these news sources is contingent upon their celebrity status, leveraged through fame and wealth produced through global cultural industries.

Communication

The political economy of the development industry highlights the emergence of private sources of funding, through individuals, foundations, corporations, and other agencies acting outside of the state. While there are many industries contributing to the wealth of a global elite, here I consider global communication industries as a resource creating the fame of female celebrities, who then use their status to attract and channel resources to selected development initiatives. Working to promote girls' education is a relatively savvy, uncontroversial development goal, allowing celebrity donors to be associated with what can be projected as altruistic acts.

The communications industries producing wealth and fame are global in distribution and revenue. Global film revenue was projected to reach US$ 88.3 billion in 2014, while global television revenue exceeds that of film at US$ 428.1 billion (Statistica, 2015a; 2015b). Global music recordings are falling in revenue, but still valued at US$ 15 billion in

2013 (Smirke, 2014). Along with even more profitable videogames, these industries create wealth for owners and stars as capitalist enterprises.

Celebrities in global development

Celebrities are believed to benefit the work of global development by raising awareness of issues, helping nonprofit organizations secure access to leading politicians and power brokers, and attracting financial resources to support their causes and foundations. Against the backdrop of these potential highlights, others raise concerns with the use of celebrities in global development work, as sanctifying donors, glamorizing poverty, and naturalizing extreme inequities in wealth. Celebrity engagement with the global development industry may serve to perpetuate modernization models based on neoliberal ideologies, detracting from dialogue about social justice and basic needs.

Building on their status as stars of the global music, film, and television industries, media celebrities participate in philanthropic work in a variety of ways, from being passively composed in public relations stunts to actively engaged in strategic advocacy (such as Peter Gabriel in the work of Witness; Pedelty, 2013). The connections between wealthy owners and celebrities reinforce the status of this global elite produced by the profits of global communications industries. These profits create the financial and social capital to promote particular approaches to global development (Kapoor, 2013). Capitalizing on these global industries that allow them a broad geographical reach and on celebrity cultures that ascribe status and credibility to those with star power, celebrities are becoming increasingly involved in global development (Cooper, 2008; Tsaliki et al., 2011).

Although the economic structure of these industries can be considered global, the reference privileged is that of Anglo, English-language cultural contexts (Cooper, 2008). The foundations celebrities fund, the gala events they host, the networks they leverage, all in the interests of development, tend to be centered in Northern Western territories, where their fame grants them voice in speaking on behalf of communities in the global South. Particularly in the case of those in wealthy countries who are less in tune with political news, celebrities are able to attract their attention (Couldry et al., 2010; Curran et al., 2009).

While raising broad awareness of global problems may assume a pluralistic model of transition in which individual media consumers actively determine what causes to support and which products to purchase, critical models of social change recognize that celebrities have more political capital in their ability to select global concerns for public attention than their audiences. Many charitable organizations, such as the Red Cross and Oxfam, rely on celebrities for public outreach as well as political access (Colapinto, 2012b). This political capital intersects with economic capital through elite networking in which those earning fame and fortune through profit are able to maintain proportionally high earnings through tax exemptions or low tax rates. Promoting philanthropic work has the added bonus of projecting humanitarian concerns onto those who fund and appear in public relations for foundations and programs (Kapoor, 2013; Tsaliki et al., 2011). Celebrities build on fame as capital in ways that enable them to structure development narratives.

The discursive power of media celebrities extends beyond an ability to select one concern, such as education, over others, to perpetuating the underlying narrative explaining the causes of, as well as solutions for, development problems. These narratives tend to simplify complicated conditions, ignoring complex historical contexts (Dieter & Kumar, 2008), and even worse, perpetuating a depoliticized version of events. By obscuring the messy politics of problematic conditions addressed through development work, intervention can more easily be framed as a technocratic or managerial concern (Escobar, 1995; Kapoor, 2013). In this unidimensional frame, we are presented with victims who are to be pitied, rather than communities with dignity who deserve justice (Boltanski, 1999). Turning our attention away from justice, with its structural implications, encourages us to consider how we as individuals can take action to come to the aid of those who appear to us to be victims.

Individual choices then become concentrated on consumption as a way not only to contribute to development causes, but also to mark ourselves as visible in doing so. The RED campaign (Richey & Ponte, 2011), marketing designated products in the color red to finance the Global Fund, as well as the many philanthropic causes represented by bracelets in particular colors, illustrates how these purchasing choices are connected to identifying individuals as caring for particular causes. The idea that through our individual consumption we can change our world benefits the corporations owning products as well as the reputations of celebrities. Relevant to this discussion of how individuals contribute to development, Goodman (2010) describes the "consumer, like the very act of consumption . . . (as) literally re-cast as a/the 'savior' whose power to promote development the world over has become paramount" (p. 105). If consumption is the answer to global development problems, we need not concern ourselves with exploitation and inequities (Boykoff

& Goodman, 2009; Kapoor, 2013; Rasmussen & Richey, 2012; Richey & Ponte, 2011; Street, 2012).

Focusing on the role of celebrity takes the argument that privatization in development reinforces global neoliberal capitalism even further: celebrities promoted through global media as "humanitarians" doing "charity" work are "integral to the neoliberal global order" (Kapoor, 2013, p. 3). Even scholars sympathetic to the efforts of celebrities to draw attention to global poverty recognize that media attention to celebrity philanthropists reinforces neoliberal ideologies (Njoroge, 2011; Tsaliki et al., 2011). Whether the intentions of celebrities are sincerely altruistic or strategically motivated toward improving their images is not the issue. Instead, the concern is with the broader systems of global capitalism that sustain an elite network that restricts the possibility for development to support participatory or advocacy practices engaged outside of a neoliberal paradigm (Tsaliki et al., 2011).

While many celebrities become engaged in global development work, in this analysis I build on discourse surrounding the girls' schools supported by female stars, whose fame and fortune have been accrued through their profitable work in the global television, film, and music industries. Concentrating on well-known female celebrities allows us to explore feminist concerns with the patriarchal foundations of development, problematizing the complex nature of women engaged as donors as well as recipients of the aid process.

Development

Although the literature on development tends to focus on projected beneficiaries of targeted campaigns or on communities engaged in participatory planning and implementation, broadening our scope we can envision development donors and intermediary organizations as integral to the process of development intervention. Development agencies constitute an incredibly varied population of organizations, foundations, and other collectives, operating through government, multilateral, private, or other sources of funding, each with its own particular restrictions and agendas. In this analysis, I focus on individual private donors, who use their fame as capital to leverage funding as well as their own wealth to fund projects as well as foundations. The few women able to participate in an exclusive club of wealthy donors do so through their celebrity status. After considering how the three women identified in this study contribute to development more broadly, I focus on their specific programs in the field of girls' education.

Women acting as agents of development, through their work as donors, complicate a more simplistic framework that connects hegemonic domination with patriarchy. Some fortunate women have benefited greatly from global capitalist industries, though typically through their mediated commodification. Emerging through the global production of television, music, and film, have used their wealth and status to become visible agents of the development industry. These analyses build on critical approaches to development communication that recognize the importance of political-economic conditions and feminist concerns.

The three celebrity women highlighted in this case study are purposively selected as significant contributors to global development through their contributions to building schools for girls (Wilkins, 2014). Various indices attest to their status in global venues (Forbes, 2007; 2009; 2012; 2015). Among these three, Oprah is the wealthiest (US$ 3 billion in personal wealth in 2015, earning US$ 82 million in 2014). Oprah ranks highly, as fourth on the 2014 Forbes list of the most powerful celebrities in the world (Fyer-Morrel, 2014), as well as 14th among the world's most powerful women and 14th among the world's most powerful entrepreneurs.

Madonna comes close to Oprah's rank, as the fifth most powerful celebrity according to Forbes (though in 2013), and was earlier noted for being the world's best-selling female recording artist and the fourth wealthiest woman in entertainment in 2012. Her estimated net worth of US$ 800 million in 2014, though, is but a fraction of the wealth accrued by Oprah. Angelina's net worth, at US$ 145 million in 2015, is less than that of Madonna's, and she is also much farther down the list of the world's most powerful celebrities (73rd) and most powerful women (50th). Forbes estimates "power" through indices assessing finances, media presence, influence, and impact. Given these calculations another woman highly influential in global development, Melinda Gates, ranks third on the 2014 list of the world's most powerful women. Although Angelina appears much farther down this list, her additional claim to fame comes from being on the list of the world's most beautiful women in earlier rankings. Going back to the time period more proximate to their building of girls' schools, 2009 rankings list Angelina, Oprah, and Madonna as the top three most powerful celebrities (Finlay, 2011, p. 196). Building their status through their glamor, talent, and ownership, Angelina, Madonna, and Oprah have gained wealth through their successful navigation of and commodification in the global film, music, and television industries.

These three celebrities not only make their own individual contributions to their own and other foundations, but also collaborate with various philanthropic organizations and networks. Established in 2007 by Trevor Neilson, the Global Philanthropy Group, formerly with the Gates Foundation, brings together many celebrities, including Madonna and Angelina, although the latter cut ties with this network after learning of Neilson's arrogant gossiping about his celebrity clients (Colapinto, 2012a; 2012b). It is worth noting Neilson's interest in working with Oprah's OWN television network on creating a program on the glamor of global philanthropy (Colapinto, 2012b). The particular causes as well as the broader development goals become part of the public relations narrative (see Chapter 1). Bearing in mind the financial and social capital afforded these three women given their fame and fortune based on the global communications industries, next I explore their work in girls' education.

Building girls' schools

Each of these celebrities has brought visibility and funding to girls' education. Oprah attracted widespread media attention with her initiative to build a private school for girls in South Africa. Madonna's attempts to stimulate a similar program in Malawi were met with controversy and serious obstacles. Within a broader portfolio of issues and territories, Angelina elected to fund girls' education in Afghanistan. Next I explore the context of their development work in order to situate these specific interventions within their broader social change missions.

Oprah

Oprah has been cited as the most charitable celebrity in the US (Porter, 2010), allocating US$ 41.4 million for philanthropy in 2010. In addition to her own foundation, she funds a variety of programs addressing health, children, and women's issues. The Oprah Foundation also serves as a central venue for her philanthropic work. Formerly known as the Oprah Winfrey Leadership Academy Foundation, the Oprah Foundation adds to her own investment with contributions from individuals, corporations, and other donors. The Oprah Foundation itself was estimated to be worth about US$ 172 million in 2012. An earlier manifestation of a connected volunteer nonprofit organization, Oprah's Angel Network, closed down in 2011, at the same time she ended her 25-year television talk show. Prior to this decision, though, she (along with Al Gore) was listed as being among the most "influential" celebrities on global issues in four countries (Boykoff & Goodman, 2009, p. 400).

This was the period in which Oprah leveraged her influence to build a school for girls in South Africa. While it was designated as a Leadership Academy in 2007, Oprah's foundation established a girls' school for grades 7–12, south of Johannesburg. This single, exclusive school was allocated US$ 40 million, benefiting a few hundred fortunate girls. In keeping with the nurturing role of women, Oprah reportedly described herself as "one proud mama" when the first class recently graduated from this academy, as reported in the British press (Smith, 2012). This Leadership Academy for Girls still operates, focusing on grades 8–12, offering "a nurturing environment for academically gifted girls who come from disadvantaged backgrounds" with the aim of developing "a new generation of dynamic women leaders" (OWLA, 2013).

Earlier visions of this school were criticized for their ideological approach, emphasizing individual responsibility, as well as logistical concerns. First, privileging individualism does not do justice to recognizing the critical conditions of poverty that are beyond personal control. The central message guiding the ideology of Oprah's charitable initiatives begs women to take personal responsibility, highlighting individual empowerment at the expense of recognizing social inequities that constrain opportunity (Peck, 2008). Next, the extremely high funding of this one school contrasts poorly in cost–benefit analyses with spending by other charities, such as Catholic AIDS Action, allocating US$ 80,000 for 1500 children, or the Rwanda Community Development Organization, spending US$ 300,000 on 50,000 orphans (Peck, 2008, p. 218). But Oprah was not the only female celebrity to invest in girls' education in the African region.

Madonna

While Madonna differs from Oprah in that she is not contributing as much financially to global development, they share an interest in funding schools for girls, with Madonna supporting one in Malawi to match the other in South Africa. But before exploring Madonna's efforts, it is worth noting the broader context of her global development giving. The central targets of her global charitable work include orphanages in Malawi; vulnerable children who have lost parents or have contracted HIV/AIDS; programs on HIV/AIDS and malaria; poverty; and education (Friedman, 2012).

Madonna established her foundation, Raising Malawi, in 2006, "to bring an end to the extreme poverty and hardship endured by Malawi's 1.4 million orphans and vulnerable children once and for all" (Raising

Malawi, 2015). Public information on this foundation does not report an operating budget, but does admit to working with community and academic organizations in Malawi, along with the Clinton Foundation, Millennium Promise, the corporation Bingham McCutchen, and others. Assets for this foundation were estimated at about US$ 2.7 million in 2012. Working with Michael Berg, the co-founder of this foundation, Madonna leveraged her own US$ 11 million contribution by helping to raise US$ 18 million (Nagourney, 2011).

Madonna's six-minute film on her work in Malawi (http://www.youtube.com/watch?v=NfQQAnQEs6I) opens with visual shots of people crying and burying children. Against this backdrop of despair and death, her melodious voice asks: "How do we break this cycle?" The resounding chorus, featuring different individuals, such as Reverend Tutu, sings of our power to change ourselves and our nations, and that we share "a common fate." We are then told: "We have a choice." Madonna then asks herself rhetorically: "Why did I choose Malawi?" She answers herself: "I didn't. It chose me" (Madonna, 2008). This rhetorical slant may be intended to counter criticisms of her foundation's approach to development as being "top-down."

In the end, the Raising Malawi Foundation did not build the $15 million school intended to admit 400 girls (Nagourney, 2011). Some blamed this wasted expense on mismanagement and corruption, pinpointed on the boyfriend of Madonna's former trainer (Nagourney, 2011), while others noted bad advice from consultants such as Neilson (Traub, 2008) or unfortunate connections with the Kabbalah Centre, itself the focus of an IRS investigation due to the shady financial dealings of the Berg family who ran it (Ryan, 2011). As a result of the reputed corruption in the Kabbalah Centre and her foundation, Madonna fired the board of advisers for Raising Malawi, but continued to fund the construction of schools (Raising Malawi, 2015).

Government officials in Malawi have accused Madonna of being more concerned with her public image than with working collaboratively to invest in the education of their country (Reuters, 2011). Private funding such as that of Raising Malawi becomes particularly important to poor nations when foreign aid, in this case 40% of the nation's budget, is suspended, as happened when Malawian police killed protestors (Reuters, 2011). Mapondera and Smith (2012) give voice to those in villages who gave up their homes to make space for these schools, leaving empty land that later became designated space for a cemetery for the national heroes of Malawi. The tension between the government of Malawi and the work of this celebrity-sponsored foundation remains a challenge in this specific case, but also illustrates the broader dynamics that highlight the critical role of political agencies in negotiating aid between donors and recipients.

Schools later built in Malawi through Raising Malawi in partnership with buildOn enrolled both girls and boys, with fellowships helping to support girls in completing their secondary education. Madonna's more recent initiative, promoted as a "revolution of love," funded a "dream school" for girls in Pakistan, intending to replicate this school later in Afghanistan (Bakker, 2014). To draw attention and raise funds in support of projects in this region, Madonna sold her painting by Fernand Leger for US$ 7.16 million, thereby funding her new organization, the Ray of Light Foundation (Battersby, 2013; Madonna, 2013). The homepage of this foundation's website now boasts in white letters, across a photograph of light-skinned Madonna surrounded by many darker-skinned children's faces: "Let's Start a Revolution" (Ray of Light, 2015). The explanation reads:

> My Revolution has nothing to do with bloodshed or violence. It is a revolution where we support one another regardless of race, religion, or gender. A revolution that promotes peace and demands equality. I don't accept injustice. And neither should you. I invite you all to join my Revolution of Love! – Madonna.

The central initiative awards grants to artists through an Art for Freedom program. The mission of this foundation moves away from a focus on girls, though with explicit references to gender and justice. This shifts her work away from the failed intervention in Malawi. Although there have been no public statements as to what might have happened since, in 2013 there was extensive coverage of Madonna's plans to build schools in Pakistan, more visible because of the public attention toward Malala Yousafzai's shooting by Taliban men. Malala's plight attracted attention from many global celebrities, not only from the three studied here, but also from Hillary Clinton, Bono, and others. A Pakistani news source repeated in several other news venues raised concerns that Madonna "might be putting the teenager even more into harm's way," through "her relentless self-promotion, envelope pushing and obsession with her body," tapping "right into extremist ideas about 'Western freedom' and what happens when women gain power, not to mention an education" (Daum, 2012). Coverage of Madonna shifted to Pakistan and Afghanistan, the latter of which was already the site of a school project supported by Angelina.

Angelina

Compared with Madonna, Angelina Jolie plays a somewhat different role on the global development scene, cast as a more collaborative team player, through her service as a "goodwill ambassador" for the UN, special envoy of the UN High Commissioner for Refugees, and Citizen of the World, according to the award given by the UN Correspondents Association. In sharp contrast to the political resentment Madonna's attempt at building schools left among government leaders and citizens in Malawi, Angelina was awarded honorary Cambodian citizenship in 2005 in recognition of her work there.

In addition to volunteering her time to the UN and the Clinton Global Initiative, co-chairing the Education Partnership for Children of Conflict, Angelina contributes funds to several organizations, such as the UN High Commissioner for Refugees (UNHCR; US$ 5 million since 2001) and the Namibian Wildlife Sanctuary (US$ 2 million; UNHCR, 2012). Funds are concentrated though, combined with the resources of Angelina's partner Brad Pitt, toward the foundation they established in 2008 with a US$ 8.5 million investment (Philanthropy News Digest, 2011). In contrast to the more conformist role played by Audrey Hepburn as goodwill ambassador for UNICEF following her acting career, Angelina's ambassadorship for the UNHCR during her film career drew public attention to her private life with her partner (Cooper, 2008), helping to transform her previously wilder image into that of a more stable mother (Wheeler, 2011).

Explicitly recognizing family members through naming, the Maddox Jolie-Pitt Foundation (MJP), based in Cambodia and Los Angeles, describes its mission as being "dedicated to eradicating extreme rural poverty, protecting natural resources and conserving wildlife. MJP promotes sustainable rural economies that directly contribute to the health and vitality of communities, wildlife and forests" (Maddox Jolie-Pitt Foundation, 2012). Among many projects devoted to environmental, health, and children's concerns, in 2008 this foundation joined Microsoft in support of the Kids in Need of Defense (KIND) fund, providing free legal counsel to immigrant children without their parents in the US. Focusing on children is a central theme for Angelina. The issues she addresses through her philanthropic work include people displaced by conflict, such as refugees; environment, conservation, and agriculture; children's concerns, such as caring for orphans and education; poverty, such as microcredit; and health, such as HIV/AIDS (Maddox Jolie-Pitt Foundation, 2012).

Only recently did Angelina join the chorus of her peers and open a school for girls, but hers is in Afghanistan rather than the African region (with additional support for the Malala Fund for girls' education and empowerment in Pakistan). These initiatives are being funded by a new jewelry line, in collaboration with designer Robert Procop who designed her engagement ring from Brad Pitt in 2012 (Reuters, 2013). Recent media attention to Angelina's schools for girls outside of Kabul relates this program to schools funded by Oprah in South Africa and Madonna in Malawi, noting the latter's controversy over "costs and mismanagement" and the former's school staff member who was "arrested on charges of assault and abuse of students" (Reuters, 2013). It is worth noting that a story first distributed by Reuters news service was excerpted in some of these stories as well in the UK and the US.

When the school was described by sources within the region, most news attention recalled that she had opened an earlier school in 2010, but that the newer construction in 2013 was different in that it would be funded by sales of jewelry created in the style noted above. Most published an estimate of 200–300 girls expected to attend, but one article explained that of the 400 students they would "mostly" be girls. These articles described the schools as being of value to children, sometimes in terms of their "need" and sometimes as in terms of their being victims of "conflict."

Explicit attention to gender imbalances in the country was mentioned in only a few of the articles, describing the area outside of Kabul as "a region that traditionally favours boys' education over girls';" so that a school such as this would need "to counter-balance a cultural bias that values boys' education over girls'," particularly in a "conservative country where tribalism and traditionalism are deeply rooted...parents ...prefer their girls to stay at home." Recognition of this site as a residence of many refugees was articulated in about one-third of these stories, with one article connecting the issue to "rebuilding after the collapse of the Taliban." Constructing the nature of beneficiaries in development is also complemented by attention to what might propel social change processes.

Communication for development

Although most of this literature does not explicitly reference the role of the media in development, it is worth exploring the few $(n = 8; 6\%)$ that do. These three celebrities clearly use their access to the television, film, and music industries as avenues to promote their voices in development, whether through particular television programs or stations in the case of Oprah, online news about Angelina, or documentary films by Madonna. It is worth referencing Madonna's dedication of a song to Malala, the now well-known Pakistani girl shot as signal of protest against girls' education: the press in Pakistan were "bemused" when during the song Madonna "performed a striptease that revealed Yousufzai's first name, Malala, written across her back" (*Right Vision News*, 2012). Although access to global media is a form of capital leveraged by celebrities on behalf of their chosen causes, here I concentrate on the role of communication technologies in educational programs as explained in public discourse.

Typically media appear as indicators of perceived modernity. One key description noted that "cinema was banned (1996–2001 under Taliban) and girls were prohibited from attending school," connecting gender inequity to restrictions of popular culture. The article also notes that most girls interviewed for the story preferred Bollywood to Hollywood, and had little access to television at home (AFP, 2013). Issues of access were not raised by North American news sources.

Access to cellphones, though, was seen as a problem in distracting girls from being successful at school in early coverage of Oprah's school in South Africa. According to local news about this enterprise:

> Oprah Winfrey has confiscated the expensive cellphones she gave her South African private school pupils as gifts after she learnt that only half of them had passed their June exams.

> America's Queen of Talk discovered that the girls at her exclusive academy at Henley-on-Klip south of Jo'burg did poorly in their June exams because they were spending too much time on the cellphone chat service, Mxit.

> [Parents] said the girls' Samsung E250 cellphones have now been replaced by the more modest Nokia 1200, which doesn't allow access to Mxit.

> (Ajam, 2008)

Alternatively, digital media can be articulated clearly as an educational tool, either for those in wealthier countries who know little about the world around them, or students who might benefit from access to sources of information beyond what is available in their schools. In the first-world scenario, we are invited to appreciate the value of digital media in "raising awareness and money for causes such as education, sex trafficking and forced prostitution" through the Half the

Sky Movement promoted by Kristof and WuDunn (Westhead, 2013). They encourage "the Facebook generation [who] can play online to get an insight into the hardship and obstacles women in the developing world face." In this discussion, Westhead (2013) includes Kristof's use of tweets to celebrate celebrity involvement, such as "Angelina Jolie opens girls school in Afghanistan financed by her jewelry. Kardashian, your turn."

Digital media also complement educational initiatives for girls, when technological structures and access are considered as well as building schools. Only Madonna's educational programs were partnered with telecommunications in public reviews, in several articles across regions. In the Canadian, press we see this connection between education as building and as telecommunication:

> Madonna laid the first brick of her new girls' academy near Malawi's capital on Tuesday, in which she encouraged Malawian girls to "dare to dream," according to the inscription on the brick.... At the same event, Madonna also launched a telecommunications and fundraising initiative that aims to provide education to children around the world by offering secondary school scholarships and by supporting schools in developing countries in accessing the internet. "Kids will be able to connect with kids from the other parts of the world," the singer said. "This will promote peace throughout the world." Telecommunications giant Ericsson will donate computers to various schools in 11 African countries through the United Nations Millennium Village initiative, where model villages are established to demonstrate how the quality of life in African rural areas can be improved through community-led development.
>
> *(Guelph Mercury*, 2010)

The *Daily News Egypt* published a similar story, connecting Madonna's "telecommunications and fundraising initiative" with the work of Jeffrey Sachs and the telecommunications corporation Ericsson on a "Connect to Learn Initiative" (*Daily News Egypt*, 2010).

A few days later Sachs (2010) published his own editorial on this program in the *Pittsburgh Post Gazette*, promising "a planetary break-through," through "the reality with Connect to Learn (www.connectto learn.org), a new initiative to ensure that all children on Earth can attain at least a secondary education." As a well-known development professional, it is worth sharing his perspective on the power of telecommunications technology to drive educational programs:

The revolution in information and communications technology is surely the most powerful single force for economic development in the world today. Not just in New York, Shanghai or Paris can you find a mobile telephone in the hands of every passerby. These days, you'll see mobile phones in Nairobi taxis and among camel-herders in northern Kenya. There are now 4.6 billion mobile subscribers, and the numbers are soaring. An estimated 250 million subscribers live in Sub-Saharan Africa alone.

The spread of 3G (and soon 4G) offers the prospect of a technological breakthrough in education. Suddenly, even remote schools can connect to the Internet and to other schools through a solar panel, low-cost computers and wireless access. A school that lacked even rudimentary supplies suddenly can have access to the same global store of information as any other place in the world. . . .

We are seeing such rapid changes throughout Africa. Impoverished communities are cheering the prospect of a rapid ramp-up in girls' education, if meager resources permit.

On a sunny day in Malawi recently, Madonna and the CEO of Ericsson, Hans Vestberg, attended the groundbreaking for a girls' school to launch the new global education initiative. On the horizon in two directions stood the mobile towers to connect the school with the world. The promise was not lost on the national government. The education minister committed to scale up education nationally as rapidly as resources would permit.

In short, the links between education and reduced fertility, faster economic development and lower environmental degradation are powerful and obvious.

Connecting kids around the world in shared online curricula and facilitating "social networks" of kids around the world at an early age will yield far-reaching educational benefits.

Across the work of these three women as development donors, we can identify central themes in the construction of women as agents of development who use their fame as leverage for global communication, and as a vehicle for their voices, as well as using their industries to accrue status and wealth. Public discussion of their educational programs, when addressing the role of the media, tends to consider digital media as complementary to building infrastructure, as distracting from serious study, or as emblematic of modernity. While girls are the target of the educational interventions described here, female celebrities have the opportunity to appear as development donors. Next I explore how women are cast in this role, connected with gendered constructions of helping relationships.

Gender

The role of women

In this section I consider how women are constructed within this projected agency as donors in the development enterprise, through published documentation and news sources. In public discourse concerning these three celebrities, their value is projected as connected to their roles as virtuous donors, capitalizing on their leverage as nurturing mothers, ensconced in their commodification as beautiful, glamorous women. As donors, their role also contributes to the sense of mission, conventionally portrayed in public discourse with religious themes (Wilkins, 2007). The roles cast for these women as donors characterize them as virtuous saints or fairy godmothers with mystical powers, as nurturing mothers with cross-racial global appeal, or as glamorous queens, either dramatically diva-like or elegantly regal.

Virtuous saints

Manifesting their glamor in the projected light of missionary zeal, Christian references dominate public attention to their charities, building on their constructed identities. Casting these celebrities with the appearance of purity begins with their very names. Madonna, with her codified celebrity moniker, offers an ironic and iconic articulation of virtue and sexuality in popular culture. Angelina's name offers a diminutive reference to a pure and helpful angel, and like the name of Madonna, references biblical narratives that value women as pure, virtuous, and giving, for the greater good. Even Oprah has a historical connection with biblical texts, having originally been named Orpah, for the sister of Ruth, which she reportedly changed later because of difficulties in pronunciation. A similarity across these women, then, is that they all have names that reference biblical narratives that suggest women earn their worth when acting as virtuous maternal figures, particularly without the nastiness of conception or messiness of childbirth.

Attention to Madonna's work in Malawi relied frequently on these references, calling her "Saint Madonna of Malawi," whose "appearance was described by local politicians as a "gift from heaven," even referring to the history of the land she purchased to build a school as previously owned by "David Livingstone, the British missionary, [who] first brought Christianity almost 150 years ago" (Malone, 2011). In another South African newspaper, a "young orphan" supported by her foundation was quoted as confessing to Madonna: "You are our god. Where could we have been without you?" (*The Star*, 2009). While less dominant in coverage, occasional references to Angelina (such as her "big Christmas gift," *Namibian*, 2011) and Oprah (quoting her school's principal referring to a "blessing in disguise" Omar, 2011) have integrated Christian missionary themes. However, Madonna seems to be most frequently cast in this missionary capacity, even incorporating technological solutions within a metaphor of religious radiance: "The 51-year-old also promised electricity to a local village." Speaking in Mphandula, the singer said: "I know you work in darkness. I will bring you electricity" (*Daily Mail*, 2009). While Madonna's appeal is projected in terms of religious mission, Oprah's framing relies more on metaphors of magic and gifts.

References to Madonna's spirituality are eclectic, positioning her as transcending the Christian icons of her earlier fame. A South African source extends her imagery with a crucifix to explorations of Kabbala and Islam (*Cape Argus*, 2013):

> It is almost 25 years since she first sang Like a Prayer, but it seems the intervening years have done little to help Madonna (pictured) decide exactly whom she is praying to. For it appears the queen of re-invention may be on the verge of one of her most startling changes yet, after she revealed she was studying the Qur'an. The 55 year old was raised a Roman Catholic, but for the past 17 years she has been a devout follower of Kabbalah, a mystical offshoot of Judaism.

> Now the singer, whose partner Brahim Zaibat, 25, is a Muslim, has begun investigating Islam. She said: "I am building schools for girls in Islamic countries and studying the Qur'an."

Although one might appreciate Madonna's interest in learning more about the cultural contexts with which she might engage, this characterization verges more on the side of ridicule. Assertions of Oprah as more magical, though, appear to be more appreciated.

Fairy godmother

Oprah's philanthropic work in global development takes on this nurturing role as she epitomizes the "fairy godmother" to African girls, building schools, funding orphanages, and supporting programs for children. Similar to surprising audience members of her television show with new cars, her inclusion of a select few girls to attend her comparatively luxurious school privileges the idea that chance, rather than merit, channels mobility. Just as fairy godmothers bestow gifts through magic, Oprah bequeaths schools and vehicles with enough spectacle to detract from questions that might reveal Oz behind the curtain. Several news articles from the South African press feature the idea of her contributions as "gifts," such as the "vegetable patch for a school with hungry children, playground equipment for a rural orphanage and 11 brick houses for shack dwellers in Orange Farm feature on a gift list given by girls at the Oprah Winfrey Leadership Academy" (Gifford, 2008); and Oprah's "gift to build a dream on" (Gifford, 2008). The idea of Oprah as fairy godmother features in descriptions of her school, whose "conception is like a fairy tale" (Omar, 2011), and which was praised by Nelson Mandela as offering "opportunities to some of our young people they could never imagine had it not been for Oprah" (*The Star*, 2007). Central to this characterization of a fairy godmother is the idea of a celibate maternal figure, neither sexual nor physical in connections with other adults or children. Madonna and Angelina, in contrast, stake their claim as actual mothers, through childbirth and adoption.

Nurturing mothers

Valuing women as mothers even when they are donors fits a broader development discourse, in which women as recipients of aid become visible in their roles as mothers and caretakers of families (Wilkins, 1997). As donors, these three women privilege children in their giving strategies over many other valuable causes. While all three devote resources towards philanthropy designed to benefit children, only Madonna and Angelina themselves are described in terms of their direct status as mothers to named children: about half of all articles (55% of those covering Madonna and 45% of those addressing Angelina) explicitly refer to the children of these two celebrities.

Best known in global philanthropy for her role as an advocate and actual transnational adopter (Kapoor, 2013), Angelina gains status through her focus on children and her connection to handsome partner Brad Pitt. Chouliaraki explains this "tension in Jolie's humanitarian persona between a 'universal' discourse of motherhood, inviting identification with Western publics, and a discourse of intense particularity including glamorous looks and legendary wealth, setting her apart as an object of popular fantasy" (2012, p. 10). The magic of glamor resonates with the fairy godmother image, further reinforcing hierarchies across national and racial lines given their tendencies toward transnational adoptions.

These adoptions reinforce the celebrities' positions as "global mothers," eloquently articulated by Shome (2011) as a manifestation of the power of white transnational femininity. Both Madonna and Angelina have adopted children, in addition to birthing their own. Madonna has adopted both a son and a daughter from Malawi, perhaps finding inspiration in Angelina's adoptions in Cambodia, Ethiopia, Vietnam, and Namibia. Sandra Bullock and Charlize Theron have joined this exclusive club of Caucasian female stars bringing home African babies. Unlike the welcome Angelina was granted during her adoptions, Madonna's attempts were met with controversy. Her decision to adopt Mercy in 2009, following her adoption of David Banda in 2008, was initially rejected by a local court in Malawi, but a supreme court in the country allowed her to process this adoption upon appeal (Finlay, 2011; Kapoor, 2013). These adoptions fit a broader trend of US families adopting children from the region, particularly from Ethiopia (BBC, 2012). The African Child Policy Forum reports that in this region international adoptions have risen dramatically, quadrupling between 2004 and 2012 (BBC, 2012).

While many support these adoptions for providing family support for children in need, as well as financial support to orphanages and children's services, others raise concerns about the commercialization of this process, their fear for children's safety, and their concern with trans-continental and trans-racial adoptions. Some children's advocates encourage adoptions within cultural and national communities for the sake of the child. In the African region, some children are given into adoption even with one parent living (BBC, 2012). In the US, almost twice as many light-skinned children in orphanages, with no living parents, have been adopted as those with darker skin (Jaye, 2012). In the African region, the Child Policy Forum has raised the concern that many countries do not have adequate procedures to ensure children are well cared for post-adoption, or even to guarantee against child trafficking. Apart from these logistical and safety concerns, Tchouaffe (2007) believes that these trans-racial adoptions by wealthy Americans of African children cause harm by reinforcing the idea that white benefactors are needed to rescue helpless Africans. On the other hand, these expensive adoptions do help to fund orphanages and children's services to support many other children in need. For example, the Home of Hope orphanage that Madonna supports in Malawi helps to finance families that help care for children so that they have homes outside of orphanages (Dugger, 2009).

Glam queen

While both Angelina and Madonna have earned their fame in part through their glamorous appearances, Madonna appears to suffer from a Madonna/whore dichotomy that characterizes the image she has projected throughout her musical career. Both though are framed in media coverage through this glamorous lens. Angelina is referred to in the South African *Sunday Times* as "the world's busiest, most beautiful star...whose glamour can bear comparison with the screen idols of 1950s Hollywood" (2011). While Madonna also attracts attention to her glamorous persona, her characterization appears less secure, and is at times competitive with male figures. In the South African *Star*, Madonna is "used to being the centre of attention, but on Thursday Madonna was most definitely upstaged – by her adopted son David" (2009).

Not only has Madonna's entrance into global development excited controversy within the North American press, but within the African press as well, in which media attention has been much less flattering toward her than that devoted to Oprah and Angelina. Within this news coverage, Angelina controlled her representation by dominating those given voice to reflecting on her work, as did Oprah. In contrast, news covering Madonna's schools and adoptions was more likely to be negatively disposed. Madonna was criticized not only for not being sensitive to national laws regarding adoption, but also for a lack of accountability for the corruption in her project to build schools.

While the press felt Madonna was acting in her own interests, which might have been constructed more positively as a male characteristic, they were more defensive of Oprah. The South African *Daily News* suggested that the Malawian government "has declined to work with the singer on her foundation's latest construction plan, with a spokeswoman saying: 'We now feel like this is all about propping up her global image and not in our interest'" (2012). In contrast to that coverage of Madonna, the South African *Star* blamed criticism of Oprah on racism. It states that "the world's media cannot resist portraying us as just another African country threatened by bureaucratic corruption assisted by an inherent amorality," in that for those "who cannot resist that sort of thing, the story of Oprah's poor black girls behaving badly was a chance to lay bare their true feelings about race," and quotes a website posting that "Black people are not civilised" (2009).

More than the others (it only appears in one reference to Madonna), Oprah is cast explicitly as a "queen," either of "television" broadly or of "talk" shows more specifically (in four of the articles reviewed). Instead of asserting her status as a financial owner and industry leader, these constructions situate her as royally feminine. This status has clear hierarchical value even if it is perhaps neutered through this gendered portrayal.

Angelina's status was more typically ascribed to her perceived beauty. Most of these narratives featured Angelina most prominently as an actress, some with attention to her being an "American" or "Hollywood" film actress particularly. News attention in India and Pakistan reminded readers that "acting is controversial in the country, with many conservative Afghans associating it with un-Islamic behavior and even prostitution," but that this "beautiful American lady... [was] very humble. She sat on dust. She did not behave like a movie star" (*Right Vision News*, 2013). Publications in the Asian region excerpted from an originally released Reuters report extolling the comparative virtues of Angelina: "Jolie is not the first celebrity to open schools in faraway places. Both Oprah Winfrey and Madonna have funded the building of schools in South Africa and Malawi. Madonna's project provoked controversy over costs and mismanagement, while a staff member at Winfrey's school was arrested on charges of assault and abuse" (Reuters, 2013).

Among these three celebrities, attention to Angelina's work in global development has been the most favorable, with Madonna's being the most controversial. While Oprah's schools have experienced serious problems, her role as fairy godmother may have saved her from more substantial criticism.

The role of men

Despite the fame of these women, within the global elite men still dominate in terms of wealth and power, allowing men such as Bill Gates and George Soros, both global financiers and initiators of nongovernmental organizations, to emerge "as celebrities, partly for their status as two of the richest people on earth, and partly for their spectacular generosity" (Kapoor, 2013, pp. 48–49). The very endowment of the Gates Foundation, at US\$ 60 billion, exceeds the GDP of many countries (Kapoor, 2013, p. 50).

Much like Yunus in the microenterprise narrative, these men are cast as saviors, following the religious metaphors, matched by women as pure saints and mystical mothers. While men find themselves in the spotlight by their heroic actions as lone figures, women rise to hero-ism when sacrificing on behalf of their families and children, earning applause for their compassion. Benefiting from U2's fame, Bono holds a role as a prominent spokesperson in several development projects, such as the RED campaign (Richey & Ponte, 2011), which was launched on Oprah's television show in 2006.

Highly visible in development, Bono has been credited with build-ing "the superhighway between Africa and Hollywood" (Traub, 2008). Within public discussions of development, Bono and Bob Geldof earn attention for being able to connect with the business world, but Angelina and Madonna must be "more empathetic and 'caring'" (Kapoor, 2013, p. 17). Analogous to the glorification of Mother Theresa, women gain status through their nurturing roles, through caring for children whether they conceive them or not; and when women do not birth children, they are expected to play the role of mother through adopting children or supporting orphanages.

The portrayal of Oprah, Madonna, and Angelina in relation to men differs dramatically. Oprah, as fairy godmother, does not attract media attention in relation to men (only 7% of articles connect her with a male partner), and perhaps therefore is more likely to be portrayed as "heroic," as the mother of one of her school's students called Oprah, also declaring that "her favourite TV programme was the Oprah Winfrey Show" (Moeng, 2009). While Angelina's relationship with spouse Brad Pitt attracts quite favorable and frequent coverage in almost two-thirds (64%) of all articles concerning her philanthropic work (even when we are reminded explicitly of ex-husbands Johnny Lee Miller and Billy Bob Thornton), "heroic" references remain the domain of Pitt, who is also described as "an intelligent man and physically he's a real man, in all things that it means" (Lawrence, 2011). As a couple, Angelina and Brad are said to "understand the power of family" (*Cape Argus*, 2010). Focusing on news published in the Asian region specifically referencing Angelina's schools in Afghanistan, partner Brad was rarely mentioned, but instead the focus was on her connection to jeweler Robert Procop, her collaborator on the creation and sale of jewelry designated to offer financial support for these schools.

In contrast, Madonna's ex-husbands appear as competitors and her estrangement from them is portrayed as instability (mentioned in 14% of all articles on Madonna): as an explanation for her work in Malawi, the *Daily News* in South Africa suggests that: "Of course, Madonna may have something to prove. Her ex-husband, Sean Penn, has earned inter-national attention for his relief work in Haiti" (*Daily News*, 2012); and

Malawi's *The Tribune* wrote that her "quickie divorce" from Guy Ritchie was making it "very difficult for international pop diva Madonna to adopt another child from Malawi" (2013). Male allegiance seemed to be needed during her difficult times, and came from Ashton Kutcher, who responded to criticism of "Madge" by claiming that she was one of the most "generous" people he knew (*Cape Argus*, 2013). Asserting legitimacy through male companions neither values women in their own right nor problematizes gendered norms.

Gender

In this attention to girls' schools as an educational intervention, presumably valued due to assumptions made about girls and boys learning in shared classrooms, visibility of gender is largely absent (less than 3% of articles) in published news. It is the longer articles authored by men, Sachs (2010) and Kristof (2010), in their discussions of girls' education more broadly that allow space to explore the gendered context in which girls and boys study and work. Another notable article for articulating the gendered contexts of learning comes from South Africa (Magome, 2009), interviewing Anne Van Zyl as the new head of Oprah's school.

In addition to the importance of gender in understanding programs designating schools for girls, articulations of female and male roles in philanthropy donors implicate gendered assumptions. In Moraes' (2011) description of Oprah's final celebratory television episode of her eponymous series, Madonna pays tribute to Oprah as a source of personal inspiration, calling her "a self-made woman ... at the top of her game ... [with] male genitals ... [and] a wealth of compassion." This assertion of mixed metaphors suggests a transgendered image that complicates more dichotomous masculine/feminine framing. While overall gender may be fairly absent from the conversation about girls' schools, gendered norms tend to structure associations of girls with victimhood and women with being compassionate mothers, whether as perceived development targets or as donors.

Accountability

Accountability can be conceived in terms of the effectiveness of building girls' schools as a development intervention, of educating girls toward improving their lives, or of promoting positive publicity for visible donors. Before addressing the public relations component of these strategic programs, I consider educational outcomes.

According to UN assessments, progress has been made in global terms, in that the number of children not enrolled fell by 3 million between 2000 and 2011, but in that latter year 57 million children, roughly representing 10% of all primary-aged children, were not participating in formal educational systems. More telling though is that the higher number of young people who are not literate (123 million of those aged 15–24) are disproportionately female, though the gender gap has narrowed (95 literate young women for every 100 men in 2010, up from 90 for every 100 in 1990; UN MDGs, 2013). While primary school has become more accessible for girls over time, secondary school remains a challenge.

Given these assessments it is not primary school but secondary that deserves resource allocation if girls' needs are taken into account. Oprah's school indeed does focus on this secondary level, and announces its success through photographs of the graduating class on its website (Palumbo, 2015). Madonna's public assessment claims that 5600 children have enrolled in the primary and secondary schools she has built since 2013, with more girls completing the secondary level through scholarships from her foundation (Raising Malawi, 2015). Her "Dream School" in Pakistan boasts of its success in enrolling 1200 students (Bakker, 2014). Angelina's school in Afghanistan focuses on education at the primary level, in partnership with the Education Partnership for Children of Conflicts and the UNHCR.

The outcomes directly related to the actual establishment of the girls' school might include assessments of the numbers of girls enrolled (particularly given the number who have applied), in relation to the cost per student given the operating costs of the program. Monitoring might also assess attendance rates, retention, and graduation. It would be valuable as well to assess the comparative rates of girls attending girls-only schools to girls attending other schools with mixed gender enrollment.

According to research reviewed by Donnelly for the *Boston Globe* (2007), critics of the luxurious program and school created by Oprah have cause for concern. Other NGOs are able to educate many more students at a much lower cost per child. What would be helpful here would be an assessment as well of learning outcomes and subsequent education and employment.

The Global Partnership for Education (GPE, 2015) targets girls' education as a central goal, intending to increase girls' enrollment in secondary school in a "safe, supportive, learning environment." Assessment then would need to monitor not only the numbers of students, but also their educational resources (such as textbooks and digital access), teachers' qualifications, and contextual factors contributing to healthy and safe learning. Global Partnership for Education (GPE) assessments have determined that most of their partner countries are approaching gender parity in primary school completion, another way to measure the success of educational programming.

Learning outcomes could include literacy, numeracy, and other life skills. In addition to being able to read and write, basic mathematical skills are important not only for potential integration into a work economy, but also to promote critical engagement as citizens. According to the GPE (2015), although enrollment in school has been increasing among children, their actual learning will be limited without better teacher training, more and better textbooks, lower teacher–student ratios, and supportive home environments.

As a development intervention educating girls is assumed to improve the possibilities for them to succeed later in life. These assumptions can be empirically tested, contrasting whether girls who have attended these schools, compared to others similar in age and relevant circumstances, are significantly initiating first marriages and pregnancies later, going to college, finding employment, and participating in their political and civic communities.

What is the effectiveness of secondary education for girls? Research suggests that girls who stay in school through their adolescence are more likely to avoid poverty, to have lower fertility rates, and to nurture healthier children (Levine et al., 2009; UNDP, 2013). The GPE (2015) cites an aggregate statistic that some countries "lose more than $1 billion a year by failing to educate girls to the same level as boys," though it is not clear which countries or how this figure was determined. It is important to note though that these studies tend to establish correlations across these conditions, and are not suggesting that formal education serves as a direct cause toward improving material or health outcomes. Still, girls' education remains a critical goal given the more direct connections between literacy/education and marriage age, fertility levels, and employment, as matters of equity, of development, and of human rights.

Another way to consider accountability, though narrowly prescribed, may be to assess the extent of sympathetic news generated concerning the celebrity or group most visible as development donor. Controversy and corruption accentuate negative publicity about these donors as well as their projects. In public assessments of the celebrities observed in this analysis, Madonna's ventures were comparatively the most vilified, while Oprah's were the most venerated. Madonna's school in Malawi was not built, and her adoptions were contested; her foundation name and approach shifted attention to more cultural programming and to interventions elsewhere. Even though Angelina's image has been historically marked in terms of more deviant and youthful rebellion against convention, her more recent attachment to Brad and multi-cultural adoptions place her more in traditionally sympathetic familial roles, in contrast to Madonna's less uniformly appreciated maternal ventures. Despite the earlier controversies faced by her South African academy, Oprah's image was able to rise above concerns and transcend challenges, through her seemingly magical touch.

Putting aside the nature of the coverage accorded to these celebrities, Oprah, Madonna, and Angelina were able to bring public attention to the issue of girls' education, even if it has been devoid of attention to gender. Their status, enabled through their commodification in and management of global communications industries, gave them both visibility and voice. Global communication provides a platform that elevates those profiting from the industry to structure neoliberal perspectives of development.

Perpetuating the neoliberal gaze

Female celebrities offer a visibility and voice in support of girls' education consonant with a neoliberal approach to global development. A neoliberal framework for development privileges modernization as an approach to social change, highlighting individual agency in achieving entrepreneurship, political rights, and mobility through education. Neoliberalism operates "as a set of ideas and practices centred on an increased role for the free market... with implications for social justice" (Willis et al., 2008, p. 1), as a hegemonic structure that challenges resistance movements and limits women's participation in development (Dutta, 2011, p. 155). Presented as an apolitical approach to social change, women are encouraged to take responsibility for themselves as individuals rather than raise a collective voice in protest over clear gender inequities in political, economic, social, and cultural resources.

Within structuring and intersecting logics of neoliberalism and patriarchy, women earn their value through their participation in market economies (promoted as a tool of individual empowerment) and their nurturing roles within families as well as through global philanthropy. Whether as development donors or recipients, the significance of this maternal role needs to be understood as part of this hegemonic development agenda. The male gaze noted by feminist scholars as dominating representation of women in popular culture is echoed here in this discussion of development discourse (Shome, 2011). The connection between neoliberal and patriarchal perspectives is critical in feminist critique building on political-economic and cultural analyses.

Feminist scholars have criticized development discourse for characterizing female beneficiaries of intervention through their status as mothers. Even when portraying donors, this maternal characterization prevails. The significance of this maternal role needs to be understood as part of a neoliberal approach to development that recognizes women's value as individuals, without referencing gender dynamics that contribute to inequities in economic resources, political rights, and social responsibilities. As explained by Shome, the "discourse of global motherhood must be situated in the context of contemporary neoliberal conditions of unequal flows of global capitalism and cultural exchanges" (2011, p. 389).

All three of the women highlighted here also contribute to services caring for children without parents. Overall, children's health and welfare appears to be a priority focus for these female stars, cementing their value as nurturers within the development scheme. Although she has not adopted children herself, Oprah reinforces the importance of this maternal role when characterizing her pride in the girls graduating from her academy in South Africa in these very terms. While all three can be criticized potentially for lack of cultural sensitivity and social accountability (stronger evaluations are needed of their programs!), their adherence to gendered stereotypes, as virtuous, glamourous donors, is sustained through public discourse. The glorification of these celebrities is tempered with the recognition of broader agendas that reinforce neoliberal ideology.

Resonating with this neoliberal agenda, Oprah has become known for her attention to self-empowerment, both within her television programming and her charitable work (Boltanski & Chiapello, 2005; Peck, 2008). Particularly among the programs supported by Oprah and Madonna, the mantra of the social change process articulated in their prized programs asks girls and women "to set themselves free," as donors "sanctify" themselves.[1]

In understanding the bases of these celebrities' resources, it is important to note that Oprah differs in important ways from the other two, since she has accrued wealth not only through the commodification of beauty, as have Angelina and Madonna, but through ownership in the very industry that has supplied her wealth. This ownership has allowed Oprah to reach a higher level of fortune and to enter the club of the most wealthy in the world, usually exclusive to men. And as such, she has become one of the most powerful and giving of individual donors in the global community. Gaining her wealth and status from the global television industry, her approach to global development then does not threaten global capitalism, but supports neoliberal logic by emphasizing individual empowerment in strategic social change.

This attention to empowerment resonates clearly with the Women in Development (WID) and modernization approaches to development. The central aim of the Oprah Winfrey Foundation is "to support, empower and educate women, children and their families all over the world" (Oprah Winfrey Foundation, 2012). Helping girls, women, and through them their families, to secure self-esteem, enabled through education, becomes the critical goal of these efforts.

Building from this exclusive attention to girls and women, Gender and Development (GAD) frameworks consider the broader dynamics within which women have rights and opportunities. The articulated goal of the Maddox Jolie-Pitt Foundation (2012) to "build healthy and vibrant communities" working with "impoverished rural villagers and local governments" approaches GAD considerations more closely by attending to the context in which political decisions are made and the role of the community as a central focus; yet, neither is gender explicitly referenced, nor are other power differences, such as class. Including financial support for environmental issues along with health, education, and poverty programs further reinforces Angelina's more comprehensive approach to social change. Madonna's development work falls uneasily somewhere within these two approaches, on the one hand echoing Oprah's empowerment of girls strategies, but rhetorically committing her foundation to working with those in the villages who best understand local problems and to working toward sustainability (Raising Malawi, 2012).

Liberal political theory and capitalism depend on this neoliberal ideology that centers agency in individuals rather than recognizing constraints in policies and structures. Limiting agency to consumption is too narrow. But in this way the neoliberal project depoliticizes social and economic issues, so that we do not question why people are poor, children are suffering, and women discriminated against in terms of pay and rights. Instead, education programs focus on this as a strategy for economic mobility, and poverty programs privilege microenterprise projects that support small-scale entrepreneurship connecting local businesses to broader capitalist interests. The neoliberal gaze accentuates the sanctity of the female donor along with the individual empowerment promoted through many of these development approaches.

Celebrating celebrity in global development spotlights spectacle, curtaining our gaze from the backstage dirt and pretending authenticity exists without rehearsal. In Kapoor's words, this approach "is not meant to help the poor as much as save the rich, that is, avoid catastrophe for revolt, and legitimate, maintain, and advance global capitalism" (2013, p. 80). Female celebrities cast as global philanthropists reinforce the gendered norms that enable their profitable commodification through global media industries, contributing to the neoliberal logic of an increasingly privatized global development enterprise.

References

AFP. (2013). Angelina Jolie, beautiful stranger behind Afghan school. *Times of Oman*, 14 April.

Ajam, K. (2008). Cellphone crackdown at Oprah's girls school. *Cape Argus*, 20 September, p. 2.

Bakker, T. (2014). Madonna's "revolution of love" builds Dream school for girls in Pakistan. *News Corp Australia*, 29 September.

Battersby, M. (2013). Madonna raises $7m from sale of Fernand Léger painting to 'make girls like Malala smile' around the world. 8 May. Retrieved from http://www.independent.co.uk/arts-entertainment/music/news/madonna-raises-7m-from-sale-of-fernand-lger-painting-to-make-girls-like-malala-smile-around-the-world-8607743.html. 13 September 2013.

BBC News. (2012). Adoption from Africa: Concern over "dramatic rise." 29 May. Retrieved from http://www.bbc.co.uk/news/world-africa-18248007. 20 October 2012.

Boltanski, L. (1999). *Distant suffering: Morality, media and politics*. Cambridge: Cambridge University Press.

Boltanski, L. & Chiapello, E. (2005). *The New Spirit of Capitalism*. London: Verso.

Boykoff, M. & Goodman, M. (2009) Conspicuous redemption? Reflections on the promises and perils of the "Celebritization" of climate change. *Geoforum, 40*(3), pp. 395–406.

Cape Argus. (2010). One for the kids. *Cape Argus*, 25 November, p. 8.

Cape Argus. (2013). Has Madonna ditched Kabbalah for the Qur'an? *Cape Argus*, October, p. 6.

Chouliaraki, L. (2012). The theatricality of humanitarianism: A critique of celebrity advocacy. *Communication and Critical/Cultural Studies, 9*(1), pp. 1–21.

Colapinto, J. (2012a). When celebrities become philanthropists. *The Guardian*. 28 July. Retrieved from http://www.guardian.co.uk/lifeandstyle/2012/jul/29/when-celebrities-become-philanthropists. 21 September 2012.

Colapinto, J. (2012b). Looking good. The new boom in celebrity philanthropy. Retrieved from http://www.newyorker.com/reporting/2012/03/26/120326fa_fact_colapinto. 21 September 2012.

Cooper, A. F. (2008). *Celebrity Diplomacy*. Boulder: Paradigm.

Couldry, N., Livingstone, S. & Markham, T. (2010). *Media Consumption and Public Engagement: Beyond the Presumption of Attention.* Revised and updated Edition. Hampshire: Palgrave Macmillan.

Curran, J. Iyengar, S., Lund, A. B. & Salovaara-moring, I. (2009). Media system, public knowledge and democracy: A comparative study. *European Journal of Communication, 24*(1), pp. 5–26.

Daily Mail. (2009). My, how you've changed! Super cool David leads the way as Madonna takes her adopted children back to Malawi. *Daily Mail,* 30 October. Retrieved from http://www.dailymail.co.uk/tvshowbiz/article-1224029/ Madonna-takes-adopted-children-Malawi.html. 20 October 2012.

Daily News. (2012). Cause: Children in Malawi. *Daily News.* 26 April 2012, p. 12.

Daily News Egypt. (2010). Connectivity for all. *Daily News Egypt,* 21 April, 2010.

Daum, M. (2012). Madonna's tone-deaf tatoo. *Pakistan Observer.* 19 October, p. 244.

Dieter, H. & Kumar, R. (2008). The downside of celebrity diplomacy: The neglected complexity of development. *Global Governance, 14*(3), pp. 259–264.

Donnelly, J. (2007). Outside Oprah's school, a growing frustration: Critics in Africa urge wider impact. *Boston Globe,* 20 January.

Dugger, C. W. (2009). Aid gives alternative to African orphanages. *New York Times.* Retrieved from http://www.nytimes.com/2009/12/06/world/africa/06orphans. html?pagewanted= all&_moc.semityn.www. 21 September 2012.

Dutta, M. (2011). *Communicating Social Change: Structure, Culture, Agency.* New York: Routledge.

Escobar, A. (1995). *Encountering Development: The Making and Unmaking of the Third World.* Princeton: Princeton University Press.

Finlay, G. (2011). Madonna's adoptions: Celebrity activism, justice and civil society in the global South. In L. Tsaliki, C. A. Frangonikilopoulos & A. Huliaras (Eds.), *Transnational Celebrity Activism in Global Politics: Changing the World?* (pp. 195–210). Bristol, UK: Intellect.

Forbes (2007). The richest women in entertainment. Retrieved from http:// www.forbes.com/2007/01/17/richest-women-entertainment-tech-media-cz_ lg_richwomen07_0118womenstars_lander.html. 21 September 2012.

Forbes (2009). The Celebrity 100. Retrieved from http://www.forbes.com/2009/ 06/03/forbes-100-celebrity-09-jolie-oprah-madonna_land.html. 27 May 2013.

Forbes (2012). The world's 100 most powerful women. Retrieved from http: //www.forbes.com/power-women/list/#page:1_sort:0_direction:asc_search: Oprah. 21 September 2012.

Forbes (2015). America's richest self-made woman. Retrieved from http://www. forbes.com/profile/oprah-winfrey/. 5 July 2015.

Friedman, R. (2012). Madonna gets off cheap building African schools. *Forbes.* 26 March. Retrieved from http://www.rickross.com/reference/kabbalah/ kabbalah275.html. 12 October 2012.

Fyer-Morrel, V. (2014). World's 10 most powerful celebrities in 2014. *Forbes.* Retrieved from http://www.therichest.com/rich-list/most-influential/worlds-10-most-powerful-celebrities-in-2014/7/. 5 July 2015.

Gifford, B. (2008). A gift to build a dream on. *The Star.* Retrieved from http: //www.iol.co.za/news/south-africa/a-gift-to-build-a-dream-on-1.421471?ot= inmsa.ArticlePrintPageLayout.ot. 8 July 2015.

Global Partnership for Education (GPE). (2015). *Learning Outcomes*. Retrieved from http://globalpartnership.org/focus-areas/learning-outcomes. 15 February 2015.

Goodman, M. (2010). The mirror of consumption: Celebritization, developmental consumption and the shifting cultural politics of fair trade. *Geoforum, 41*(1), pp. 104–116.

Guelph Mercury (2010). Madonna lays first brick for her new girls' school in Malawi, with inscription "dare to dream," *Guelph Mercury*, 6 April, p. 1.

Jaye, L. (2012). Should race be a factor in adoption? *CNN*, 21 March.

Kapoor, I. (2013). *Celebrity Humanitarianism: The Ideology of Global Charity*. New York: Routledge.

Kristof, N. D. (2010). The DIY foreign-aid revolution. *The New York Times*, 24 October, p. 48.

Kristof, N. D. & WuDunn, S. (2009). *Half the Sky: Turning Oppression into Opportunity for Women Worldwide*. New York: Vintage Books.

Lawrence, W. (2011). Queen of extremes. Angelina Jolie. *Sunday Times*, 12 June 2011.

Levine, R., Lloyd, C., Greene, M. & Grown, C. 2009. Girls count. A global investment and action agenda. *Center for Global Development*. Retrieved from lication/girls-count-global-investment-action-agenda. 18 July 2013.

Maddox Jolie-Pitt Foundation. (2012). Retrieved from http://www.mjpasia.org. 26 September 2012.

Madonna. (2008). Malawi. Retrieved from http://www.youtube.com/watch?v=NfQQAnQEs6I. 26 September 2012.

Madonna. (2013). Madonna announces support for girl's education at the Sound of Change live concert. *Madonna*. Retrieved from http://www.madonna.com/news/title/madonna-announces-support-for-girls-education-at-the-sound-of-change-live-concert. 13 September 2013.

Magome, M. (2009). Oprah Academy's new head. *Daily News (South Africa)*. 22 September, p. 7.

Malone, D. (2011). All night parties. Rooms rented for years to store her gym gear. What REALLY happened to the millions Madonna pledged to Malawi's children. *Daily Mail*, 1 April

Mapondera, G. & Smith, D. (2012). Zeroes to heroes: Madonna's defunct school in Malawi to become cemetery. *The Guardian*. Retrieved from http://www.guardian.co.uk/world/2012/jul/20/madonna-malawi-school-site-cemetery. 26 September 2012.

Moeng, K. (2009). Girl reaches for her dream. *Sowetan Live*. Retrieved from http://www.sowetanlive.co.za/sowetan/archive/2009/10/14/girl-reaches-for-her-dream. 8 July 2015.

Moraes, L. (2011). For Oprah, saying goodbye is nothing short of "Spectacular," *Washington Post*, 24 May, p. C09.

Nagourney, A. (2011). Madonna's charity fails in bid to finance school. *New York Times*. 24 March. Retrieved from http://www.nytimes.com/2011/03/25/us/25madonna.html. 26 September 2012.

Njoroge, D. (2011). Calling a new tune for Africa? Analysing a celebrity-led campaign to redefine the debate on Africa. In L. Tsaliki, C. A. Frangonikilopoulos & A. Huliaras (Eds.), *Transnational Celebrity Activism in Global Politics: Changing the World?* (pp. 233–248). Bristol, UK: Intellect.

Omar, Y. (2011). The Oprah school you might know about. *The Sunday Independent*, 11 September, 2011.

Oprah Winfrey Foundation (2012). *Oprah Winfrey Foundation*. Retrieved from http://www.oprah-winfrey.org/oprah-winfrey-foundation. 25 October 2012.

Oprah Winfrey Leadership Academy (OWLA) (2013). *Mission & Vision*. Retrieved from http://www.owla.co.za/mission.htm. 13 September 2013.

Palumbo, S. (2015). Meeting the graduates of the Oprah Winfrey Leadership Academy for Girls. Retrieved from http://www.oprah.com/spirit/Oprah-Winfrey-Leadership-Academy. 24 March 2015.

Peck, J. (2008). *The Age of Oprah: Cultural Icon for the Neoliberal Era*. Boulder: Paradigm.

Pedelty, M. (2013). Peter Gabriel: The masked activist. In M. Pedelty & K. Weglarz (Eds.), *Political Rock* (pp. 23–36). Surrey UK: Ashgate.

Philanthropy News Digest. (2011). Jolie-Pitt Foundation announces $2 million gift to Namibian wildlife sanctuary. 5 January. Retrieved from http://foundationcenter.org/pnd/news/story.jhtml?id=320400010, 5 October 2011.

Porter, M. (2010). Oprah's favorite thing. Retrieved from http://www.casefoundation.org/blog/oprahs-favorite-thing-charitable-donations. 22 December, 3 October 2012.

Raising Malawi (2015). Our impact. Retrieved from http://www.raisingmalawi.org/pages/progress. 24 March 2015.

Rasmussen, L. M. & Richey, L. A. (2012). The Lazarus effect of AIDS treatment: Lessons learned and lives saved. *Journal of Progressive Human Services, 23*(3), pp. 187–207.

Ray of Light Foundation. (2015). Ray of Light. Retrieved from http://www.rayoflight.org/. 7 July 2015.

Reuters. (2011). Malawi fed up with Madonna, slams school plans. 13 March. Retrieved from http://www.reuters.com/article/2012/03/13/entertainment-us-malawi-madonna-idUSBRE82C19N20120313. 26 September 2012.

Reuters. (2013). Angelina Jolie funds Afghan girls' schools with new jewelry line. 2 April. Retrieved from http://www.csmonitor.com/World/Latest-News-Wires/2013/0402/Angelina-Jolie-funds-Afghan-girls-schools-with-new-jewelry-line. 25 May 2013.

Richey, L. & Ponte, S. (2011). *Brand Aid: Shopping Well to Save the World*. Minneapolis: University of Minnesota Press.

Right Vision News. (2012). Pakistan: Taliban's "Radio Mullah" sent hit squad after Pakistani schoolgirl. *Right Vision News*. 13 October.

Right Vision News. (2013). Pakistan: Angelina Jolie, beautiful stranger behind Afghan school. *Right Vision News*. 16 April.

Ryan, H. (2011). The Kabbalah Centre in Los Angeles is the focus of an IRS investigation into tax evasion. *Los Angeles Times*. 6 May. Retrieved from http://articles.latimes.com/2011/may/06/entertainment/la-et-kabbalah-investigation-20110506. 26 September 2012.

Sachs, J. (2010). Broadband for all: The latest technology can deliver a secondary education to children everywhere – and remake the world. *The Pittsburgh Post-Gazette*, 25 April, p. B1.

Shome, R. (2011). "Global Motherhood": The transnational intimacies of white femininity. *Critical Studies in Media Communication, 28*(5), pp. 388–406.

Smirke, R. (2014). IFPI Music Report 2014: Global Recorded Music Revenues Fall 4%, Streaming and Subs Hit $1 Billion. *Billboard Biz,* 18 March.

Smith, D. (2012). Oprah Winfrey's South African girls' school celebrates first graduation. *The Guardian.* 13 January. Retrieved from http://www.guardian.co.uk/tv-and-radio/2012/jan/13/oprah-winfrey-south-africa-school. 20 October 2012.

Statistica. (2015a). Film industry: Statistics and facts. Retrieved from http://www.statista.com/topics/964/film/. 13 March 2015.

Statistica. (2015b). Global TV industry revenue. Retrieved from http://www.statista.com/statistics/265983/global-tv-industry-revenue/. 13 March 2015.

Street, J. (2012). Do celebrity politics and celebrity politicians matter? *The British Journal of Politics & International Relations, 14*(3), pp. 346–356.

Tchouaffe, O. (2007). Angelina Jolie, Madonna, Oprah and African children: On media fairy tales, personal blessings and the ongoing curses of Africa. *Flow.* Retrieved from http://flowtv.org/2007/01/angelina-jolie-madonna-oprah-and-african-children-on-media-fairy-tales-personal-blessings-and-the-ongoing-curses-of-africa/. 26 January. 26 September 2012.

The Star. (2007). Mandela cheers Oprah's new school. *The Star.* Retrieved from http://www.iol.co.za/news/south-africa/mandela-cheers-oprah-s-new-school-1.309464#.VZ0iMvlVhBc. 8 July 2015.

The Star. (2009). Son outshines Madonna during tour of Malawi. *The Star,* 31 October 2009, p. 6.

The Tribune. (2008). Malawi: 'Madonna can't adopt another child'. *The Tribune.* Retrieved from http://allafrica.com/stories/200812110534.html. 8 July 2015.

Traub, J. (2008). The celebrity solution. *New York Times.* 9 March. Retrieved from http://www.nytimes.com/2008/03/09/magazine/09CELEBRITY-t.html?pagewanted=1&_r=1. 23 September 2011.

Tsaliki, L., Franonikolopoulos, C. & Huliaras, A. (2011). Making sense of transnational celebrity activism: Causes, methods and consequences. In L. Tsaliki, C. A. Frangonikilopoulos & A. Huliaras (Eds.), *Transnational Celebrity Activism in Global Politics. Changing the World?* (pp. 297–311). Bristol, UK: Intellect.

United Nations (UN). (2013). *MDGs.* Retrieved from http://www.un.org/millenniumgoals/education.shtml. 18 July 2013.

United Nations AIDS (UNAIDS). (2013). HIV and AIDS Estimates. UNAIDS. Retrieved from: http://www.unaids.org/en/regionscountries/countries/malawi. 18 July 2013.

United Nations Girls' Education Initiative (UNGEI). (2013a). *Afghanistan.* Retrieved from http://www.ungei.org/infobycountry/afghanistan.html. 18 July 2013.

UNGEI. (2013b). *Malawi.* Retrieved from http://www.ungei.org/infobycountry/malawi.html. 18 July 2013.

UNGEI. (2013c). *South Africa.* Retrieved from http://www.ungei.org/infobycountry/southafrica.html. 18 July 2013.

United Nations Children's Fund (UNICEF). (2013). *Malawi.* Retrieved from http://www.unicef.org/infobycountry/malawi_statistics.html#103. 18 July 2013.

UNICEF. (2013a). *Afghanistan.* Retrieved from http://www.unicef.org/infobycountry/afghanistan_statistics.html#103. 18 July 2013.

UNICEF. (2013b). *South Africa*. Retrieved from http://www.unicef.org/infoby country/southafrica_statistics.html. 18 July 2013.

United Nations Development Program (UNDP). (2013). *Human Development Report 2013*. Retrieved from http://hdr.undp.org/en/media/HDR2013_EN_Summary.pdf. 18 July 2013.

United Nations High Commissioner for Refugees (UNHCR). (2012). *Angelina Jolie*. Retrieved from http://www.unhcr.org/pages/49c3646c56.html. 26 September 2012.

Westhead, R. (2013). Facebook games buy real-life books. *The Toronto Star,* 3 April, p. A21.

Wheeler, M. (2011). Celebrity politics and cultural citizenship: UN Goodwill ambassadors and messengers of peace. In L. Tsaliki, C. A. Frangonikilopoulos & A. Huliaras (Eds.), *Transnational Celebrity Activism in Global Politics: Changing the World?* (pp. 47–61). Bristol, UK: Intellect.

Wilkins, K. (1997). Gender, power and development. *The Journal of International Communication, 4*(2), pp. 102–120.

Wilkins, K. (2007). Confronting the missionary position: The mission of development/The position of women. *Communication for Development and Social Change: A Global Journal, 1*(2), pp. 111–125.

Wilkins, K. (2008). Development communication. In W. Donsbach (Ed.), *The International Encyclopedia of Communication* (pp. 1229–1238). London: Wiley-Blackwell.

Wilkins, K. & Mody, B. (Eds.), (2001). Communication, development, social change, and global disparity. *Communication Theory Special Issue, 11*(4).

Wilkins, K. G. (2014), Celebrity as celebration of privatization in global development: A critical feminist analysis of Oprah, Madonna, and Angelina. *Communication, Culture & Critique.* (pp. 163–181). DOI: 10.1111/cccr.12080.

Willis, K., Smith, A. & Stenning, A. (2008). Social justice and neoliberalism. In A. Smith, A. Stenning & K. Willis (Eds.), *Social Justice and Neoliberalism: Global Perspectives* (pp. 1–15). New York: Zed Books.

World Bank (2012). *Gender Equality and Development. World Development Report 2012*. Retrieved from http://siteresources.worldbank.org/INTWDR2012/Resou rces/7778105-1299699968583/7786210-1315936231894/Overview-English. pdf. 20 October 2012.

5
Advocating Accountability for Gender Justice

Development as an industry has failed to improve women's conditions coherently or consistently despite its professed intentions. This failure in part rests on an assertion of women's roles in problematic gendered stereotypes, without recognition of gendered power dynamics. Avoiding gender as a conceptualizing framework in programs for or with women builds on a neoliberal approach to development, in which empowerment becomes operationalized in ways that perpetuate global conditions that accentuate inequities. Yet if we are to be accountable in a socially significant way, we need to advocate for gender justice. It is this sense of accountability, not to a single donor or particular intervention, but to the central cause for concern, that offers hope.

Accountability is key in advocating for gender justice (Goetz, 2007). Cognizant of the varied definitions and their political implications, Goetz conceptualizes gender justice in terms of "inequalities between women and men that result in women's subordination to men" (2007, p. 31). Considering approaches to gender justice that focus on entitlements and choice, absence of discrimination, and positive rights to voice, her definition recognizes that this articulation engages a strong political stance requiring responsibility for engaging strategic change. Sen (2005) articulates gender justice as connected to but not simply congruent with social and economic justice, emphasizing the complexity through which women are oppressed in multiple sites.

Sen's (2005) reflections on struggles for gender justice position women's movements as competing against religious fundamentalism and neoliberal economic agendas perpetuated through the Washington Consensus, representing a set of free-market principles guiding a dominant approach to development. The Women's Initiatives for Gender Justice (2015) project advocates on behalf of women affected by conflict through the International Criminal Court, as one illustration of how organizations operationalize this ideal. Gender justice implies a sense of fairness within a holistic context, distinct from women's empowerment.

Before articulating an advocacy approach for development that might build toward gender justice, I would like to consider how the previous case studies, on microenterprise, population, and education, contribute to analyses of development as a discourse, the role of communication, and the articulation of gender. The three cases selected come from development areas identified as those most directly related to improving conditions for women (Kristof & WuDunn, 2009, p. 246).

The first question raised in this project concerns how development discourse constructs problems and solutions in public narratives. By narratives I refer to the structures of presentation in which actors and events, positioned over time and in space (McDonald, 2014), suggest roles for women and men in given fields. Narratives of gender and development can be asserted and transformed through power relations (Cornwall et al., 2007), seen as the structuring of options through discourse (Thomas & van de Fliert, 2015, p. 53). The three fields considered each focus on empowerment for women or girls, emphasizing individual attributes. Microenterprise programs designed to benefit women particularly emphasize entrepreneurship, though at a small scale in local settings in private markets. This model of empowerment does not encourage public service, large-scale businesses, or leadership potential. Population programs support empowerment as a way of promoting individual choice, to marry or divorce, to use contraception, to plan families – all options that might have immediate as well as long-term benefits both to women themselves and to their communities. While the reproductive rights model does value women's choices, an empowerment approach that over-emphasizes individual selection misses an important constraint, suggesting a strategic need to shift the structures within which choices are made. These structures, such as what health services are available and at what costs, and what policies prohibit and allow marriage and its dissolution, condition the potential for people to deviate from dominant norms. Educational programs, like those in population, promote empowerment as women's abilities to use their skills to find jobs, to marry later, and to have fewer children. Across these approaches, although structural conditions and norms may be offered as context, problems are conceived as belonging to individual girls and women, such that the solutions posed through development target individual change, typically of women, rather than women and men in family and social contexts.

Many types of concerns have been raised with development as an enterprise. The movement toward more participatory programs decades ago (Dutta, 2011; Huesca, 2001) raised serious criticisms of hierarchical interventions, as not only being ineffective, but also as being ethically inadequate. Recent assessments of public water pumps demonstrate the futility of aid programs that have little understanding of local contexts (Hobbes, 2014). Leslie Steeves' thoughtful analysis (2015) of the one-laptop-per-child campaign in Ghana illustrates the folly of assuming technologies work in universal ways, rather than being appropriated into use within existing gendered norms. Even former World Bank economist William Easterly (2006) finds overly centralized development programs failing to promote locally relevant strategies, though his conclusion that entrepreneurship would resolve the problems of top-down administration unnecessarily connects interest in different processes with privatization. Much of the critique of top-down development has focused on bilateral and multilateral programs, working through and with national governments to promote Western-conceived modernization. Current trends though mark the growth of social movements, nongovernmental organizations (NGOs), civil society organizations (CSOs), and other private sources as key actors in development. But while the stage has broadened to include a wider range of agents, there is still a dominant approach within a global context that challenges the possibility of alternative and resistant strategies. The strengthening of neoliberal development needs to be considered across these varied agencies and programs.

One way to consider the problems of development is to focus on the narrative of the project, particularly as a hegemonic assertion of neoliberal development. In these analyses women's empowerment as a central development goal becomes conceptualized in ways that resonate with neoliberal themes, such as self-reliance, individual choice, and entrepreneurship. The recently initiated Narrative Project, funded through the Gates Foundation, does raise significant points about the need to be more respectful in our language about development and to avoid seeing donors as heroes or saints (Wilkie, 2014). Academic studies of "helping" as a relationship (Gergen & Gergen, 1983) document the moral concerns with conceptualizing this as an asymmetrical relationship as well as problematic consequences of this unequal dynamic to both parties. But the Narrative Project fails in being overly optimistic rather than leaving room for serious empirical evaluation that might point to problems as well as solutions. This need to tell stories with happy Hollywood endings (referring to a US-centric narrative of individuals conquering problems with successful resolution) resonates clearly with a problematic idealism, which Ehrenreich (2009) identifies as overly "bright-sided." Her witty and insightful characterizations of the ways in which misplaced optimism can be harmful, such as the encouraging of cancer patients to believe they are in control of their health outcomes, demonstrate the horror of asserting artificial happiness. If we truly care about the development problems we identify, accountability toward our communities is what matters, not glossy public relations summaries.

The next research question concerns the role of communication within the development narrative. Whereas the development communication field mostly focuses on communication for development (C4D), critical approaches emerging from anthropology, communication, and geography encourage analyses of development as discourse, signifying underlying assumptions about the nature of problems, solutions, and processes. In analyses of microenterprise programs, we see narratives emphasizing the telephone as a vehicle for women to earn income. Communications technologies become part of education programs as well, in ways that accentuate their more "modern" character. Even in population programs, communication is conceived as enabling individual empowerment, to choose contraception and to make choices. Across these narratives we see communication asserted as a technology, conceived as enabling profits through business, connectivity with families, and learned skills for employment.

This project connects development more closely with political economy, articulating global communication industries as a development resource, which is particularly important in understanding the emergence of wealthy private donors and foundations, and of celebrity philanthropists. The global film, television, music, computer, telephone and other communication industries produce expansive private capital, which is justified through narratives that focus on individual achievement rather than structural inequities. Narratives then perpetuate the ideologies that service the interests of global communication industries, precluding alternative attempts to consider gender justice.

Communication as discourse recognizes the importance of connecting gendered articulations to broader practices and resource allocations. It matters then that the dominant representations are of women, and not women in relation to men or broader communities and additional identities. Moreover, the particular ways in which women become visible are themselves gendered. Microenterprise identifies women as being more responsible than men for their families. Population programs still rely on women as primary targets for contraception decisions rather than focusing on men's reluctance to use condoms. Women leaders of reproductive rights movements and events are relatively ignored in the broader public conversation about key development issues. Female celebrities are valued in terms of their projected maternal, magical qualities when contributing to development programs.

Although women are being envisioned in development, women are not envisioning – at least not in this narrative. The women who could be conceived as leaders in global conferences, leaders in philanthropy, or leaders of countries or large enterprises, get far less attention. Women as leaders are trivialized when a broader mediated conversation projects a more sustained and dominant representation of women as victims and as helpless. We have moved from epistemological denial to presence, but this presence is problematically represented. And worse, women's voices are restricted in these conversations, yet it is their voices that are necessary for effective civic engagement. Women can receive loans through the microenterprise programs described, but if women are involved in making decisions with banks about the type and designation of those loans, we do not see that. Women can find contraceptive and health services, but the few women who have strongly advocated for reproductive rights are overshadowed by other women acting in their maternal capacities. Very few women have achieved the highest levels of global wealth, with those fortunate few doing so mostly through their marriages, inheritances, or commodification: those who have contributed substantially to development are subjugated to narrowly gendered roles. So although there are more women actively involved at many levels, their contributions and potentials are not respectfully considered in public discourse.

A central criticism of these articulations of development, of communication, and of gender is that they are all overly narrow. When development narratives support neoliberal initiatives, we miss opportunities to consider the structures and norms within which individuals make decisions. When we consider communication only as technology with apolitical and universal appeal, we miss the contextual considerations of everyday practice, as well as communication as process, as discourse, and as resource. And when development programs focus on women, we miss understanding gender as a critical condition in social relationships, connected with other identities and associations.

In order to broaden these scopes, communication needs to be considered as a global resource, connected both with neoliberal development as a hegemonic approach and with the potential for communities and movements to offer resistance. This means moving

from an empowerment model focusing on individuals to a social justice framework (Melkote, 2012) that considers the importance of gender
inequality as a way of understanding why women still do not have the
same status, pay, or opportunities as men. This broader framework is
necessary if we are to consider accountability in a different way.

Accountability for gender justice

Accountability toward gender justice means understanding evaluation
as a socially significant project, foregrounding context in assessment.
Accountability can be seen as counter-productive when conducted as
a bureaucratic monitoring exercise with funding consequences to programs. Some would argue that innovative initiatives take time to work,
such that outcome assessment conducted too early could stop an oth-
erwise potentially valuable program. Others point out concerns with
legitimacy in evaluation, particularly when an organization or individual's success is tied to results. Accountability can also be seen as an
overly managerial approach to understanding complicated programs,
missing the more nuanced textures of social issues. What I am proposing
here is different: accountability is necessary if we are to steer our efforts
toward the project of social justice.

This perspective relies on Gallagher's (2011) belief that accountability, which she sees as "inherent in social justice arguments," can make
research a critical tool in transformative processes (pp. 139–140). The
Global Media Monitoring Project she describes is a comprehensive
study of mediated news meant to support advocacy on gendered access
and media analysis. Research such as this informs more comprehensive approaches to social justice, or in this case gender justice, seeking
significant structural change.

Accountability that addresses justice necessarily needs to consider
gender differences, over time, bringing context directly into this framework. Focusing on gender justice calls for assessing different goals than
those of women's empowerment, which can be measured through individual changes over time or differences across groups of women. Gender justice would consider contrasting circumstances across men and
women, accounting for class, ethnicity, and other power differences relevant to context. Questions would not concern merely whether women's
choices have changed over time or as a result of a program, but whether
status and conditions across men and women have changed over time,
given a host of interventions, policies, and other factors. Normative
conditions, demographic changes, and other shifts such as increased
education or better access to clean water and toilets might contribute

to decreasing inequities, making it difficult to make a direct empirical connection between a program and desired outcome. Broadening this assessment though allows us to consider context more directly, as well as unintended consequences.

Although I agree with Kristof and WuDunn (2009, p. 247) that programs need to be evaluated with rigorous methods, I would argue that doing so is not about bureaucratic needs but about serious concern for using scarce resources to improve our conditions. Creative assessments need to consider questions that speak to the problem posed, not the project implemented, addressing broad concerns with inequities. Critical questions can be asked about the underlying narrative and its resonance with other agencies and ideologies; how resources, conceptualized broadly, are spent comparatively on projects, such as schools, health services, and loans; and potential unintended consequences.

Rigorous evaluations could assess the comparative resources spent on groups of interventions sharing common themes. For example, are schools for girls resulting in different learning outcomes, educational experiences, or subsequent schooling or jobs compared with mixed-gender schools? And what type of school with particular faculty–student ratios, expenses on resources, or other conditions, results in specified outcomes? What are the consequences of attracting funding to reproductive health services following global conferences? Are these global events valuable in mobilizing key groups to attract new or different kinds of funding? And are health conditions any better? More intensive assessments of women and men, as well as families in loan programs could do more to assess the cost of the banking program relative to specific outcomes, as well as the opportunity, financial, and social costs to loan recipients.

Unintended consequences are under-examined in evaluation literature in the development field. With microenterprise, we see that loans tend to multiply over time with high interest rates, that women receiving loans may be more likely to experience domestic violence, and that the cost of reaching women may be higher than that of men. Whether as individual consumers of contraception or as individual leaders, women being represented in terms of their individual choices and status takes attention away from the collective power women might have when mobilized as part of a movement or engaged as a community of citizens. By focusing population programs on contraception behaviors, attention to the rights of women to control their bodies, in other aspects such as violence or genital mutilation, is missed. Female celebrities may achieve the building of schools devoted to girls' education, but at the expense of perpetuating their own images through a gendered lens that diminishes their accomplishments. And by focusing on the individual empowerment of girls, these narratives detract from discussions of the patriarchy that enables the commodification of women to contribute to global profit, enhancing the wealth of a few at the further expense of others.

Expanding our vision of accountability also means working toward answering questions more typically considered within critical scholarship, but doing so with strong empirical evidence. Critical scholarship reminds us of the importance of considering power dynamics in context. In this project, these dynamics are foregrounded in terms of gender, but necessarily connected with ideological assertions, such as neoliberal and Orientalist approaches that help shape the development narrative. Critical scholarship can contribute to shifting dominant narratives through advocacy.

Advocacy communication

Working against a hegemonic neoliberal approach to development that asserts women's empowerment as a privileged stance, I consider how an advocacy approach might offer avenues for resistance in the spirit of gender justice. In doing so I need first to articulate the role of advocacy in communication, and in development approaches to social change.

A recent special edition of *Communication Theory* (2015) offers a portfolio of the most recent and innovative considerations of how communication theory contributes to our understanding of social change. Although previous journal editions have explored significant theories guiding development and social change (Enghel & Wilkins, 2012; Wilkins & Mody, 2001), this is the first to identify advocacy as a central theme in this literature. Previous discussions had moved the field from being centered on mainstream bilateral and multilateral programs toward recognizing the emergence and importance of NGOs, social movements, and activists as additional actors engaged in strategic transition. The expanding literature on social movements contributes strong theoretical work and evidence to our understanding of political transition (Downing, 2011; Gumucio-Dagron & Tufte, 2006; Hemer & Tufte, 2005; Stein et al., 2009; Wilkins et al., 2014). Explicitly recognizing politics as a way of theorizing development allows us to interrogate the cultural, political, and economic contexts of strategic social change.

Explicating politics as inherently part of intervention, and articulating advocacy as central to development builds on theories of political communication that presuppose critical models of transition, instead of falling into idealized pluralist notions of a public sphere. Based on the understanding that power dynamics facilitate different potentials for domination and resistance, strategic advocacy might build on multiple sources of capital, including human, social and cultural, as well as financial and political resources. While advocacy communication engages with politics explicitly, the history of the field demonstrates that communication about development often attempts to "depoliticize" the work of development institutions (Dutta, 2011; Sparks, 2011) in order to justify limited approaches to social change that do little to question the underlying processes that perpetuate inequities.

A critical vision of the public sphere recognizes the importance of structure in creating possibilities and challenges for civic engagement. Within political and economic structures, we need to understand the social and cultural contexts in which people actively voice their perspectives (Couldry, 2010; Williams & Delli Carpini, 2011). Couldry et al. (2010) illustrate how public connection has the potential to enable informed and active participation in the public sphere. Civic engagement need not only refer to formal political structures, but could also engage informal collective movements, particularly when the formal leadership has lost its legitimacy with citizens. Including social and political movements as part of the public sphere therefore means that we are talking not just about voting, but about more broadly based acts of strategic engagement (Downing, 2011; Huesca, 2001; Stein et al., 2009).

Focusing on development advocacy steers our attention to the norms and structures that guide transition, away from individual empowerment, potentially allowing room for alternative narratives to those dominating discourse. If neoliberal development is indeed dominating as a structuring narrative, then a framework of gender justice may serve as a competing frame. An underlying social justice orientation conceptualizes communication as a dialogic process, facilitating praxis, combining thoughtful reflection with informed action (building on Freire, 1983). Advocacy communication balances an interest in participatory communication with a recognition that political and economic conditions are constraints on engaging in dialogue and activating resistance (Wilkins, 2015).

From this perspective communication does not become aligned with hierarchical diffusion of information, or even horizontal connections across communities, but instead with facilitating activist strategies. Communication then represents more than a social construction, embedded in a political process of contesting meaning in a particular historical context. Connecting advocacy with communication is meant to convey the idea that communication can represent not just collective agreement, but also political resistance, with dignity and not subservience. This resistance is important in a framework that works to assert the rights and voices of those who are marginalized and oppressed, through supporting processes that promote justice and equity.

There are several ways in which communication might facilitate advocacy, recently emerging as a "key term in development discourse" (Servaes & Malikhao, 2012, p. 229). Communication can help us to witness and comprehend problems, as well as potential solutions, among those engaged in the collective effort as well as those targeted, such as public constituencies or policy makers. Contrary to a pluralist understanding of political engagement, advocacy frameworks recognize that differences in access to resources create spaces through which some groups have more power than others to assert their perspectives. Working within a recognized hegemonic process, advocacy communication enables the potential to negotiate and work toward changing conditions for a public good through leveraging political resources and opportunities (Thomas & van de Fliert, 2015).

Critical scholars connect these inequities to global capitalism, as a comprehensive system that dominates economic exchange and supplies ideological narratives that glorify individual consumption and imply benign free markets (Mattelart, 2011). Taking global conditions and concerns with gender inequities seriously, we need to consider how global conditions contribute to the rise of private global capital and the intensity of poverty. In response advocacy considers communication strategies as dialectic, both asserting dominant visions as well as allowing the potential for oppositional perspectives. As a collective enterprise, communication might represent this resistant rhetoric working to engage in structural and normative change to benefit marginalized and oppressed communities. Normative change involves creating a climate conducive to shifting relevant attitudes and assumptions. Structural change means creating beneficial policies and decisions within organizations and governments that structure actions. Changing the rules of the game at these levels of power is critical in order to create more equitable and just playing fields (Wilkins, 2000).

Advocacy for gender justice

Advocacy devoted to gender justice re-positions dominant perspectives of women's empowerment through foregrounding policies, structures, and norms. Microenterprise programs targeting women's small-scale entrepreneurship raise important concerns with material resources and financial capital. Advocacy strategies would work to change policies that require equal pay and that restrict women's inheritance rights or divorce settlements, programs that offer meaningful employment, and norms that challenge gendered roles and support flexible opportunities for work–life balance. Education programs for girls promote empowerment through skills and knowledge that are believed to enable healthy choices, paying jobs, and civic responsibility. Advocacy strategies might focus on civic engagement, using critical analysis skills strengthened through educational experience to understand choices and their consequences, as well as the potential to change the range of choices through collective action. Population programs envision empowerment for women also as a set of choices over contraception, health, and families. Advocacy programs might perhaps integrate civic engagement with attention to collective action for women's reproductive rights. An advocacy approach would require a comprehensive framework including multiple strategies working toward gender equality.

Gender equality, like women's empowerment, commands attention in development discourse. But just as key concepts such as "participation" and "sustainability" have been co-opted over time after being initially proposed as ways of significantly revisioning development, we need to be careful of the ways in which "gender equality" becomes used. The World Bank's 2012 Development Report opens with the first main message that "gender equality matters for development" (p. 1). While asserting gender equality as a "core development objective," they justify this as "smart economics," echoed in their subsequent report (Klugman et al., 2014). And while recognizing key disparities across gender in terms of preventable deaths, "unequal access to economic opportunities," and "differences in voice," the prescription given is "globalization" (World Bank, 2012, p. 2). Globalization is described as beneficial given "cheaper information and communication technologies... which have the potential to reduce gender disparities by connecting women to markets and economic opportunities, reshaping attitudes and norms among women and men about gender relations, and encouraging countries to promote gender equality" (World Bank, 2012, pp. 2–3). Following a quote from Pakistani heroine Malala Yousafzai on the importance of the media, a World Bank report decides that these information and communication technologies are "amplifying women's voices, expanding their economic and learning opportunities, and broadening their views and aspirations" (Klugman et al., 2014, p. xii).

"Voice" is partnered with "Agency" in the title of this World Bank report (Klugman et al., 2014), though the latter is operationalized in terms of individual empowerment to make decisions. Recognizing the power of social norms in prescribing expectations around women's and men's behavior, strategic attempts to change discriminatory policies and to promote more flexible gender roles are justified in terms of economic costs. In contrast, the underlying mission proposed here is not justified in terms of cost or efficiency, but in terms of gender justice. Central to this gender framework is asserting women's and men's rights to control their lives, as healthy and engaged citizens. A strong economic foundation is necessary to enable the provision of services and status that will foster these conditions.

Advocacy calls for a different track than typically engaged in the development industry. Many bilateral donors, such as the US Agency for International Development (USAID, 2014), highlight "gender equity" along with "women's empowerment" as core development objectives. While USAID's justifications tend to be articulated in terms of economic efficiency and individual rights, the Swedish International Development Cooperation Agency (SIDA) articulates a mission for gender equality that details "fair distribution of power" as well as concerns with poverty, the environment and climate, and discrimination (Byron & Ornemark, 2011). Although nearly as large a donor as USAID, the Japan International Cooperation Agency (JICA, 2013) allocates less funding specifically for women, but does include "gender and development" as one of its development themes, articulated in terms of "gender mainstreaming" within existing national systems. Overall, however, JICA's rhetorical deference to women's issues does not command as many specific allocations of funding or active engagements with a variety of domains as other bilateral institutions (Wilkins, 2003). While most bilateral agencies recognize gender concerns as part of their missions, particularly since the 1995 Beijing Conference, their approaches differ widely.

Multilateral institutions within the UN system offer a set of development agencies that includes those specifically devoted to women's role in development. Although several UN agencies, such as UNFPA and UNICEF, address women's issues, the organization most directly related to these topics is the UN Entity for Gender Equality and the

Empowerment of Women (formerly UNIFEM), which was created in 2010 (UN Women, 2011).

Nongovernmental organizations (NGOs) have more flexibility in determining their missions given their potential separation from the agendas mandated through government funding. Attracting approximately US$ 18 million from various donors in the fiscal year ending in 2014, the Global Fund for Women (2015) conducts "advocacy" through raising awareness, strengthening partnerships and mobilizing resources. Although the fund accepts corporate donations, which represent about 2% of its total budget compared to 29% from individual donors and 53% from private and family foundations, other NGOs consciously avoid corporate collaboration. The Global Fund for Women highlights social justice rhetoric in its public mission statement, working for a "just, equitable and sustainable world in which women and girls have resources, voice, choice, and opportunities to realize their human rights" (Global Fund for Women, 2015). Advocacy targets include policy changes such as criminalizing domestic violence against women, ensuring women's right to inherit property and creating laws to prohibit sex trafficking.

This attention to advocacy to protect marginalized groups from the consequences of injustice and inequity is echoed across several other NGOs in their work. ActionAid connects women's issues to their disproportionate probability of living in poverty, advocating on issues directly related to violence against women and girls, economic rights, mobilizing women, and women's control over their bodies (ActionAid, 2015). The African Women's Development Fund (AWDF, 2015) restricts its contributions to the African continent, supporting over 800 women's organizations across 42 countries. The group sees itself as working for "social justice, equality and respect for women's human rights." Through another venue, the International Women's Health Coalition (IWHC, 2015) uses its independent voice to "recognize women's and girls' human rights, health and equality... [as] essential to social, environmental, and economic justice." Its overarching goals are designed not only to change policies at the national level in order to reduce discrimination and violence and enhance access to justice, but also to promote policies and voice within the UN. Development Alternatives with Women for a New Era (DAWN, 2015) mobilizes networks of feminist scholars, researchers, and activists from the global South to promote women's rights, in its vision of "a world where inequalities and discrimination based on gender and all other identities are eliminated," including issues related to "bodily integrity and security" as well as inclusion in decision making in order to respect and realize human rights. The Women's Environment and Development Organization (WEDO, 2015) envisions its work as "a global women's advocacy organization," working for "human rights, gender equality and the integrity of the environment." Through these articulations of their missions, these NGOs are contributing to a gender justice approach.

Communicating gender in global development

In this section I explore how gender is articulated in development programs featuring the female body. The right to bodily integrity is compromised when girls and women are subject to violence and violation. Recent attention to gender-based violence (GBV) in development discourse, along with more public concern over female genital mutilation (FGM), offers an opportunity to consider how women's bodies become communicated as contested sites subject to harm. Advocating rights to safety and health for women necessarily becomes situated in broader gender dynamics when considering the policies and norms that ignore sexual violence and unnecessary surgeries. In this section, I consider how GBV and FGM are conceptualized as development issues, with implied frameworks for social change, articulations of gender, and assumptions about communication, which can be constructed within a human rights and social justice rather than neoliberal approach to development. How advocacy becomes explicitly integrated into programs and accountability contributes to learning will be addressed as part of development discourse following attention to constructions of social change, gender, and communication.

The WHO estimates that approximately one out of every three women in the world has experienced some form of sexual violence (World Bank, 2014). GBV serves as quite a broad conceptual category, defined across reports as "an umbrella term for any harmful act that is perpetrated against a person's will, and that is based on socially ascribed (gender) differences between males and females" (Holmes & Bhvanendra, 2014). USAID emphasizes an individual focus in its articulation of GBV as "violence that is directed at an individual based on his/her biological sex, gender identity, or perceived adherence to socially defined norms of masculinity and femininity" (Menon et al., 2014, p. 1). Across UNFPA, World Bank, UK-funded and USAID documents, there is a shared recognition that women and girls are more likely to be subject to GBV given female subordination and vulnerability. Along with other forms of GBV, including female infanticide, sexual exploitation and abuse, and honor killings, FGM practices are integrated into this framework that connects human rights with health and safety protection.

Development agencies build on WHO definitions of FGM as "all procedures involving partial or total removal of the external female genitalia or other injury to the female genital organs for non-medical reasons" (such as UNFPA & UNICEF, 2012, p. 13). WHO estimates (2015), though based on challenging attempts to gather data on such a sensitive topic, calculate that about 100–140 million women and girls have been subject to this practice on a global scale, with the highest prevalence in Somalia, Guinea, Djibouti, Mali, Sudan, Egypt, Eritrea, Gambia, Sierra Leone, Mauritania, and Ethiopia (UNFPA, 2014a). Although this practice may be most prevalent in the African region, there are communities in the US, the UK, and other Northern, Western regions also seeking and finding practitioners of FGM (USAID, 2014). FGM involves surgery that is not necessary for medical reasons but has serious physical and emotional health risks, such as infection, pain, difficulties in childbirth, intercourse and urination, and psychological trauma (Berg & Denison, 2012).

Justifications for the practice of FGM refer to cultural norms about female purity and interests in controlling women's sexuality, in order to increase girls' perceived attractiveness to male suitors for marriage (Kristof & WuDunn, 2009, p. 222). Although some might want to dichotomize this issue into a battle between suggested universal values of bodily integrity and human rights versus local cultural practices, it is much more complex. In development frameworks, cultural relativity can play an important role in considering how best to replicate programs in different ways that might be effective, balancing attention to local context with institutional missions. And within local contexts values held are not monolithic, across or within gender or generation. Yet this is a particularly compelling illustration of yet another case in which women's bodies are literally contested sites over how best to engage in development.

Discourse engaged in terms of "abandonment" of this practice focuses on this as "mutilation" (though previously it had been described as female circumcision, Kristof & WuDunn, 2009), whereas those concerned with approaching local communities cautiously have been adjusting their language to "mutilation/cutting" or FGM/C. Most of the UNFPA, UNICEF, and USAID missions have considered their work within the FGM/C framework, although more recent reports from these UN agencies (2015) dropped the "C," whereas "cutting" is the only description used in the German development report reviewed (Deutsche

Geselleschaft, 2015). Focusing on this as "mutilation" alone was more evident in the work of local NGOs in Egypt, the NGO Wallace Global Fund, and national news sources in the US and UK (such as the *Guardian* through French, 2014 and in *Newsweek* through Westcott, 2015).

Parallel to arguments about GBV, advocates against FGM situate this practice as an infringement to human rights (Berg & Denison, 2012). UNFPA (2014) defines "a human rights-based approach to FGM" as "placing the practice within a broader social justice agenda – one that emphasizes the responsibilities of governments to ensure realization of the full spectrum of women's and girls' human rights." These UN reports clearly situate human rights in connection with gender dynamics, arguing that avoiding "gender discrimination" is central to "preserving life, [and] to physical and mental integrity, including freedom from violence" (UNFPA, 2014). Gender equality is promoted as a central principle in advocating against FGM as a matter of human rights (UNFPA/UNICEF, 2014a). When programs build from this attention to gender in mission statements, they include boys and men as well as girls and women as agents contributing to gendered expectations (UNICEF, 2013). Integrating gender equality with attention to human rights enables a more holistic conceptualization of social change with potentially more effective ways to support significant change in policies and in norms.

The development industry has been including "women" in development discourse since the 1970s, but FGM has not been as prominently displayed as a central development issue until more recently. Previous attention to FGM had been embedded in discussions of women's health and GBV, in UN statements and global meetings such as the Committee on the Elimination of Discrimination Against Women (CEDAW) in 1992, the World Conference on Human Rights in 1993, and subsequently a USAID Commission on the Status of Women (USAID, 2014). Situating FGM as not only a health risk but also as a feature of gendered violence broadens the development scope beyond the responsibilities of individuals to that of policies and rights.

Participants in the 1994 ICPD conference, discussed in more detail in an earlier chapter, included attention to FGM concerns, and along with the UN asked member states to legislate for the elimination of this as an officially sanctioned practice (UNFPA, 2014a; UNFPA/UNICEF, 2012). Egyptian advocates, inspired and supported by the 1994 meeting, formed a task force soon thereafter, resulting in the criminalization of FGM in the country in 2009. Overall national governments have passed legislation in 17 African countries, as well as in many others including the US and nine European nations (Wallace Global Fund, 2015).

Specific attention to GBV has been growing since 2012. The World Bank (2014) notes that it has supported 12 new projects exclusively or primarily focused on GBV in the subsequent two years, in addressing gender equality in order "to achieve goals of ending poverty and boosting shared prosperity." This was the year that the US government issued its own declaration, reported in a joint publication from the US State Department and USAID:

> Under the leadership of President Obama and Secretary Clinton, the United States has put gender equality and the advancement of women and girls at the forefront of the three pillars of US foreign policy – diplomacy, development, and defense.
>
> (US State Department, 2012, p. 5)

Positioning GBV as a "cornerstone" of its foreign policy, the US government proposed to allocate funding for intervention, to work with other public and private partners (including CSOs, NGOs, and the business community), and to engage in "public diplomacy," publicizing reports and events with the aid of noted celebrities. One such illustration of a key event was "Zero Tolerance Day," 6 February 2012 (UNFPA, 2015; UNFPA/UNICEF, 2012), celebrated at the US Department of State with public declarations by then Secretary Hillary Clinton (USAID, 2014). Growing attention among development donors resulted in an increasing number of programs and agreements articulating FGM as a "violation of women's health and rights" (Wallace Global Fund, 2015). Although USAID claims have supported abandonment of FGM since the 1990s, only in the past few years did this concern mobilize more attention, particularly connected with GBV, with new partnerships and reports issued in 2012. Similar to other dominant development agencies, this bilateral agency sees FGM as "not only a public health concern but also a human rights issue that violates a woman's right to bodily integrity" (USAID, 2014, p. 2). Even the World Bank (Klugman et al., 2014) sees GBV as a "global epidemic" (p. 3) that is "associated with social norms and expectations that reinforce inequality" (p. 5).

The partnership between UNFPA and UNICEF, initiated in 2008, worked in its early phase on FGM in 15 African countries (UNICEF, 2013), more recently proposing to expand their programs to include new sites for work and to support CSOs (UNFPA/UNICEF, 2014a). Unlike the other programs reviewed, USAID was more interested in working with the private sector in their GBV programs, believing in the "power and potential of harnessing the private sector in robust partnerships to tackle issues of gender-based violence" (US Department of State, 2012, p. 30).

Consonant with development approaches applauding these public-private partnerships, USAID attention to GBV focuses on a goal of "empowering women and girls by using tools and resources for strengthening their ability to make safer life choices" (Menon et al., 2014, p. 9). Some of the indicators used to assess female empowerment, connected under the same heading as "gender equality," include women's reports of their own sense of self-efficacy and "target group" beliefs that men and women should have equal access to similar social, political, and economic opportunities (p. 29). A goal shared across reviewed reports is in changing public perception concerning the acceptability of GBV. Changed public perception, particularly within pluralist models of transition, is believed to be necessary to engage in advocacy.

Advocacy

Advocacy not only engages particular strategic programs, but also builds on coalition building and networks. The African Charter on Human and Peoples' Rights on the Rights of Women in Africa, known as the Maputo Protocol (African Union, 2012), illustrates a significant example of a regional network of national governments, NGOs, and CSOs working with the African Union on behalf of women's rights. Adopted in 2003 by the African Union, in the following ten years 36 countries in the region ratified this charter. Current strategies are working to implement these policies in other countries that had not yet ratified the charter by 2014, including Egypt, Algeria, Botswana, Burundi, Chad, Ethiopia, Sierra Leone, South Sudan, Sudan, and Tunisia (SOAWR, 2012). Having declared this as the African Women's Decade (2010–2020), the network of organizations engaged in implementing and assessing the protocol is also working to create awareness and compliance in countries where the charter has been ratified and to ensure that women's lives have improved.

Described as "a progressive legal instrument that gives a diverse range of rights to African women and girls" (Makau, 2013), this comprehensive framework outlines a broad range of issues relevant to improving gender conditions in the region, including promoting political and economic rights, as well as preserving health and dignity. A detailed assessment (edited by Kombo et al., 2013) admits that the protocol is "useless" unless there is significant change. Moreover, this change needs to be understood as being rooted in gender dynamics and not merely about women: "The Protocol offers us a tool for transforming the unequal power relations between men and women that lie at the heart of gender inequality and women's oppression" (p. 39).

Solidarity for African Women's Rights (SOAWR) was created in 2004 to help implement national policies that facilitate the agenda of this regional protocol, bringing together the work of 36 CSOs. In order to change national policies, SOAWR sees communication as helping to inform and mobilize constituents, and to shift norms about the importance of gender inequality. This coalition receives support from the Global Fund for Women as well as ActionAid International, the African Women's Development Fund, Open Society Institute, Oxfam, and many other agencies. Their values statement includes explicit attention to "defending and upholding women's voice, agency, dignity and rights across the African continent" and in "the importance of courage to confront patriarchy." Recent documentation (SOAWR, 2012) outlines its current campaign as focusing on the elimination of discrimination and harmful practices against women; and on rights to dignity, health and reproductive rights, bodily integrity and security, marriage, divorce, and inheritance.

The issue of FGM surfaces in relation to eliminating violence against women, defined as "all acts perpetrated against women which cause or could cause them physical, sexual, psychological, and economic harm" (Lawyers Circle & Oxfam, 2014, p. 26). This recent report concerning work in Kenya connects FGM with several articles outlined through the protocol, describing FGM as "an acute form of sexual violence that affects a significant proportion of women and girls in Kenya" (Lawyers Circle & Oxfam, 2014, p. 30). One of the recommendations of this assessment, to offer free medical treatment and psychological support, is relevant more broadly to all those suffering from gender-based violence. Although the Kenyan government passed legislation in 2001 through a Children's Act, along with stronger policies prohibiting FGM in 2011, CSOs need to promote awareness of the designation of this practice as a criminal offence. Although necessary if policy change is to have any influence, Kombo, Sow, and Mohamed's (2013) report recognizes that education campaigns are not in and of themselves "sufficient to end FGM as in the final analysis, FGM has to do with gender power control" (p. 57).

Changing gender expectations is particularly challenging given resistance to doing so, not only in local cultures but also in transnational and global spheres. The protocol itself met with resistance from other politically conservative groups, such as Human Life International (2011), working against women's sexual and reproductive rights (Open Society Foundation, 2013). These rhetorical challenges can have devastating consequences when enacted in policies that inhibit women's potential for decision-making, whether in private or public spaces. Pamment's (2015) case study of a British campaign to end sexual violence in conflict demonstrates a strategic intervention attempting to create "new international norms regarding how both perpetrators and victims of sexual violence in fragile states are treated" (p. 2). Attention to competing discourses is critical to understanding the broader contexts in which strategic advocacy needs to work.

An advocacy model points us to an interest in shaping policy as well as social norms, recognizing the importance of structural incentives as well as cultural expectations in reinforcing policies. The UN argued that states have responsibilities to protect rights and to enforce that protection, through creating clear and enforced policies with adequate funding for implementation, monitoring, professional training, and support for CSOs (UNFPA, 2014). In the Egyptian projects reviewed (Barsoum et al., 2009; 2011), advocacy programs mobilized public support of national policies through religious leaders and youth volunteers. Mobilizing collective support for national policies was an explicit part of other programs as well, such as a USAID (2014) project in the Sudan and UNFPA/UNICEF programs (2014b) in several countries.

Public support may be mobilized by advocacy strategies designed to leverage political will to create specific policies criminalizing FGM, as well as educating the public once these policies have been created. Funding the networks needed to mobilize citizens, communities, and organizations toward sharing strategies to effect legislation and awareness can be seen as part of clearly articulated advocacy strategies. The Wallace Global Fund (2015) illustrates how one globally engaged NGO sees their work in "advocacy and resource mobilization" to work to build "political support needed to achieve impact at a meaningful scale to accelerate the abandonment of FGM/C" through partnerships with several NGOs working in Egypt, Kenya, and other African communities. Related to the previous chapter on girls' education, the Wallace Global Fund supports a Kenyan girls' school that admits students whose families have publicly pledged not to allow their daughters to be cut. USAID reports on GBV also declare the importance of "advocacy," to US Congress and other NGOs in finding ways to leverage political support for these interventions (Menon et al., 2014; US Department of State & USAID, 2012).

Another component of a more broadly based advocacy strategy includes attention to training and capacity building to support health professionals in their work (USAID, 2014), particularly in connection with community organizations (GIZ, 2015). A bilateral intervention funded by Germany and implemented in Guinea supports community organizations in hiring consultants to engage in dialogue with women and with men. Recent interventions in Egypt also work to change medical training to educate future health professionals in the risks of FGM (Westcott, 2015). In addition to supporting training, development programs work to shift community engagement, through supporting volunteers, educational programs, and initiatives such as the declaration of villages as "FGM-free" in Egypt, or the launch of "girls' awareness week" in an Ethiopian project (USAID, 2014).

Normative conditions have the potential to reinforce existing practices as well as to support new ones. Even if legislation is in place, and communities are aware of them, social expectations may enable practices to be maintained despite the threat of punishment. UNFPA's (2015) work in Tanzania, which has an estimated 15% FGM prevalence rate, builds on this concern that although FGM is illegal it is still happening. The clear normative change that needs to occur is from perceptions of FGM being a "tradition" to it being a "crime," possible when people actually witness public enforcement of existing rules. Another normative shift is called for in moving the issue of violence against women from a private to a public concern, whether we consider FGM, domestic abuse, or partner rape.

Many assume that the cultural norms supporting FGM are rooted in religious teachings, although official discussions of Islam and of Christianity do not sanction this practice. In addition, historical accounts suggest that FGM may have been in practice prior to the advent of Islam and Christianity (Westcott, 2015). Many of the programs reviewed call upon Christian and Muslim leaders to participate in public workshops and declarations against FGM (USAID, 2014; Westcott, 2015).

Recognizing the potential significance of maturation rituals, a constructive approach may go beyond only challenging FGM toward promoting alternative "rites of passage," as engaged by a UNFPA program in Kenya. Another program in Senegal recognizes the family context in which rituals gain importance, highlighting the role of grandmothers as potential agents of influence in decisions made about the health and status of girls (USAID, 2014). The PEPFAR initiative offers another useful illustration of how programs can explicitly include and address gender norms with and about men (US Department of State & USAID, 2012).

Social norms are clearly part of the "community level transformation" and "advocacy" strategies promoted by USAID (2014). Given the complexity of family dynamics and cultural contexts, interventions would be better informed through intensive research in local sites. Understanding development discourse as multi-layered through institutional as well as local practices is critical in this process. Next, I consider the role of communication in development discourse on FGM and GBV.

Communication

Apart from the dominant C4D approach that privileges psychological orientations of social marketing, other models highlight sociological contexts in which social change might be engaged, structured through political and economic conditions. Advocacy approaches incorporate attention to policy and to attitudes, conceptualizing communication as potentially supporting broader shifts in development discourse, in this case toward eliminating FGM (UNICEF, 2013). The normative shifts advocated are on several levels, from demanding attention from the development industry to community expectations around gender and sexuality.

Some programs consider media campaigns to be integral to shifting public perception, as in an Egyptian project relying on television, radio, print, and digital sources to inform citizens of harmful risks and consequences. The Generations Dialogue program in Guinea, though, found through its research with community consultants that most people were already aware of the risks involved, but through stories from family and friends and not necessarily from mediated campaigns (GIZ, 2015, p. 3).

A model integrating sociological processes with political engagement takes this attention to attitudes a step further, highlighting the importance of dialogue, partnered with action. UNFPA (2014) programs in Burkina Faso and Ethiopia rely on radio programs, broadcasting interviews with key figures, to stimulate local discussion and advocacy. Similarly, the Generations Dialogue leveraged its work with dialogue sessions in Guinea to inform a subsequent program in Yemen, where community groups decided to push for policies prohibiting girls from marrying before they turn 18 years old, connecting political change with community dialogue (GIZ, 2015).

Working against GBV, some programs target men through media to promote "awareness" (Holmes & Bhvanendra, 2014; World Bank, 2014), particularly relevant given the escalation in violence during conflict (Wilson Center, 2014). An alternative to targeting men directly, hoping for an attitude change that would somehow result in their deciding not to rape or harm women, offers media as a tool for women's awareness about where might be safe to walk in public spaces. Activists in Egypt, at least those with access to digital media, are able to use "harassmap" crowdsourcing to pinpoint through GIS locations where sexual harassment is occurring, so if there are any avenues open women with this knowledge have the opportunity to change direction and keep moving (Fahmy, 2015).

In advocating for policy change, one path prescribed by scholars of media advocacy (Wallack et al., 1999) calls upon communication strategies to work to attract media attention, seeing coverage as a critical intermediary goal, functioning between movement actions and government recognition. Some of the UNFPA and UNICEF (2012) projects described specifically document media attention, in terms of the amount and nature of press releases and coverage, television and radio programs, and professionals trained. Recent UNFPA documentation (2014) quotes UN Secretary-General Ban Ki-moon on the importance of media in reporting on the "damaging public health consequences of FGM, as well as on the abuse of the rights of hundreds of thousands of women and girls around the world." Partnering with the *Guardian*, this UN program offers a reward for constructive reporting to a media professional working in Kenya, with the prize being two months of training in its London office.

Another development program, initiated in the UK and funded through its Department for International Development, claims to be based in human rights but appears to be more in line with social marketing strategies. Initiated in 2014, "The Girl Generation: Together to End FGM" program is being implemented in ten countries in the African region. The program director explains this as using "innovative marketing and communications approaches to accelerate an end to this human rights violation" (Davis, 2014). Working with Ogilvy and Mather, one of the largest, most profitable marketing corporations in the world, their communication strategy is designed to support change in FGM practices, particularly through the use of British female celebrities, who converged upon the London Eye for this public event. The use of public celebrities is also evident in other public discourse on this issue: a film starring Somali actress Safa Idriss Nour, based on Waris Dirie's 2011 publication, leveraged their fame to attract attention in Djibouti, where there is an estimated 98% prevalence of FGM (French, 2014). In each of these cases, these celebrities were called upon to recognize the issue of FGM not only in other regions but also within the UK. As in the case of girls' schools established by other global female celebrities, relying on women's fame may attract visibility, but meaningful dialogue and substantive political change is another thing entirely.

Accountability

Distinct from an approach to public relations monitoring, accountability integrates recognition of the value of empirical evidence with transparency in documentation, to inform people positioned to enact policy as well as to engage communities. UNICEF (2013) suggests enhancing the capacities of CSOs to engage in documentation (though they talk about this as "surveillance"), in support of national laws and policies, as well as of medical professionals and FGM practitioners who may need to find other sources of income. UNFPA literature (2014) on FGM points to the importance of governments taking responsibility for their policies as well as ensuring public accessibility to information. Without sharing their data, the value of their evidence, and of the resources dedicated to its accumulation, is lost.

The legitimacy of evaluation depends on perceptions of the agencies and agents commissioning, conducting, and communicating assessments. This legitimacy can be contingent upon the reputations of noted researchers and their organizations, the agendas of funding and implementing bodies, and the interests of communities. Although not all independent evaluating teams automatically earn this sense of credibility, donors typically structure outcome evaluations through independent agencies. In some projects USAID (2014) worked with Nairobi University as a research center, just as its German bilateral counterpart (GIZ, 2015) encouraged community organizations to keep detailed records of dialogue sessions in conjunction with independent consultations. UNFPA and UNICEF's (2012) documented evaluation builds on work commissioned by the Harvard School of Public Health Program on International Health and Human Rights to develop a monitoring and evaluation plan. The latter UN agency (UNICEF, 2013) indicates that it maintains its accountability through the work of its country offices.

Program evaluations tell us not only about documented effects, but also about the ideal success motivated by assumed models of social change. Some of these programs hope to inspire direct interpersonal discussion on subjects donors assume to be sensitive. Impact evaluations in Mali demonstrate significant differences between those in intervention groups being more willing to discuss "female genital cutting" with family members than those in comparison communities (GIZ, 2015). These programs see familial communication as an intermediary step to shifting social norms.

Many of these evaluations, though, follow the more classic hierarchical knowledge–attitude–practice model rooted in targeting individuals to change their behaviors, once they are informed and feel supportive of the directed change. Barsoum and colleagues' (2009; 2011) evaluations of Egyptian programs contrasted intervention with matched comparison communities, conducting surveys in each. They conclude that men and women in intervention sites learned more about negative health risks of FGM than those in other communities, and that while knowledge and attitudes, such as whether the practice is believed to be sanctioned by religious authorities, are susceptible to change, what matters most to these evaluators is that women in intervention areas were six times less likely to intend to take their daughters for FGM. Intention is often used as a proxy for behavior, but clearly validity concerns surface if these women learn what to say in response to research questions with little bearing on what they actually do.

Berg and Denison (2012) have conducted a systematic review of research studies with strong designs, examining data before and after interventions between intervention and credible comparison groups. Examining results across eight studies, they find evidence for program effectiveness in changing 19 of the studied 49 outcomes, with high variation. They cautiously suggest that there is some limited evidence of effectiveness of these interventions in changing knowledge, attitudes, and practice (whether as direct experience or stated intention), but raise concerns over the weak quality of the data. One of the challenges they raise is with the lack of connection at times between funded interventions and cultural contexts, noting that significant shifts in practice would not be sustainable, despite potential intermediate effects, without cultural relevance. Relying on interviews and surveys with mothers remains a concern for validity as well, given the potential disconnect between what people say and what people do.

It is this concern with what people do that underscores interest in prevalence, meant to document the proportion of women in particular age groups who have actually experienced FGM. UN assessments demonstrate varied success in changing prevalence rates, though they admit that the collection of data on this subject, done through different methodological means with varying levels of success, makes it difficult to use this documentation as a confident source for accountability (UNFPA/UNICEF, 2012). Some of these evaluations also include interviews and focus groups, which can be useful in attempting to ascertain potential measurement validity concerns with self-reports and to contribute contextual understanding.

Development agencies such as SOAWR and UNFPA agree that stronger documentation of compliance and practices is necessary if we are to understand the potential value of the Maputo Protocol in effecting change (SOAWR, 2014; UNFPA, 2014). UNFPA reviews of this protocol recognize that more needs to be done to strengthen enforcement, with better monitoring and evaluation of practices and sanctions, and the political will to ensure change (UNFPA, 2014). SOAWR asks the critical question as to whether women are indeed better off than prior to the initial African Union agreement. One might also ask whether countries that did ratify this protocol subsequently witnessed changing conditions relative to other countries that did not.

Recognizing the difficulties in seeking reliable and valid data across countries, despite their reporting obligations, some surveys have been able to document decline in FGM prevalence over time (Kombo et al., 2013). Intermediary outcomes suggested for documentation include mapping compliance, chronicling implementation processes, and tracking media coverage. Similarly, reports on GBV realize the importance of having research to improve a nascent field of intervention (Menon et al., 2014), but also raise concerns over the sensitivity of these issues and the safety of survivors and researchers in the process of data collection (Holmes & Bhvanendra, 2014; Menon et al., 2014).

Existing documentation does indicate that women are increasingly vulnerable to violence in crisis and emergency conditions (Holmes & Bhvanendra, 2014), with one-third of all maternal deaths worldwide occurring during conflicts (Wilson Center, 2014). USAID mission statements though attempt to broaden this focus from crisis situations to include valuable attention to prevention (Menon et al., 2014).

Makau (2013) makes the case that CSOs need to support assessment as a way of making governments accountable. Accountability here refers to ensuring that policies have significant effects on social change, not just on public relations of programs. What is relevant is the content within the Raising Her Voice report, not merely the publicity accorded the London reception applauding it, with attention to celebrity Annie Lennox making a statement through videolink (Coppens, 2014). Increasing accountability means including space for voice in dialogue and negotiation, and disseminating information that can inform decision making (Klugman et al., 2014, p. 169), using data sources such as those gathered through agencies like the UN on FGM

(Klugman et al., 2014, p. 183). Genuine accountability to the underlying concern of changing gender inequities is what matters.

Most development programs work directly with the development industry allocating resources to improve existing systems; by changing policies not governments, such as women's rights to inherit property or marry at an older age; or changing services, such as those devoted to maternal and reproductive health. Work to support the Maputo Protocol, for example, fits this approach. Working against the development industry, social movements attempt to argue against development programs challenging the dominant rhetoric in order to enact change. Accountability, while recognized as critical to informing anti-GBV interventions, needs to be conceptualized, engaged with and shared in ways that move beyond a bureaucratic monitoring function. Smaller development agencies as well as social movement organizations might attempt to work in parallel with the development industry, working on smaller-scale programs more directly with communities on changing norms, for example, about expected gender roles in families and in work. While specific agencies and communities can take these different strategic approaches, working to change a system, to fight against or in parallel with dominant approaches, their networks of funding and collaboration make such advocacy approaches more intertwined in practice than can be neatly categorized in theory.

Many of the issues to consider in a call for gender justice would benefit from integrated strategies that advocate on many levels. Addressing gender-based violence, for example, calls for structural change in creating and enforcing laws and providing access to health care and legal counsel, as well as normative change in shifting attitudes about the severity of these events (Usdin et al., 2000). The World Bank (2014) notes a Jordanian program supported by the Japanese Social Development Fund offering legal aid that benefits women (as the majority but not exclusively engaged group), in learning about their rights. These cases of development devoted to GBV and FGM have been included here to inform further consideration of how development narratives consider the role of communication and the potential for accountability. If we are to move from women's empowerment as a central theme to that of gender justice, we will need to privilege fairness over individual gain.

Advocating accountability for gender justice

Advocacy for gender justice demands attention to the implications of patriarchy privileged through neoliberal agendas of dominant global agencies, with accountability towards understanding the practices and consequences of strategic interventions. Women do need to be supported in protecting their rights to dignity and choice about their own bodies, but a gender justice approach means doing more than offering reproductive health services, or loans for businesses, or single schools. The context in which inequities constrain potential includes men and masculinity, as well as heteronormativity and racism, exacerbating serious and intensifying material inequities.

A justice framework considers our relative ability to contribute to our worlds, through voice and vision. Couldry (2010) positions the value of voice and the need for investing in structures to enable voice against the challenge of neoliberal political culture. Gilligan's early work (1982) on voice established the importance of taking voice seriously, influencing theoretical revisioning in many of our academic disciplines. One central shift meant seeing empathy and care as human strengths, recognizing that an ethic of care is *feminist*, but not necessarily *feminine* (Gilligan, 2014). Gilligan positions this feminist project as something more than observing the differences between men and women, instead struggling against patriarchy. An ideology of patriarchy is strengthened through narratives privileging women's empowerment as a neoliberal project of development.

This book project began with a puzzle: why have we not done better in improving women's conditions given the visibility and resources appropriated for this purpose by the development industry? The key to solving this disjuncture may be in understanding the limitations of the dominant development narrative. Focusing on women's empowerment at the expense of gender equality privileges neoliberal attention to individual achievements as somehow universal, transcending historical and cultural context. But what good is it for women to gain self-esteem if that confidence is artificially induced? Why would we highlight choice as a central feature of empowerment if the overly narrow structures within which decisions are made make choice, like participation, merely an illusion? Who benefits from asserting women's empowerment in these constricted ways? Those who would rather avoid serious critique of intensifying political and economic power in the global sphere appreciate an underlying model of social change that blames individuals for their perceived lack of confidence and ill advised choices.

When women have the potential to lead, not only to be seen as leaders but also to have voice in decisions that actually matter, what happens to their positioning in this discourse? As entrepreneurs women are infantilized as able to handle only small business. As prominent leaders of public sectors and NGOs in global development conferences, these women's voices are overshadowed by attention given to other women as development targets. And as wealthy donors, female celebrities are constrained by overly gendered expectations of their roles as pure and compassionate rather than as strong heroes.

The dominant development narrative is also limited when conceptualizing communication as just a technology, without attention to the structures of production, distribution, and reception through which some groups have more voice than others with consequences as to how we understand our world. Seeing communication as more than a technology meant to integrate us into a global capitalist market, the narratives that contribute to development discourse shape the possibilities for serious revision of how we engage in thoughtful strategic change. Seeing communication as an industry within a global context also helps us to see how it is that certain narratives are privileged over others, connected with profit and power.

What would happen if we were to take gender gaps seriously? We would need to engage policies and programs, supportive of shifting norms and structures, that see justice as a fundamental principle, whether aligned with gender identities, political affiliations, or any other distinctions that separate us according to access to resources.

In this final chapter, I have considered some ways in which we might work to approach gender justice as a central framework. This framework would require advocacy in working to change policies as well as norms, with reducing inequities as a central goal. Accountability to our communities is absolutely essential if this is to be a serious project. Advocating for gender justice, through thoughtful, informed strategic intervention that builds from a narrative of equality rather than empowerment, should offer a different discourse. That is my hope.

References

Action Aid International (ActionAid). (2015). *Women's Rights*. 15 April 2015. Retrieved from http://www.actionaid.org/what-we-do/womens-rights.

African Union. (2012). *Protocol to the African Charter on Human and Peoples' Rights on the Rights of Women in Africa*. 29 December 2012. Retrieved from http://www.africa-union.org/root/au/Documents/Treaties/Text/ Protocol%20on%20the%20Rights%20of%20Women.pdf.

African Women's Development Fund (AWDF). (2015). *About AWDF*. 15 April 2015. Retrieved from http://www.awdf.org/our-work/about/.

Barsoum, G., Rifaat, N., El-Gibaly, O., Elwan, N. & Forcier, N. (2009). *Toward FGM-Free Villages in Egypt: A Mid-Term Evaluation and Documentation of the FGM-Free Village Project*. Cairo: Population Council.

Barsoum, G., Rifaat, N., El-Gibaly, O., Elwan, N. & Forcier, N. (2011). *Poverty, Gender, and Youth*. *National Efforts Toward FGM-Free Villages in Egypt: The Evidence of Impact* (Working Paper No. 22). Cairo: Population Council.

Berg, R. C. & Denison, E. (2012). Effectiveness of interventions designed to prevent female genital mutilation/cutting: A systematic review. *Studies in Family Planning, 43*(2), pp. 135–146.

Byron, G. & Ornemark, C. (2011). *Gender Equality in Swedish Development Cooperation*. Stockholm: SIDA.

Coppens, K. (2014). African women's rights project launches in Dechert's London office. *Dechert, LLP*. 15 April 2015, Retrieved from http://sites.edechert.com/10/4004/landing-pages/african-women-s-rights-project-launches-in-dechert-s-london-office.asp.

Cornwall, A., Harrison, E. & Whitehead, A. (2007). Gender myths and feminist fables: The struggle for interpretive power in gender and development. *Development and Change, 38*(1), pp. 1–20.

Couldry, N. (2010). *Why Voice Matters: Culture and Politics after Neoliberalism*. London: Sage.

Couldry, N., Livingstone, S. & Markham, T. (2010). *Media Consumption and Public Engagement: Beyond the Presumption of Attention*. Basingstoke: Palgrave Macmillan.

Davis, A. (9 October 2014). New campaign to end female genital mutilation in Africa. *London Evening Standard* (UK). Retrieved from http://www.standard.co.uk/news/london/new-campaign-to-end-female-genital-mutilation-in-africa-9784134.html. 15 February 2015.

Deutsche Gesellschaft für Internationale Zusammenarbeit (GIZ). (2015). *How to Organize Generation Dialogues about Female Genital Cutting: A Guidance Note for Community-Based Organisations and for Agencies Providing Funding and Technical Support*. 15 April 2015. Retrieved from http://www.intact-network.net/intact/cp/files/1388306556_A%20Guidance%20Note%20for%20Community-Based%20Organizations%20and%20for%20Agencies%20Providing%20Funding%20and%20Technical%20Support.pdf.

Development Alternatives with Women for a New Era (DAWN) (2015). *Vision*. 10 April 2015. Retrieved from http://www.dawnnet.org/feminist-resources/about/vision.

Downing, J. (Ed.) (2011). *Encyclopaedia of Social Movement Media*. Thousand Oaks: Sage.

Dutta, M. (2011). *Communicating Social Change: Structure, Culture, Agency*. New York: Routledge.

Easterly, W. (2006). *The White Man's Burden: Why the West's Efforts to Aid the Rest Have Done So Much Ill and So Little Good*. New York: Penguin Press.

Ehrenreich, B. (2009). *Bright-Sided: How Positive Thinking is Undermining America*. New York: Picador.

Enghel, F. & Wilkins, K. (Eds.). (2012). Communication, media and development: problems and perspectives. *Nordicom. Special Issue, 31*(17/18).

Fahmy, A. (18 March 2015). Tackling Egypt's gender-based violence with crowdsourcing. *Open Democracy*. Retrieved from https://www.opendemocracy.net/openglobalrightsopenpage/amel-fahmy/tackling-egypt%E2%80%99s-gender-based-violence-with-crowdsourcing. 30 March 2015.

Freire, P. (1983). *Pedagogy of the Oppressed*. (M. B. Ramos, Trans.). New York: Continuum.

French, M. (16 February 2014). How supermodel Waris Dirie saved girl from female genital mutilation. *Guardian*. Retrieved from http://www.theguardian. com/society/2014/feb/16/supermodel-waris-dirie-female-genital-mutilation-fgm/. 15 February 2015.

Gallagher, M. (2011). Feminism and social justice: Challenging the media rhetoric. In S. C. Janse, J. Pooley & L. Taub-Pervizpour (Eds.), *Media and Social Justice* (pp. 131–144). New York: Palgrave Macmillan.

Gergen, M. M. & Gergen, K. J. (1983). Interpretive dimensions of international aid. *New Directions in Helping*, *3*, pp. 329–348.

Gilligan, C. (1982). *In a Different Voice: Psychological Theory and Women's Development*. Cambridge: Harvard University Press.

Gilligan, C. (2014). Moral injury and the ethic of care: Reframing the conversation about differences. *Journal of Social Philosophy*, *45*, pp. 89–106.

Global Fund for Women. (2015). *Global Fund For Women*. 10 April 2015. Retrieved from www.globalfundforwomen.org.

Goetz, A. M. (2007). Gender justice, citizenship and entitlements: Core concepts, central debates and new directions for research. In M. Mukhopadhyay & N. Singh (Eds.), *Gender Justice, Citizenship and Development* (pp. 15–57). Ottawa: IDRC.

Gumucio-Dagron, A. & Tufte, T. (Eds.), (2006). *Communication for Social Change. Anthology: Historical and Contemporary Readings*. South Orange, NJ: Communication for Social Change Consortium.

Hemer, O. & Tufte, T. (Eds.). (2005). *Media and Glocal Change: Rethinking Communication for Development*. Göteborg, Sweden: Nordicom.

Hobbes, M. (2014). Stop trying to save the world: Big ideas are destroying international development. *The New Republic*. 17 November. Retrieved from *http://www.newrepublic.com/article/120178/problem-international-development-and-plan-fix-it*.

Holmes, R. & Bhvanendra, D. (2014). *Preventing and Responding to Gender-Based Violence in Humanitarian Crises* (Network Papers No. 77). Retrieved from http:// www.odihpn.org/hpn-resources/network-papers/preventing-and-responding-to-gender-based-violence-in-humanitarian-crises. 15 February 2015.

Huesca, R. (2001). Conceptual contributions of new social movements to development communication research. *Communication Theory*, *11*, pp. 415–33.

Human Life International. (2011). *The Maputo Protocol: A Clear and Present Danger*. 15 April 2015. Retrieved from http://www.maputoprotocol.com/about-the-protocol.

International Women's Health Coalition (IWHC). (2015). *Our Vision*. 10 April 2015. Retrieved from http://iwhc.org/about-us/.

Japan International Cooperation Agency (JICA). (2013). *Gender and Development*. 24 January 2013. Retrieved from http://www.jica.go.jp/english/our_ work/thematic_issues/gender/index.html.

Klugman, J., Hanmer, L., Twigg, S., Hasan, T., McCleary-Sills, J. & Santamaria, J. (2014). *Voice and Agency: Empowering Women and Girls for Shared Prosperity*. Washington DC: World Bank Publications.

Kombo, B., Sow, R. & Mohamed, F. J. (Eds.). (2013). *Journey to Equality: 10 Years of the Protocol on the Rights of Women in Africa*. SAWR: Equality Now.

Kristof, N. D. & WuDunn, S. (2009). *Half the Sky: Turning Oppression into Opportunity for Women Worldwide*. New York: Vintage Books.

Lawyers Circle & Oxfam. (2014). *Raising Her Voice: Implementing the Protocol on the Rights of Women in Africa: Analysing the Compliance of Kenya's Legal Framework*. 15 April 2015. Retrieved from http://policy-practice.oxfam.org.uk/publications/implementing-the-protocol-on-the-rights-of-women-in-africa-analysing-the-compli-333065.

Makau, K. (2013). The Maputo Protocol 10 years on: How can it be used to help end child marriage? 11 April 2015. Retrieved from http://www.girlsnotbrides.org/the-maputo-protocol-10-years-on-how-can-it-be-used-to-end-child-marriage/.

Mattelart, A. (2011). *The Globalization of Surveillance*. Cambridge: Polity Press.

McDonald, D. G. (2014). Narrative research in communication: Key principles and issues. *Review of Communication Research, 2*(1), pp. 115–32.

Melkote. S. (2012). Development support communication for social justice: An analysis of the role of media and communication in directed social change. In S. Melkote (Ed.), *Development Communication in Directed Social Change: A Reappraisal of Theory and Practice* (pp. 15–38). Singapore: AMIC.

Menon, J., Rames, V. & Morris, P. (9 May 2014). *Toolkit for Monitoring and Evaluating Gender-Based Violence Interventions Along the Relief to Development Continuum*. Washington DC: USAID.

Open Society Foundation. (2013). International Women's Program. Retrieved from http://www.opensocietyfoundations.org/about/programs/international-women-s-program. 16 January 2013.

Pamment, J. (2015). Digital diplomacy as transnational media engagement: Aligning theories of participatory culture with international advocacy campaigns. *New Media & Society*. DOI: 1461444815577792. Online publication. First published March 23 2015. Retrieved 1 April 2015.

Sen, G. (2005). *Neolibs, Neocons and Gender Justice: Lessons from Global Negotiations* (Occasional Paper 9). Geneva: UNRISD.

Servaes, J. & Malikhao, P. (2012). Advocating communication for peacebuilding. *Development in Practice, 22*(2), pp. 229–243.

Solidarity for African Women's Rights (SOAWR). (2012). Solidarity for African Women's Rights. 29 December 2012. Retrieved from http://www.soawr.org/en.

Sparks, C. (2007, reprinted 2011) *Globalization, Development and the Mass Media*. London: Sage.

Steeves, L. (2015). Give a laptop, change the world: The story of the OLPC in Ghana. 10 April 2015. Retrieved from https://www.youtube.com/watch?v=wfVrTSq_iKc.

Stein, L., Kidd, D. & Rodriguez, C. (Eds.) (2009). *Making Our Media: Global Initiatives Toward a Democratic Public Sphere*. New York: Hampton Press.

Thomas, P. & van de Fliert, E. (2015). *Interrogating the Theory and Practice of Communication for Social Change: The Basis for a Renewal*. New York: Palgrave Macmillan.

UNFPA. (6 November 2014). Media to play key role in eliminating FGM in Kenya. *UNFPA*. Retrieved from http://www.unfpa.org/news/media-play-key-role-eliminating-fgm-kenya.

UNFPA. (6 February 2015). The start of a movement: Girls rising up against FGM. *UNFPA*. Retrieved from http://www.unfpa.org/news/start-movement-girls-rising-against-fgm.

UNFPA/UNICEF. (2012). *Joint Programme on Female Genital Mutilation/ Cutting: Accelerating Change. Annual Report.* New York: UNFPA- UNICEF.

UNFPA/UNICEF. (2014a). *Abandonment of Female Genital Mutilation/ Cutting: Accelerating Change. Phase II. Funding Proposal.* New York: UNFPA–UNICEF.

UNFPA/UNICEF. (2014b). *Joint Evaluation of the UNFPA-UNICEF Joint Programme on Female Genital Mutilation/Cutting: Main Results.* New York: UNFPA.

United Nations. (2010). *Millennium Development Goals: At a Glance.* New York: UN Department of Public Information.

United Nations Children's Fund (UNICEF). (2013). *Female Genital Mutilation/Cutting: Statistical Overview and Exploration of the Dynamics of Change.* New York: UNICEF.

United Nations Population Fund. (UNFPA). (2014). *Implementation of the International and Regional Human Rights Framework for the Elimination of Female Genital Mutilation.* New York, NY: UNFPA.

United States Agency for International Development (USAID). (2014). The US government working together for the abandonment of female genital mutilation/cutting. *USAID*. Retrieved from http://www.usaid.gov/sites/default/files/documents/1864/USGEffortstoEndFGM.pdf. 15 February 2015.

UN Women. (2011). *United Nations Entity for Global Equality and the Empowerment of Women*, 12 October 2011. Retrieved from http://www.unwomen.org.

US Department of State & USAID. (2012). *United States Strategy to Prevent and Respond to Gender-Based Violence Globally.* Washington DC: US State Department.

Usdin, S., Christofides, N., Malepe, L. & Maker, A. (2000). The value of advocacy in promoting social change: Implementing the new domestic violence act in South Africa. *Reproductive Health Matters, 8*(16), pp. 55–65.

Wallace Global Fund. (2015). *Ridding the World of Female Genital Mutilation/Cutting.* 6 April 2015. Retrieved from http://wgf.org/stop-female-genital-mutilation/.

Wallack, L., Dorfman, L., Jernigan, D. &, Themba, M. (1999). *Media Advocacy and Public Health: Power for Prevention.* Newbury Park: Sage.

Westcott, L. (17 March 2015). How to end female genital mutilation in Egypt. *Newsweek.* Retrieved from http://www.newsweek.com/2015/03/27/how-end-female-genital-mutilation-egypt-314264.html.

Wilkie, C. (3 September 2014). Internal memo recommends major global charities adopt new outreach strategy. *Huffington Post.* Retrieved from http://www.huffingtonpost.com/2014/09/03/gates-foundation-memo_n_5761990.html.

Wilkins, K. (2003). Japanese approaches to development communication. *Keio Communication Review, 25*, pp. 3–21.

Wilkins, K. 2015. Editorial. In K. Wilkins, & J. Servaes (Eds.) Advocacy and Communication for Social Change. *Communication Theory Special Issue*, 25(2), pp. 117–122.

Wilkins, K. & Mody, B. (Eds.). (2001). Communication, development, social change, and global disparity. *Communication Theory Special Issue, 11*(4).

Wilkins, K., Tufte, T., & Obregon, R. (Eds.). (2014). *Handbook on Development Communication & Social Change.* IAMCR Series. Malden, MA: Wiley-Blackwell.

Williams, B. & Delli Carpini, M. (2011). *After Broadcast News: Media Regimes, Democracy and the New Information Environment.* Cambridge: Cambridge University Press.

Wilson Center. (20 November 2014). Addressing maternal health and gender-based violence in times of crisis. 12 April 2015. Retrieved from http://www.worldbank.org/en/results/2014/04/14/mainstreaming-initiatives-to-tackle-gender-based-violence.

Women's Environment and Development Organization (WEDO). (2015). *Our Vision and Mission.* 10 April 2015. Retrieved from http://www.wedo.org/about/about-us.

Women's Initiatives for Gender Justice. (2015). *Who We Are.* 11 April 2015. Retrieved from http://www.iccwomen.org/.

World Bank. (2012). *Gender Equality and Development.* Washington, DC: World Bank.

World Bank. (14 April 2014). *Mainstreaming Initiatives to Tackle Gender-Based Violence.* 12 April 2015. Retrieved from http://www.worldbank.org/en/results/2014/04/14/mainstreaming-initiatives-to-tackle-gender-based-violence.

World Health Organization (WHO). (2015). *Female Genital Mutilation and Other Harmful Practices.* 8 April 2015. Retrieved from http://www.who.int/reproductivehealth/topics/fgm/prevalence/en/.

Notes

1 Communication, Gender, and Development

1. Trends in mortality and poverty have been showing improvement but they have not reached MDG targets at the time of this publication.

4 Communicating Gender in Education Development

1. Simple Minds, *Sanctify Yourself*. Retrieved from http://www.lyricsdepot.com/simple-minds/sanctify-yourself.html. 25 October 2012.

Index

Europe, 15
European Union (EU), 29

Facebook, 114, 149
Female Genital Mutilation (FGM), 116, 176, 183–6, 188–96
feminism, 22–4, 26–9, 35, 56, 135, 141, 162, 182, 197
feminist scholarship, 4, 85, 100
film, 137–8, 140–1, 147–8, 173
Ford Foundation, 49, 99
Foreign Direct Investment, 12
France, 5, 14–15
Fraser, Nancy, 27
Freire, Paulo, 178

Gallagher, Margaret, 2, 26–7, 175
Gambia, 184
Gandhi, Indira, 54
Gandhi, Sonia, 54
Gates, Bill, 19, 156
Gates, Melinda, 141
Geldof, Bob, 157
Gender and Development (GAD), 23, 163
gender justice, 170–1, 173, 175, 177–8, 180–1, 183, 196–7
Gender–Based Violence (GBV), 98–9, 116, 183, 185–9, 191, 195–6
Gender–Related Development Index, 92
Generations Dialogue Program, 191
Geometry of Development, 11
Germany, 5, 13–15, 29, 190
Ghana, 119, 172
Gilligan, Carol, 197
Girard, Bruce, 120
girl generation, 192
global fund, 139
global fund for women, 182, 188
global industry, 34, 36
Global Media Monitoring Project, 175
Global Microcredit Summit 2006, 49, 60
Global Partnership for Education (GPE), 159, 160
Global Philanthropy Group, 142
Global Summit of Women, 108

Global System for Mobile Communications (GSMA) Fund, 73–4
globalization, 9–10, 12, 25–8, 31, 35, 63, 180
Goetz, Anne–Marie, 170
Goodman, Michael, 139
Google, 99
Grameen Bank, 34, 44, 46, 48–51, 57, 59, 61, 63–4, 69–70
Gross National Income (GNI), 14, 45
Guardian, 101
Guinea, 184, 190–191

Haiti, 157
Half the Sky Movement, 148–9
Harrison, Elizabeth and Whitehead, Ann, 24
Harvard School of Public Health Program on International Health and Human Rights, 193
Hatch, John, 51
He for She, 109
hegemony, 28, 32, 179
Hepburn, Audrey, 146
Herman, Edward & Chomsky, Noam, 20
Hogan, M. C., 96
Hollywood, 148, 156–7, 172
Hollywood Narratives, 90
Home of Hope, 154–5
Human Life International, 188

Index of Gender Equality, 92
India, 9, 14–15, 20, 25, 30, 34, 43–8, 50, 54–5, 58–9, 62, 66–7, 73–4, 76–7, 79, 96, 110, 118, 156
Indian Service Reliance, 59
Indonesia, 21, 30
Intel Tech, 110
Inter–Parliamentary Union, 54
International Center for Research on Women (ICRW), 67, 117–18
International Conference on Population and Development (ICPD) in Cairo 1994, 35, 85–6, 93, 95, 97–8, 100–4, 106–7, 114–15, 117, 119–21, 185

Lightning Source UK Ltd.
Milton Keynes UK
UKOW06n1846060716

277811UK00003B/13/P